Amish
in
Wisconsin

An Anecdotal Journal

Richard Lee Dawley

Richard Dawley

Amish Insight
New Berlin, Wisconsin

AMISH IN WISCONSIN

Published by Amish Insight
Edited by Joan Meznarich, Amy E. De Jarlais, Shelly Hall
Line drawings by Barbara Wiltz
Front cover photograph by Bob Schaap
Back cover author's photo by Scott Dawley
Back cover photo of Jakob Ammann's residence in 1698
  by Hans Kern, Eggiwil, Switzerland
Photos by Cindy Pekrul, Gavin Donaldson, and author
Typeset by Judy Dawley, J.D. Graphics
Endorsements by:
•Donald B. Kraybill, author of *The Riddle of Amish Culture, The Amish and the State, Amish Enterprise, Anabaptist World USA,* and *On the Backroad to Heaven.* Professor of Sociology and Anabaptist Studies at Elizabethtown College, Elizabethtown, Pennsylvania 17022
•John E. Sharp, Director of the Mennonite Church USA Historical Committee and Editor, Mennonite Historical Bulletin, Goshen College, Goshen, Indiana 46526
Permission from:

About the Author
Richard has traveled extensively in the U.S., Canada, and Europe for his research. Retired after 31 years, as a school counseler, he now teaches sociology at a technical college and courses on the Amish.

Preface
To know is to understand, to enlighten, and to gain insight. My obervations and experiences being with these "plain people" as described in this journal, are designed to inspire you to become an advocate for the Amish, and to help others appreciate their diverse and unique culture.

Disclaimers
Humility is prized by the Amish. Using their names in this book could draw attention to themselves. At their request, I have substituted fictitious names in those cases. "English" is the term used in this book for all persons other than Amish.

Contact: Amish Insight
2249 S. Calhoun Rd.
New Berlin, Wisconsin 53151
Phone/fax: 262-797-1858
Email: dawley@voyager.net

Table of Contents

PART I Wisconsin Settlements

Chapter 1

KINGSTON, DALTON, AND PARDEEVILLE
"And be not conformed to this world." Romans 12:2

Warm weather and 50 mph winds suddenly sucked the plastic Mylar roof off the Amish Salemville Greenhaus that had just been erected. The wind jostled my car. We had just stopped at a stop sign on our way home when an Amish woman ran toward us battered by the wind, frantically waving her arms urging us to stop and help. She feared for her three small children as debris was blowing violently about. One 2"x 8"x 10 foot beam had smashed against a metal shed 20 feet away. A student on my tour, Mary, helped mother and children into the back seat of my car and we drove them to her grandparent's house nearby for safety.

All the plants in starter flats needed to be evacuated, so we drove to the wholesale Amish greenhouse keeper, Paul, for help. With him in the car, we returned to the devastated greenhouse. He knew a man with a semi-truck that could house the flats out of the wind before more of the structure collapsed. Fortunately, I had a cell phone for Paul to make a call. When we arrived, Amish men from the nearby cheese factory were helping and the truck had arrived. Gavin, another student on my tour, was also there to help rescue the begonias that would become the Amish family's income for the year. We all felt rewarded by helping the young family. We will buy plants on our next visit.

Having visited the Amish community near Kingston on prior occasions, I knew that going there would be a great experience for some of my University of Wisconsin-Waukesha class members. It would give them a chance to witness firsthand the Amish way of life. It's one thing to hear about their culture in class, see slides, videos, etc, but quite another to come face to face with a culture and way of existence that has withstood time and resisted the hurried ways of our modern world.

HOMEMADE AMISH MEAL

On a warm, sunny September day, we made our way through the scenic farmland of central Wisconsin, with its beautiful rolling hills and winding roads, arriving at the Amish home of our host near noon. Emma and her daughter Laura prepared and served us a meal that would easily have received a 4-star rating had it been written up by Dennis Getto, the guru of good food and restaurants in and around Milwaukee. Since she lived alone with her daughter, serving lunch meals to visitors provided them with much needed additional income.

Twenty-eight of us were seated in two long rows at tables with chairs and "church" benches. These same benches are used on Sundays for home church as well as for weddings, funerals, and other special occasions. They are transported from one farm to the next in a specially constructed horse drawn wagon as needed. After a moment of silence before the meal, we marched to the kitchen where the daughter directed us to a serving table. There we piled our plates with mashed potatoes and gravy, skinless chicken, meat loaf, dressing, corn, Jello, and coleslaw. There was plenty of food, more than enough for a second helping. Baskets of home baked bread were on the tables, along with water, milk, and coffee. As we finished, we returned to the kitchen to scrape our plates, reminiscent of a summer camp, and then had to decide among seven pies for dessert. Most of us sampled more than one! I tried cherry pie tart enough to make my salivary glands ache.

Other matters now needed attention. But where was the outhouse? To everyone's delight and surprise, the indoor bathroom was adequately equipped with a toilet commode, tub and shower, and wash sink. It was just like home! Some had observed that a small gasoline engine outside in the pump house was running. This provided power for the water pump to fill a pressure tank and constant running water for the house. Others leisurely strolled through the living room that was modestly furnished with a few chairs, a couch, and table, the only heat source being a wood and coal-burning stove. Grates in the ceiling allowed heat to rise and warm the upstairs. A traditional bent-hickory rocking chair was covered with a brightly colored blue and white hand knit throw. The floors, made of hardwood oak, were well varnished and reflected the bright light from several windows in the room. A large wooden-dowel drying rack held two bed quilts and several small wall hangings that were for sale, all made by local Amish women. A few Amish-styled bonnets and other small items, such as a wooden telescoping and fold down basket and a faceless Amish doll, were purchased. The sale of quilts and small items, as well as serving lunches, provides the main source of income for our host.

By 1:00 p.m., we bid farewell to our host and daughter and started our afternoon tour that included the Salemville Cheese Co-op, Susie's quilt shop, two furniture stores, Pleasant View bakery, Mishler's bulk food store, and the cemetery. Our first stop was disappointing since the cheese factory was closed. Amish men ran it and used electricity from the public power grid. However, the building owner, who lived out east, enabled the Amish to work in the rented plant. An Amish man, Ezra, who was working there, said they got their electricity from the "currant" bush outside.

SUSIE'S QUILT SHOP
Our caravan of 15 cars followed me to our second stop at Susie's quilt house. It was in the grandparent's house called the "daudy haus." Susie's husband, Ray, was walking along

the drive as we "snaked" past him and parked. He went on to the corncrib where his son was grinding feed. Susie was inside the house showing a customer some of the quilts she had for sale. I asked if we might spread out into the rest of the rooms while she finished her business, to which she agreed. One student, Mary, saw two rag-dolls with faces sewn on and seated in a small child's rocking chair. She questioned the faces, as most Amish-made dolls are usually faceless. Gavin, another student, observed the birthday "logs" on the wall of the two sides of the residents' families. These logs contained the names of family members for several generations and their birthdates. The *Budget* newspaper was visible in a rack on the floor. This is a newspaper containing the weekly accounts of Amish and Mennonites from their respective settlements. A person designated as the "scribe" writes the news and "gossip" and mails it to the *Budget* office in Sugar Creek, Ohio. Here it is compiled, printed, and mailed to the subscribers on a weekly basis.

Susie's customers finished their purchases and she greeted our large group. She began to unfold the large quilts that were stacked on the couch near the door. I had seen one quilt earlier that morning when I met with her to arrange our visit. It was the Wisconsin Star pattern and I had to have it. So, I bought it knowing part of the money would be going to the settlement's emergency fund handled by the deacon to pay for large medical bills. One current need was the $240,000 hospital bill for an Amish girl's treatment and a premature twin delivery. Nobody else bought a quilt or wall hanging, but two other students bought pillowcases that were hand decorated by Susie's sister who lived next door. One of the students, Barbara, had heard me tell in class of the plight of the deacon in the settlement who is responsible for raising money for these kinds of emergencies. She offered a monetary donation of her own to the deacon, which he accepted.

Furniture Shop

Then it was on to Moe's furniture and cabinet-maker's shop. The two owners and workers greeted us and showed us the varnish drying room where there were many "on order" furniture items. Our host said he had back orders that would take three months to fill. One couple in the group was enthralled with the quality of what they saw and wanted to buy a dining room table on the spot. The gliding rocking chairs caught the eye of several who admired the workmanship. Then Moe took a few interested persons to the next large room that contained all the machinery for woodworking. Power for the tools was supplied by a diesel engine that drove a shaft in a floor recess. To this shaft, each piece of equipment attached a pulley and belt for its power source. Another large room was the receiving and storage room for the lumber and unfinished furniture that would be "finished" in the shop. On the way out the long driveway, an Amish crew was cutting silage and blowing it up into the silo using the silo-filling machine that was powered by a portable diesel engine. Wagons pulled by a team of beige-colored Belgian horses carried corn shocks to the silo filler.

Mishler's Bulk Food Store

Mishler's bulk food store was the next stop. This large metal building contained spices, canned goods, jars of jams and jellies, and all kinds of pickled delights. One was chow-chow, a pickled assortment of corn kernels, cucumbers, celery, green beans, cauliflower, baby lima beans, carrots, kidney beans, yellow beans, red bell peppers, and the rest of the ingredients to make it sweet and sour. It is a product of a processor from Ephrata, Pennsylvania, which is near the well-known Lancaster Amish settlement. Everything you would need was in Mishler's from sticky flypaper you hang from the ceiling to Amish cookbooks and the *Ausbund*, a collection of Amish hymns from the 1500s printed in German.

The place was jammed mainly with "English" folks, i.e., non-Amish. This may be partly the result of the closing of the grocery store in Kingston after the owner retired and no buyers were forthcoming. Our lunch host, Emma, worked at Mishler's on weekdays, and the male Amish schoolteacher, Homer, was working this Saturday. He told me he had not been teaching for a while due to throwing his back out while he played baseball with "scholars" (Amish term for students) at recess. He had married one of the Mishler daughters earlier in the year. Mr. Mishler told me last spring about the tragic loss of his young son in an accidental drowning in a neighbor's pasture water pond. His sadness was deep.

One peculiarity about the store hours should be explained. All Amish celebrate their faith on Sundays and do not carry on any work or business on the Sabbath. But, Mishler's is also closed on Thursdays. One explanation I have heard is that as the business began to grow larger and larger, concerns were expressed that it was beginning to be "too large" for an Amish family and Amish values, or the Ordnung. This proved to be a myth, verified by a reliable person. The Ordnung is usually an unwritten set of rules established by the community over many generations that everyone is expected to respect and observe. The religious leaders, particularly the bishop and deacon, are charged with maintaining, guarding, and teaching the Ordnung. As the story goes, one other non-business day had to be selected so as not to interfere with the traditions and commitments of the settlement. Thursday was selected because most weddings are held on Thursdays. This was a convenient and acceptable solution for all involved.

LILAC FURNITURE SHOP

The Lilac Furniture Shop, just down Barry Road, was our next stop. The Amish owner, Floyd, was in his shop helping customers. There was barely enough room to walk through the three rooms jammed with wood products. Some of the items were jewelry boxes, dining room tables, and a potty chair with a bookrack and toilet paper holder on the side, an amenity all us English would enjoy. Outside there was lawn furniture such as chairs, gliders, lighthouses, and wishing wells. The owner's wife, Clarita, helped at the checkout where the manual 1940 style adding machine when cranked sounded like crinkling cellophane paper, and where their older son, Alvin, about 13 years old, handled the money and sales slips. His clothing was neat and clean with a black felt hat and a new looking denim jacket. I had seen him grow over the years since they opened the store, and he exuded confidence by answering customer's questions and handling large sums of money. We chatted one time about his school math class that helped him in his new role as "checkout clerk." He had also visited the local Amish greenhouse as part of a school field trip to observe Amish using arithmetic in their lives and work. The owner not only has a large greenhouse, but also does custom mechanical engineering and fabricating of special parts. What better way to learn math than to see it being used in the real world?

PLEASANT VIEW BAKERY

By now, people on the tour were getting hungry again. Down Barry Road to Kiefer, turning south about a half mile, we came to Pleasant View Bakery. The Amish owners had their names printed on their business card. It was late in the day, and nearly all the bakery was sold out. There were no pies or cookies left, and only a half-dozen loaves of bread sat on the metal wire racks along the cinder-block basement walls. The owner explained there was a run on bakery because he had been closed for two Fridays and Saturdays in a row, and his regular customers had run low on their stock of bakery. Nonetheless, our group bought quite a few loaves of bread and marveled at how good they looked and smelled. Three Amish children and an adult were on the porch being read to. One member of our group commented that it would have made a wonderful photograph. I agreed, but did not take one out of respect for their beliefs not to be photographed.

After my tour group had made their purchases, I stayed behind to talk with the owner concerning a letter I had sent to him. I had been referred to him to help me find an Amish family in the Kingston settlement that might be open to the idea of taking on an English boarder, me, for a short period in their home. My intent was to observe and experience daily life in an Amish home and settlement. He was less than enthusiastic about the idea because some years ago a newspaper reporter from Milwaukee had interviewed several Amish folks and showed them her written report, which met with their approval, only to find that it was published with alterations that offended those interviewed because the quotes were not as they had been given. The owner said there was lasting caution about any more newspaper reporters or persons doing interviews in the settlement. My disclaimer was that I was not looking to quote Amish folks, but rather to observe, understand, and describe the lifestyle, customs, and values the Amish hold dear.

CEMETERY

With this idea of finding an Amish family to have me as a boarder nearly dead, we drove to the Amish cemetery. It was located near a sawmill and casket-maker's shop. Parting the barbed wire, the group entered a grove of trees and a small clearing where a substantial wire fence surrounded the dozen-or-so tombstones. These markers appeared to be cast concrete with embedded inscriptions with the name, birthdate, date of death, and the number of days, months, and years of life of the departed. The nearest marker was that of a son of the deacon. It was an endearing moment for me. My relationship to that family had run full circle, their life and now death of one of their family members. It was also the first Amish cemetery I had seen. There were no new graves evidenced as grass covered the entire area. Michelle noticed several stillborn baby markers and some early child markers.

This ended our tour, but some stayed on to have a buffet supper at the Kingston House, some refreshing beverages, and a recounting of the day's experiences before heading for home, back to "civilization."

ELDERHOSTEL TOUR 2000

AMISH SCHOOL SESSION

It was on another field trip late in August that I witnessed an Amish school in session. By special arrangement, an Elderhostel group was allowed to observe this Kingston school, the Log Cabin School. It was originally built with solid logs, but inexperience caused it to deteriorate after 20 years, and it was replaced with a clapboard structure. There are six schools in the settlement serving 140 families. A new one will be built in the northeast section. Amish students are addressed as "scholars," and there were 40 in this one room. No American flag was yet unfurled. Bookshelves were filled with encyclopedias, dictionaries (both English and German), old textbooks from English schools, and classic books such as *Black Beauty*. An old mimeograph machine was still in use for duplicating hand-created worksheets. A ping-pong table was folded up with some sand-faced and some rubber-faced paddles nearby.

The present male teacher, Homer, wore a light blue broadcloth button-down commercial shirt, dark denim broadfall trousers, and suspenders. (Broadfall trousers have a long history. They are still worn by Navy enlisted men in dress blue uniforms. A front "broad" flap has about a dozen buttons. "They are a pain when you have to relieve yourself," said one sailor I spoke to in an airport. The British navy in Admiral Nelson's fleet wore them. The boy on Cracker Jack boxes wears them. So did the Pilgrims and early American colonists.) Homer had small living quarters in the rear of the classroom with only modest accommodations. Having quarters in the building may have been one way to insure the classroom would be comfortably warm in cold weather. A wood-burning stove was along the classroom wall bordering the living quarters. Above it hung a wire drying rack for mittens and other wet items.

Our forty-five minute visit was encouraging. Scholars from grades one to eight sat attentively during our stay. The teacher gave some quiet directions in German to a few students. Others seemed as curious as we were, and were polite, courteous, and respectful to the teacher by responding to his softly spoken directions without hesitation. It was a reassuring sight I had not witnessed in my 31 years employed in the public school setting, especially the last 10 years. Times are changing with sophisticated technology in the public setting, perhaps losing some of the human aspects. The Amish, on the other hand, are hesitant to embrace the technology, but instead nurture more of the human aspects. Which is really progress?

MILLER BUGGY SHOP
On a later field trip, three men from my class were able to observe work being done in the Miller Buggy Shop. The young Amish man, Albert, was welding and welcomed us confidently with a strong voice, firm handshake, and smiling face. He was building a Meadow Brook cart. It was a two-wheeled cart constructed with poplar, hickory, and ash.

The metal parts and some wood parts were part of a kit purchased from Indiana. The "shafts" had been bent in a process of steam heating and bending to conform to the horse's dimensions. The single side-by-side seat was split in order to raise one side. This enabled one to enter the rear part of the cart to fetch groceries or other objects. Cushioned upholstery would be added later along with the traditional black paint. There was no cover or top to the cart, but the Amish man did not call it a "courting" buggy. Those would sometimes have four wheels and no top.

The shop was both new and large. A small office section was enclosed with particleboard leaving the rest open for workspace. Welding and painting stalls were in another room. Winches were attached to the 4" by 8" by 12-foot wooden ceiling beams with unique pinching or scissors grapples that held it to the wood beam. The more weight that was lifted, the more the grapples pinched into the beams. A continuous link pull chain on the winch enabled one person to lift heavy objects easily. A small gasoline 4-cycle engine was running and powering a long "line" shaft located below floor level to which was attached "v" belts to drive individual pieces of machinery along one wall of the shop. The exterior walls were corrugated prefabricated white metal. The roof was interlocking metal sheets along with large corrugated plastic sheets for skylights. The area was well organized, clean for a shop, with plenty of light and ventilation from an abundant number of windows on all sides of the shop. The owner, an older Amish man and wheelwright, waved to us as he entered the house and we departed.

ELDERHOSTEL TOUR 2001

Lucille LaDue led our group of 48 Elderhostelers through the Kingston, Dalton, and Pardeeville settlement on a bright sunny Tuesday in late August. She and her husband had done this many times and had a long history of friendship with the community. She had commandeered several Amish men to repair furniture for the Green Lake Conference Center, on the grounds of the American Baptist Assembly. Over the years, she befriended many in the settlement.

On the last day of our five-day program, she arranged for an Amish family to sell their homemade bakery at the Center to raise money for their school budget. The year before, Lucille arranged for the same family to sell their baked goods to raise money to pay hospital expenses for an infant grandchild. Amish have no hospital or medical insurance. What may seem like an absurd idea has its purpose. It binds people together in the community of Amish. The deacon at two church services collects alms each year to help pay medical emergencies, not only for their community, but others as well when help is asked.

KINGSTON FIELD TRIP SEPTEMBER 22, 2001

THE HARNESS SHOP

Brilliant warm sunshine filled the car as we pulled off to the side of the macadam County Road. Gavin Donaldson, who assisted in the University of Wisconsin-Waukesha class "Amish Cultures," led us to the harness maker's shop. His assignment was to ferret out new settlements for the class field trips, and sites within the settlements to visit. On this day, we saw the Salemville cheese plant, two quilters' shops, a wheelwright, a bakery, a furniture shop, and a bulk food store. It took the whole morning.

An Amish man approached us from a field adjacent to the road. He had been working a team of Belgian horses cutting down groves of Canadian thistles along the road near his long white hen house. He was dressed in black oxfords, dark blue broadfall denim trousers suspended by narrow black suspenders over a drab, rust-brown short sleeve shirt with white buttons. The shirt had no pockets. His traditional domed straw hat was weathered and remained atop his head for most of our visit. When it was not on, black wavy "haar" (German word for hair) covered his ears and upper forehead. His eyeglasses were rather stylish (but not by current standards) with squarer shaped lens. Gavin asked him if we might see his harness shop and he obliged by escorting us to a low-pitched roof building with faded and peeling red paint and saloon-style doors in the middle of the front of the shop with small 8 by 12 inch windowpanes.

Once inside, our eyes required time to adjust to the darkness. A series of single sash windows lined the walls just below the low 6-foot ceiling providing the only light. A routered name sign on the wall spelled out "Harold Miller." He showed us the oil bath where a leather harness was drip-drying after its 20-minute dip in the preserving oil. "It keeps the leather from cracking and becoming brittle and should be done annually," he said. This contrasted with the Amish harness maker in Bonduel who dipped only every two years. Both used a new synthetic plastic material for harnesses, but Harold found it rubbed the hair and shaved skin off the horse.

"Have you ever seen a machine like this?" Harold bellowed. The massive cast iron frame and polished metal parts defied an answer. It was a sewing machine for leatherwork. Without electricity, of course, this contraption had a foot treadle to put in motion with three treadle pedals. Harold sat down and demonstrated the two positions the operator can sit; one was directly in front of the needle, and the other slightly to the side to enable the pieced work to pass by the operator. Thus, the offset pedals accommodate the operator's shift.

A series of cams, shafts and rods all worked in unison

quietly clicking. It was the proverbial sound of a well-oiled sewing machine. One unusual adaptation was the positions of the needle. Instead of moving like traditional sewing machines, it was stationary and below the table, while a movable awl was above the table and pre-punched a hole in the leather for the needle to easily pass through and make its stitch. The machine was outdated for non-Amish use, but very useful to the non-electric Amish.

When asked if there were divorces in the Amish culture, Harold exclaimed, "Well, it happens. We don't like it to happen, but it does." He said if a married man leaves the settlement, he is shunned and will have to file divorce papers in civil court. The woman will have a lawyer represent her in court. She may not remarry until the ex-husband dies, Harold explained.

Harold talked about raising children and curbing any anger at a very early age and thereby establishing authority and self-control, submission, and obedience to the parents and Ordnung of the settlement as well as biblical teachings. He named the seven schools in the district, and said that the "lot" (the manner in which religious leaders are chosen) selects the church bishops. "Deacons," he said, "can never be bishops." (A reliable source said that is the norm, but there are exceptions.) I asked if he had ever been in the lot and he said no, and glad of it. It is an awesome responsibility, and there is much weeping by the family if it happens to you. First, it is for life. Secondly, the task of raising money and organizing auctions is challenging. Third, it takes away from family time and responsibilities.

A customer had waited in the doorway for some time, and I excused us to allow Harold to tend to his business. However, the English man said not to hurry as he was listening and learning, too. He brought in a Western style saddle to the shop as we left. Harold said most of his work was for the English. I shook his hand and thanked him for the visit and reemerged into the brilliant sunshine.

THE SAWMILL

We heard the sound of a buzz saw as we emerged from our cars at the entrance to the sawmill. Rough-barked logs lined the path to the building that covered the machinery. A youth group of 20 teenagers had assembled as part of a tour, and a mill owner, Milo, was demonstrating the equipment.

A large, 20-foot log lay on a toboggan-like conveyer that slowly moved past the saw blade with a 3-foot diameter. A slab was cut from one side of the log and it was rolled over onto its flat surface, and another slab cut. The log tumbled over again for the other two sides to be trimmed. Then the same machine cut four beams, 4 inches by 8 inches, to be used as ceiling beams for a customer's shed roof.

Then each of the slabs was maneuvered by Milo one at a time onto a "planer." First, it smoothed the rough cut of the saw blade. Next, it cut the slabs into 1-inch thick, 6-inch wide planks and Milo turned them over to plane the other side. This completed the demonstration, and the diesel engine power source was brought to an idle and shut down. The silence was deafening.

I asked a young Amish boy who had assisted Milo if caskets were made here. He said they were not, that they were handmade at a carpenter's shop near the settlement's bakery. He did not know what kind of wood was used for the coffin. He said a hand-made wooden container for the coffin was used as well, in place of our concrete vaults. Milo said they worked in the sawmill in winter until it got down to 10 degrees. It is easier to "skid" logs in winter over the frozen ground. Although the sides of the mill were open to the weather, drifting snow could easily be shoveled away from the equipment.

I had taken several photographs of the saws and planer for use in my classes, and when the group leader called for a voluntary collection of money to cover the expended gas and energy of the work crew, I gave generously. Milo and I exchanged business cards, and I began to imagine plans for our next field trip to include an operating sawmill.

DECEMBER 1, 2001 EXPEDITION

The early morning fog was somewhat unusual for this month of the year. But this was an unusual year for weather in Wisconsin. It was much milder all over the northern part of the globe. The forecast was for clearing and a high of 50 degrees, a good day for our expedition to Kingston.

Gavin had made an appointment with the sawmill owner and the harness maker, and a dozen other stops planned. He drove his four-wheel-drive vehicle that reminded me of adventurous paleontologists driving across the Sonora Desert is search of dinosaur eggs. Our search was for more current living people. We traversed Hwy 49 through the Horicon Marsh flyway and Waupun (home for the state's maximum prison, but no Amish there) to County Road AW or County Line Road. At the top of a hill west of Hwy 73, we came to the Hilltop Woodworking Shop. Several newly constructed buildings were on the site, but it was closed. We found out later that the owner had suffered a stroke that morning. In the Amish community, information is transmitted quickly even without telephones.

COUNTY LINE CHAIR SHOP

We stopped at the next woodshop on the same road, County Line Chair Shop. As we parked next to the white aluminum-sided building, an Amish man came out of the house, motioned to us to enter the front door while he went in the back door. A tall man, Dan wore a black felt-domed winter hat. Several layers of coats were visible including the hook and eyes on the inner coat and snaps on the outer coat.

There were no buttons, an ancient tradition from the 1500s when English buttons were highly decorative and too worldly for humble Anabaptists. Besides, the military that imprisoned Amish also wore brightly decorated embossed buttons. Who would want to be reminded of those times? We explained our purpose for visiting the settlement that established a relaxed atmosphere. His modest sales office included several sample chairs and a gray metal Army surplus type, single-pedestal desk. He did his craft in the next room.

A band saw and planer were energized by what is called an in-line shaft. A long shaft under the floor with an access hole near each machine is turned by a diesel engine beyond the wall. Each machine is then connected to the shaft with a pulley for the power to run it. Creatively engineered clutches are often made to activate only those machines needed at one time. Dan had an order for 60 swivel bar stools made from oak. With help, they could make 10 a day.

Gavin asked if he could photograph the machines in the room. Permission was granted reluctantly only because the room was not cleaned up, Dan said, as he stuffed several wood spindle pieces for the bar stools in a bag along the wall out of the way. Then our conversation turned to the wind damage to the Salemville Greenhaus last spring.

"Gavin and I were there shortly after the plastic roof was ripped off by 50 mile per hour winds," I said.

Dan replied, "So you're the ones who helped out! We never found out who you were." Our acts were noticed and remembered and gave Gavin and me satisfaction.

Our visit ended, I gave Dan my Amish Insight business card, and he reciprocated with several of his to each of us. We thanked him for his time, shook his massive hand, and said good-bye.

SALEMVILLE GREENHAUS

As we made our way through the settlement, we stopped at the Salemville Greenhaus on Hwy GG. The young owner, Gid, lost much of his family's yearly income when it was damaged the previous spring.

He was pleased to see us, recognizing us as two of the many who helped him on that depressing day. His street sign advertised brown eggs for sale. When I asked for a dozen, he gave them to me as a token of gratitude for my help and refused payment. Such is the way of content, happy, and generous Amish folks. He gave each of us half a dozen business cards. We shook hands and headed for our next stop.

SALEMVILLE CHEESE CO-OP

Two cheeses are produced in this plant, blue cheese and gorgonzola. The plant is located at W4481 on Hwy GG east of Salemville Road. A commercial truck was parked next to the building unloading 80-pound cans of milk collected from Amish farms. Heavy electrical wires ran to the building along with a phone line. This building is run by the Amish, but owned by an English man, enabling electricity and phones to be used. A phone number is printed on their business card, 920-394-3433. Most of their blue cheese is shipped to New York State. Cheese making takes place on Mondays, Tuesdays, Thursdays and Fridays.

Gavin and I bought our cheese and said we would be back in spring with class members on our field trip to the settlement.

QUILT SHOP

Emma and Laura, code-names for this Amish mother and daughter, were home at their shop on Salemville Road south of County Road X. Emma greeted us at the door with a smile as usual, and said, "I suppose you're here to schedule a visit with your Amish classes." I assured her I was, and she invited us in.

The half dozen quilts displayed on tables in the shop were on consignment from other Amish women. Emma escorted us to the linoleum kitchen area where she planned to serve lunches. It provided income. The room would hold 50 persons. She also worked at the bulk food store in the settlement during the week. Four years of working together spring and fall made our friendship engaging. I gave her my new Amish Insight business card, and in return, she gave me the card of the caterer with whom she worked.

PLEASANT VIEW BAKERY

There is always a line of customers at this Amish bakery on Friday and Saturday morning, the only days it is open. Two puppies were for sale in a small doghouse surrounded by a chicken wire fence just off the winding walk to the bakery door. It seems there are always pups for sale here.

Inside the cramped, cinderblock basement, wire racks on the walls were filled with breads, cookies, pies, preserves, fresh donuts, and sticky pecan breakfast rolls. Amish women in the kitchen were cleaning up after a morning bake. Huge, 4-foot square doors closed on wood-fired ovens. I greeted the owner, who asked if I had brought another class tour to the settlement. I assured him not until next spring. Gavin and I made our purchases, sampled a few fresh frosted donuts, and went on our way.

HWY 22 RESTAURANT AND AUCTION

A crowd had gathered at this conglomeration of wild llamas, ewes, Amish horses and buggies and trucks and cars. An auction was in progress, but Gavin and I were in search of tasty nourishment. Several Amish men were seated at tables inside this crude log cabin having coffee with

English men. Service was slow and the ham and cheese sandwiches we ate were not to our liking. "People watching" was interesting. Several Amish men went downstairs and retrieved one gallon buckets of frozen ice cream to whisk home for their families. I suspect one man was a wannabe Amish (somebody who wants to be somebody else). He had the typical black hat and denim coat, but pants with large patch pockets on the legs are hardly a new Amish style. He even sported a goatee, not very characteristic of real Amish.

MILLER HARNESS SHOP

This was our second visit with Harold, our cryptogram name for him. Gavin had written to him in advance, and we both agreed his shop was more orderly and less cluttered than our first unannounced visit. It was a sign of hospitality, we told each other. We found out that Emma, the quilt shop owner, is his sister. Family ties are strong in Amish communities.

Gavin asked Harold if he could photograph some machines and equipment in the shop. He responded with a quiet and casual nod of approval. He told us about the seven schools in the settlement on our last visit, but Gavin asked if he would name them again so they could be written down. One was unnamed and yet to be built, and we had seen the Log Cabin and Rocky Ridge schools. The others were Meadowview, North Pine, North Scott, and Salemville.

The saloon-style front door to the shop opened and an Amish woman entered and spoke a few words in Pennsylvanian Deitsh (Deutsch), Low (Platt) German, with a few English words sprinkled in, then left. A loud crash outside was heard following the buzz of a chain saw. Harold's boys were cutting down a large dead elm tree for winter firewood. As we all left the shop, Harold's wife was outside and spoke a few words to him and returned to the house. He seemed to take all these directives in stride, just as he accepted our request to visit with him. He strolled casually in the direction of the fallen tree as we drove out the driveway to our next stop.

SAWMILL OWNER AND OPERATOR

Our class fieldtrip to Kingston last spring was able to witness the operation of Milo's sawmill. His affirming reply to my letter asking to meet with him included his reminder to leave our cameras at home. One of the groups touring the sawmill did not honor the no-photographs request, and we thought he might have wrongly connected us with that group. I admitted I did photograph the equipment, but not the Amish boys or him. This seemed to satisfy him that we know and respect the "graven image" rule.

Milo was working with a crew of Amish men stocking firewood for the school. Six flatbed horse-drawn wagons loaded with dried oak pieces were being stacked up inside a shed near the building. Approaching the group, I jokingly asked if the "expert sawmill operator" was around. Milo responded in kind by turning away, saying he did not know anybody like that. Four other Amish men present joined the laughter. The icebreaker set the tone for our visit, ridding cautiousness on the part of the Amish men.

After establishing the ground rules for our fieldtrip to his sawmill next spring, Gavin asked if he might be able to see the inside of the school. Milo agreed and went off to a nearby house to get the key to unlock the door to the new building. The key was not there, so we drove him to another house where the key might be. He found it, and on our return Gavin asked if he might photograph the inside of the classroom for our classes in Waukesha. He agreed, now almost enthusiastically.

The new classroom was immaculately clean. Books and materials were neatly piled up along the window

ledges. On the slate blackboard were Monday's assign-
ments for all eight grades. Movable desks were in straight
lines. Books, pencils, rulers, crayons, and other tools inside
were neatly organized. A dozen windows on the walls provided light. A heating stove was in the cinder block basement below the teacher's desk in the front of the room.
Modest living quarters for the teachers were in an elevated
section above the entrance foyer. The foyer was five steps
below the classroom floor level. Here was the coatroom and
shelves for baseball gloves and lunch pails. A small wash-
basin was in the rear corner of the classroom. Water was
supplied by gravity from an aboveground cistern next to the
windmill at the house nearby. A well maintained, but ancient
mimeograph machine was on a worktable at the front of the
room. There was orderliness about the place reflecting self-
discipline and simplicity—hallmarks of the Amish culture.

Milo munched on a Macintosh apple as we shook his
hand and thanked him for his efforts.

The Casket Maker

The Trappist monks in Peosta, Iowa used to sell garden
vegetables to supplement their budget for the New Melleray
Abbey. When the local civilian folks heard about the beautiful handcrafted wooden caskets that the monk carpenter
made for departed brothers, they began to place orders for
caskets. This was a new entrepreneurial opportunity for the
monks.

In Kingston, the Amish have a carpenter, Edwin,
who builds caskets for their own folks, but not for the
local citizens, like the Trappists do. His shop is modest,
filled with pieces of colorful red planks leaning against
the walls. The outside of the wooden structure is also
red, but paint is flaking with age. On warm days like this
one, he works on the screened porch across the front of
the structure. It reminds me of a summer cottage on

Lake Keesus that I owned two decades ago.

As we spoke with him, he was gluing six pieces of ruler-sized wood together on a small worktable. A rotund short man, he deftly applied the liquid to the edges of the pieces and placed them between two clamps. A young boy came in and sat nearby, perhaps a son, relation, or apprentice. Edwin's father was a casket maker before him, handing down the art of woodworking and service to the community.

Another Amish man in the settlement handles the funeral arrangements. He brings the needed measurements of the corpse for Edwin to construct the casket and wooden vault. The vault receives the casket at burial. With help, he can produce both in 24 hours. The casket, made of oak, cherry, birch, or other wood, is lined with white muslin. No other padding, springs or pillows are used. Metal pallbearer handles are bolted to the sides of the casket. A solid plank covers the foot of the casket, but the head has two hinged doors that fold back for viewing at the wake and perhaps just before internment at the cemetery. The cemetery is on Amish-owned land in the settlement.

Casket making is not the only enterprise for Edwin. He specializes in "kitchen and dining room furniture, also cedar chests and crafts," according to his business card. Furniture and cabinets are "made to order." As we drove in, we saw him working with a customer who needed an old rocking chair repaired. After an hour with Edwin, we bade him farewell and thanked him for his generous story.

Mishler's Bulk Food Store

A stop at Mishler's is always interesting. The owner's son-in-law, Homer, was working behind the checkout counter. He recognized me and asked if I had another group touring the settlement. We had spoken many times when he was one of the two teachers at the Log Cabin school. Now married, he was learning the store business. I bought cinnamon apple butter, chow-chow, and basswood honey.

GRAND RIVER BULK FOOD STORE AND KINGSTON MILL WORKS

Gavin found this new enterprise on one of his last explorations of the settlement. Located closer to Kingston, it provides condiments for the northeast district. The first Suffolk sheep I had ever seen were grazing in the nearby pasture. Gavin recognized them from his living in New Zealand. More modest than Mishler's, the store had an 8-quart kettle I had been looking for. I bought it and we left for the Kingston House, a beverage and buffet meal fit for a king.

KINGSTON AUCTION

Auction is a Latin word meaning, "an increasing." What increases is the bid amount of the item for sale. There is also an increasing excitement in the audience as they bid, oftentimes raising the bid higher than anyone expected or wanted. Such is the psychology of auctions.

Amish use auctions to raise money for a settlement to pay off bills or initiate projects, such as building a new schoolhouse or paying medical expenses of members of the congregation. In this way the congregation members are not beholden to outside agencies or institutions to remedy the cost of replacing a burned down barn. The Amish do not purchase insurance policies as a rule. Individual members contribute money when called for by the deacon, who is responsible for such enterprises.

Items such as quilts, furniture, crafts, and other hand-made articles, as well as farm implements, horse harnesses and tack, and tools are donated or consigned to auctioneers. The non-Amish also contribute to the assortment of items and receive a percentage of the gross amount collected, as do the Amish. In Wisconsin, I have attended three auctions in Albany, one each in Amherst and Bonduel, and three in Kingston. They are usually in the spring of the year, though some are in fall. Other states may be different. It becomes an opportunity to meet and even visit with people of another culture. Amish enjoy conversation, and approached with respect and sincerity they can provide insight into this society.

The Kingston auction provides an opportunity to observe Amish people in public. Seldom do you have the chance to see families with their children off the farms and be able to witness their behavior and engage in conversation with them so freely. The male teacher for one of their schools was present and chatted with me. He was in the school the previous August when an Elderhostel group was allowed to observe his class. His sister assisted him as well. He wore a button-down, blue broadcloth shirt with long sleeves common to non-Amish. Our discussion was about the Amish "special children" who were bussed to public school in the Cashton area. He had one special child in his classroom.

Fran Sieving was a student in one of my Amish classes and befriended an Amish woman, Mannie, in the Kingston settlement. I met her at the auction and reminisced about her friendship with Fran. Fran exchanged letters and visited with her.

Mannie was 66 years old with 11 children and had a sewing shop and green house. Fran was shown her root cellar, kerosene stove, and heating stove. Mannie could sew a complete man's pant and shirt and Sunday coat in about five to six hours. She said there were about 110 families in the settlement, five schools, and four churches that held three-hour services every other Sunday. She saw an influx of Amish from Indiana. Only about 10% leave the faith; a thirteen-year-old left, but only for a short time, and then returned. It is this kind of inter-connectedness that is heart-warming and informative for me and builds a trusting relationship with the Amish through the openness of the auction setting.

Reading the *Budget* newspaper helps to keep track of the news in Kingston or any settlement. Sharing that news with Amish folks lends credibility to one's interest in the Amish and not just curiosity-seeking adventure.

Another conversation at the auction was with a clock-maker from Loganville, Wisconsin. He lived in Delaware, but had found it too crowded. He has a 140-acre farm that is worked mainly by his two sons, and he hopes one of them will take it over. That means when he gets married. They raise beef cattle, which is the first non-dairy farm I had heard about. Business cards were exchanged, his being colorful with a blue background and nine different old-fashioned clocks at the top. "Closed on Sunday" was highlighted in bright yellow, and "Narrows Valley Clock Repair" in bold black letters along with his name and address. This was his semi-retirement business enterprise.

Men's shirts worn at the auction were very bright. Most had buttons and the material was acrylic, wear-resistant, and easier to sew and clean. Suspenders were varied in style that sometimes reflect the settlement tradition. For example, one pair was constructed with woven or braided leather. Most were the customary cloth/elastic, and all were of two strands in the front. Most had two in the back, but a few had a single strand connected to the pant. In some eastern states, only one strand is used and crosses from the left on the pant in back to the right in the front.

Another Amish man saw me observing the wheel-wright's nameplate on the back of a buggy. He showed me his buggy and explained the brake mechanism. It was a simple lever arrangement with a pedal inside the cab and an arm with a piece of old tire attached to it that made contact with the buggy wheel to stop or slow the buggy. He said that the hydraulic system used in Ohio had not been widely adopted in Kingston.

Belgian horses were in a corral near the barn. One was ill shod with no shoes and hoofs cracked and splintered severely. Although gentle to the curious onlookers of Amish and English alike, it became territorial and made threatening lunges at a Standardbred horse that invaded its space at the fence.

A young Amish lady sat next to me in the tent with her two-year-old daughter. She wanted to buy one furniture item but lost the bid. She said she misses her Ohio family. Brides follow the groom to the groom's family settlement. I engaged the daughter with some playful teasing (the skill of a grandfather) with a colorful handkerchief that had slipped from her hand. The mother was grateful for the brief attention and distraction for her child.

Groups of six to eight single males banded together and roamed the grounds surveying household items to be auctioned off. An older Amish man was overheard giving instruction in the family lineage to a young Amish couple. They were the only young couple seen and seemed to be in a courting mode.

A lunch was available in a large pole shed. Ham and cheese sandwiches were sold for $1.50, very modest for the mound of ham. Cherry pie was very tasty with a lump of ice cream on top. Later, I ate a bratwurst and drank a soda to quench my thirst. In the past, a breakfast was also served.

Two Amish buggies were to be auctioned in the large field. They had seen much service and were in need of repair. The 30 to 40 buggies in the parking lot were in much better condition. All were black covered buggies with windshields and windows and had the triangular red and orange slow moving vehicle sign attached to the back. The horses were tied under a line of trees for shade and stood side by side without much commotion or threat displays.

2002 AUCTION

June 8th, 2002 brought another auction to the Kingston settlement. It would raise money for the $240,000 medical bills the deacon is responsible for paying. The weather could not have been better with clear skies and moderate temperatures. Bidders' numbers went into the high 400s. I had brought students in my Amish Culture classes to this auction as well as winners in the Milwaukee public television Channel 10 auction. I donated eight guided tours through the settlement that included this quilt and furniture auction.

THE COUNTRY ROSE BED AND BREAKFAST

The night before I stayed in another Wisconsin Bed and Breakfast Association member's "The Country Rose" in Pardeeville. Innkeeper Ruth Krueger provided an elegant 1900s home with antiques and furnishings of yesteryear. The home had been her grandfather's for the 100-acre farm he worked. Then her bachelor uncle lived in it and kept it in mint condition. Ruth's father farmed the 100 acres across the road where she grew up.

In our correspondence, she told me of an Amish lady who had left the faith. The former Amish woman was living and working in Pardeeville when I talked with her by phone. She wished to remain anonymous. These contacts-by-coincidence were helpful in my research. Ruth also pointed out two neighbors' Amish farms on Haynes Road between Hwy 22 and 44 that were visible from her B&B kitchen window. The youngsters used the street to roller-blade. Amos H. Schwartz lived on one farm and had a son, Glenn, at this auction selling flowering plants from his Salemville Greenhaus in Kingston. By coincidence, Amos was at the auction, too, and I had a chance to meet him.

MORE THAN AN AUCTION
The interconnectedness of these Amish families became evident at these meetings. The auction was a means for Amish to be together and catch up on family, relatives, and friends' lives. It was becoming a social event for me, too, as well as a time for research. The settlement casket maker was at the Kingston auction and told me about an Amish casket maker in Middlebury, Indiana, by the name of Hochstetler, who was making caskets for English as well as Amish. Both used cedar shavings for the bottom of the casket "to provide a nice smell," an off-white muslin lining, and a peaked top instead of the more common flat top.

Jacob Mast was there from Wautoma with his ice cream maker. I had seen him at several auctions, and his ice cream was tasty. Preacher Freeman was there from another settlement and we talked about horseshoes. He explained the carbide tips that are put on horseshoes that seemed to bear the brunt of English complaints. The tips allegedly damage asphalt roads, but are helpful in winter to prevent slipping. He also knew about an Amish settlement in Lobeville, Tennessee, that had their church service conducted in English and had typed sermons distributed to other Amish preachers. He referred me to page eight in the *Martyrs Mirror*, a section titled "Of The Greater Danger There Is At This Time, Than In The Bloody and Distressing Times Of The Martyrs." "This Time" being 1660 and the reference made to Matthew 16:26, "for what is a man profited, if he shall gain the whole world, and lose his own soul?"

Talking with Freeman on this 90-degree day was another Amish man dressed in heat-absorbing black pants, black hat, and black coat. He said he recognized me from somewhere. We discovered it was at a wedding in Beetown when I sat near him in the service and he put his sleeping son next to me on the bench. He was a Forsinger; he led in singing some of the hymns, using a small brown-covered booklet with "shaped notes."

A preacher from the Bonduel settlement sauntered nonchalantly up to me eating ice cream. I had to take two looks before I recognized my friend. We chatted about a project he and a Mennonite preacher were involved with trying to help an African Christian witness an Anabaptist church service.

In contrast, a heavyset English man in a tee shirt, a cane, and long Amish-like white beard talked with me in the same group with Freeman about the governments of the world plotting to become one power through the United Nations with smallpox vaccinations to alter our consciousness into obedient citizens. He gave me two Internet addresses that opposed this sinister take-over of the world.

On a lighter note, the sandwiches and lunch fixings were in the schoolhouse next to the auction tent. A baker's dozen crew of young girls was glazing donuts in the basement. I peered in the window and asked if there were any free ones. It brought the desired smiles and laughter, but no free ones. Horse and buggy parking was along a tree line for shade. Waiting to use the port-o-let, I stood in front of one of the bored horses to see what it would do. It moved forward close enough to sniff my arm, and then bit the green halter rope as though trying to free it from the hitching rack and head for home for water and nourishment. Amish horses seem to exhibit human characteristics and interact confidently with their keepers in a symbiotic relationship, just as the Amish interact with the "wicked world" in a measured way, protecting their traditions yet facing the reality that total isolation from it would be unrealistic. It is this dynamic tension of being "in the world, but not of it" that tests the faith of these plain people.

In the back of the auction tent, Susie was organizing the flow of the quilts and wall hangings to the platform where the auctioneers barked out their cadence. Her husband is the deacon and organizes this auction. She was holding a 45x45 inch wall hanging I had put money down on some weeks before. She had trusted me to send the balance of the $85 cost in a check that I mailed to her. The wall hanging had a black border with a blue piping around the edge. Blocks with multicolored diagonal strips filled the center. It was more masculine than what most women might buy for $85. Inside were 16 squares with rainbow and earth colors in one-inch strips running diagonally across each square. It was a shadow pattern. When I came to their Gross Daudy house the day before, Susie was washing her hair. When I announced I was there to pick up my wall hanging, she said to come right in. She never forgets a person or a business arrangement, and is a delight to be with. As Amish get to know you and what you are up to, their trust and sincere friendship is a precious possession to have. But it takes time to show your true colors and gain that trust.

One of the couples on the tour celebrated their anniversary by buying a quilt. Others seemed happy just to witness the action and eat the food. By 2:30 p.m., the heat of the day got to my proofreader, and me, so we got into my air-conditioned car and headed for home. It had been another good auction day.

Once at home, I attended a picnic with my condominium neighbors. Two incidents there made me aware of the broad extent of interest in, but lack of understanding about, the Amish. One resident, Father Steven Amann, told me of his interest in the Amish because his name is similar to that of the Amish founder, Jakob or Jacob Ammann. My brief research, however, did not uncover any name with Steven's spelling. Steven was also not aware of his genealogy and its

European connection. It was not the custom of some past generations to talk about their heritage once they immigrated to the "New World."

A second incident involved a woman nurse's story of the Amish who accompanied their children to the Ronald McDonald House in Wauwatosa, Wisconsin. The House is provided for parents of children being treated for childhood diseases at nearby hospitals. She said the parents quickly adapted to the setting by turning on the television set and surfing the channels as well as using the microwave, telephone, and other "worldly" conveniences. It is the ownership and use in the Amish home that is forbidden in strict, conservative sects. It surprised her that Amish would use modern medicine, hospitals, and procedures. Myths and misunderstandings about the Amish still prevail in the majority of citizens of our diverse culture. It is partly due to the lack of information or interest by urban non-Amish, and partly due to the isolation and rural environment in which the Amish choose to live. Anyone different from "us" is often found to be suspect, which then generates myths to fill the void of understanding. I am hopeful that the pages of this book will fill some of that void.

DRIVING THE AMISH

The usual means of transportation for the Amish is the traditional black buggy. When long distance travel is required, they use other means, such as commercial or charter bus, train, or hired drivers, but not airplanes. One such driver in Wisconsin near Wyocena is Orlando Allen. He is known by the Amish in the area and has befriended them over the years. He is also the contact person for the annual quilt and furniture auction held in Kingston, usually in June. His name and telephone number are listed on the printed auction-advertising card, and he takes phone messages for the Amish man who organizes the auction. In the past, a pancake and sausage breakfast and a lunch were served at the auction site, with proceeds going toward the payment of medical bills for the settlement. Amish do not have commercial group or private health insurance, nor do they benefit from Social Security, Medicare, Medicaid, Workman's Compensation, or Unemployment Compensation. They rely on their own resources.

Orlando's daughter is a grade school teacher in the settlement area. An incident occurred that prompted her to teach about diversity and prejudice toward the Amish in their neighborhood. An Amish buggy was set on fire by a group of hooligans. Knowing the Amish as Orlando does, he was able to contact one to come to her classroom and tell about their lifestyle and answer questions. He was invited back several times because students found the subject interesting. The hooligans who set fire to the buggies may have been high school students or deviant adults. Peer group pressure is very effective. Such are the contributions that a resourceful driver can make to his communities, both English and Amish.

MENNONITE TAXI SERVICES

Drivers are needed to carry families to auctions, weddings, and funerals. Large 15 passenger vans serve the purpose. At one auction in Kingston, a driver brought a clutch of Amish from Indiana and displayed his availability on his license plate: "VAN GO." Most advertising is by word of mouth, however, there is a list of drivers in *The Diary* periodical for February 2002.

In some settlements, Mennonites make it their business to drive Amish around. They provide taxi services. I have not seen any in Wisconsin, but there are services in Lancaster, Pennsylvania and in Arthur, Illinois. In Arthur, the Mennonites are "falling away" Amish that have left the church to take up residence in the Mennonite brotherhood. They may stay in the area, as they are familiar with the people and businesses as well as the geography. They may also serve the Amish brothers as business agents, tax agents, and in other business related capacities. It is this melding that blurs the lines of separation between the Amish and the sinful world. It produces the push-pull between being in the world, but not of it. That tension seems to be increasing in some well-established settlements where the strength of the majority holds it together.

Such is the impact of a seemingly innocent occurrence, but, in fact, it characterizes the change that prods the church leaders to make adjustments in the Ordnung. Only the strictest of the Old Order Mennonites and Amish will resist the melding, merging, and the adjustments made to maintain their integrity and devotion to tradition. You may remember and appreciate the struggle with changes that consumed TEVYE in the classic movie, "Fiddler on the Roof."

PART I Wisconsin Settlements

Chapter 2
AMHERST
A DISBANDED SETTLEMENT

As I drove into the yard and then began walking toward the house, an Amish man and two young Amish boys came out onto a wooden deck and greeted me cautiously. I explained that I studied the Anabaptists and was from the Milwaukee area to attend the quilt auction the next day and was hoping to find an Amish family that would provide room and board for one night. The father, in a soft, slow voice said, to my amazement, that I could stay there. What providence! It would be my first night in an Amish home. It turned into a second one, as well.

Milking Time
It was milking time for 24 Red Holstein cows, sometimes called "Mennonite Holsteins," and I was invited to the barn to observe and visit. The father, Abe, easily engaged me in conversation while hand milking his first cow of the evening. His wife, Erma, was also easy to talk with as she milked, as were the older daughter, Katie, and son, Ray, and two younger boys, 10 and 12. The crude wooden and well-worn stools they sat on to milk showed their 16 years of use on this farm. A bulk tank for cooling milk was a surprising "modern" piece of equipment in the milk house. A refrigeration unit for the bulk tank not only cooled the milk, but its heat was released in a tank of water, thus providing several gallons of warm water for the milk house use.

Udder teats were washed with paper hand towels soaked in a pail of water and disinfectant, and a spray disinfectant was applied to them after milking to prevent infection.

Cows were released as they were "drained," and lazily walked out the open barn door to pasture. Chief, the dog, walked behind some that hesitated to leave and he successfully moved them out to pasture. Nothing seemed hurried except the dog. Everyone had a responsibility and routine to complete. The middle son dumped grain on the concrete barn floor in front of each cow along with a mineral supplement.

An odd, and perhaps "insignificant" observation was that no cow, while in the barn, defecated and only one urinated in the two nights I was present in the barn. In my boyhood experiences on farms in the summer, many did so, and more so when treatment of the animals was not gentle. Here the gentleness and soft-spoken talk of these "plain people" may have been contagious to the beasts. I have further seen contentment in the dog's demeanor on Amish farms in other settlements.

ABE AND ERMA

Although Abe's demeanor was gentle, kind, quiet, softspoken, and deliberate, I never heard him chuckle or laugh, but he did have a genuine smile displayed in humorous situations. Erma, on the other hand, was vibrant, active, vocal, chuckling, and quick to respond to humor, of which there was a great deal during my stay. I am prone to eliciting it, and they seemed to enjoy the novelty of having someone in the house outside their culture. I became the "novelty." Now they were the tourists, and I was the "welcome relief" as one Lancaster, Pennsylvania Amish deacon put it.

HEALTH ISSUES

Ray was said to be tired, according to his mother. This was confirmed on the drive home from the Amherst auction when he asked me if I ever got tired at the auction. This was a surprisingly personal and frank question for a young man who was very reserved, and I suspect the adolescent growth spurt and hormonal flooding may account for some of his condition, let alone the 4 a.m. trek to a void world from an unlit house to a dark barn every day, summer and winter. When I drove the parents to church in the nearest settlement, Wautoma, on Sunday morning, the mother expressed concern for the oldest son's tiredness and said they would have to do some "doctoring." Three months later when I helped them move to another farm, his mother told me he was well, and he looked well. The 18-year-old sister was observed taking supplemental vitamins at each meal. Another element for conjecture is about the influence of darkness on the human psyche. The barn had no electric lighting in it, and this was summer. What toll would winter take? The impact of seasonal affective disorder is documented medically.

BECOMING AMISH

Katie reached a milestone in her life on Sunday, August 27, 2000, the day I left. She and her brothers were picked up by an English neighbor to go to church in Wautoma. It was her day to celebrate her first communion and make her vows to commit her life to the church and be Amish, a Christian believer.

PORTAGE COUNTY FAIRGROUND AUCTION

The day before auction day, the mother was up at 2 a.m. to get ready to be picked up by a neighbor driver. She had to prepare for the coffee and donut sales table at the back of the auction tent with other Amish women. With a Coleman camping stove, she helped prepare the sales items. The mystery of how Amish women could put together a dress with straight pins and wear it was solved when she showed me the wrap-around feature of the pleated skirt part that was held together at the band with two or three straight pins. Pins also closed the vertically separated bosom flaps and the cape in front and back and around the neckline. A black dress was hanging on the kitchen door the night before, which she showed me in detail, as I had mentioned my puzzlement as to how they used straight pins. It was a new dress made for the daughter's communion.

The auction was held in a large circus-type tent at the Portage County Fairgrounds in Amherst. The forward quarter of the tent was filled with racks of quilts, unfinished quilt tops, wall hangings, and table runners, as well as wooden furniture. Quilts had a variety of designs. Among them were log cabin, star, flowered, bars, center diamond, sunshine and shadow, shoofly, and double wedding ring, as well as samplers. Furniture included bedroom sets, dining room table sets, outdoor lawn furniture, wooden knick-knacks, and other wooden items. The auctioneers were Mader and Mader, and were scheduled for two more quilt auctions on successive weekends.

KEEPING IN TOUCH

Since that visit, I have carried on a correspondence with the family. Erma's letters are informative and friendly, and do not lack frankness. She read my draft copy of this chapter at my request and made corrections and requests freely and politely. She included "smiley faces" where appropriate, as well as frowning faces where needed. They had sold their farm and were moving to the Marion area. But that is another story and chapter.

THE DEMISE AND REUNION OF A SETTLEMENT

A Journal Sentinel newspaper article stated that 70 families had lived in the Amherst settlement at one time. By May of 1997, only about 15 remained. On December 7, 2000, the day I helped Abe's family move, they were the last Amish family to leave Portage County. Several reasons were given for the exodus. One was that two of their preachers had died within a close time. One had died after his buggy went out of control and he hit a concrete abutment. The second died of natural causes. It was said that nobody would fill the empty positions. A rumor circulating in an English tavern was that one of the preachers had been a victim of a shooting. I consulted a deacon from another settlement I knew to be straightforward. He refuted the shooting theory.

In June of 2001, an English neighbor in Amherst, Wanda Tryebeatowski, advertised a reunion for former Amish residents of the settlement. About 150 showed up at the "Beer tent" (only the name for the building at the fairground, and no beer was served) for a day of eating and visiting. Word of the event was in the *Budget* and the informal grapevine network spread the message. She plans to hold another one.

PART I   Wisconsin Settlements

Chapter 3

MARION

"You can get a lot done when you do not need to take credit."....*Harry S. Truman*

A WINTER MOVE

The letter finally came, and I knew what it would say. It was time to move to another farm. My Amish friends from Amherst, the last Amish family in all of Portage County, said they would let me know when they were packing up as I had shown interest in helping and witnessing this event. But the conditions on December 7, 2000, Pearl Harbor Day, were a cold –5 degrees with light snow.

Abe, the husband, recognized me as I approached the 60-foot-long semi-truck that was being loaded. He removed his heavy work gloves and shook my hand and greeted me cordially. The dozen Amish men nearby observed this greeting in an eerie silence. They said very little until I asked what I could do to help and then began lifting boxes up to the Amish men in the truck. That helped break the ice.

LEVITY

A parade of men emptied the basement. One of them found several one-gallon glass jugs with wax paper under the cap. He removed the screw-on cap, sniffed the jug cautiously, and slowly raised it to his lips so as not to disturb the sediment at the bottom. Finding it tasty, he took a longer swig. I was curious and leaned forward to sniff it myself. It was apple cider, but not fresh enough for my liking. As he indulged in another swig, there was some chuckling and then we all went back to toting boxes of Ball jars and preserves out to the semi. The conversation was much more relaxed between the Amish men and me.

LOADING

Everything in the garage had to be dismantled and loaded, including a large water heater. The heater had a round cylinder with sheet metal on the outside, and an iron kettle two feet deep and three feet in diameter on the inside. Under the kettle was a grate that could support either a wood or coal fire. I had seen only one like it before in Cashton, but never disassembled. It took four men to lift the kettle into the semi, each man playing a role. One man had a tape ruler and measured space left in the semi for each new piece to be loaded. One of the men explained, "We've done it many times." The man of the house moved from one project to another giving direction and sharing the workload.

A large cabinet was hanging from the wall by two ordinary door hinges. A man standing on a flimsy homemade pie carrier, balancing on one foot attacked the cabinet with a crowbar to release it. I braced the makeshift stool to prevent it from tipping, and as he stepped down, he thanked me for stabilizing it. It was a friendly and observant gesture. I was useful and appreciated and part of the team.

By then, two buggies had been loaded. The cows and horses had already been shuttled to the new farm 50 miles away in several loads and the farm machinery was secured on a flatbed and ready to roll. Toward the end, six men hoisted a large, heavy tool cart up onto the semi. I expressed my concern that if the semi took a corner, the cart might shift. Several men made reassuring comments that it would not. Finally, an abandoned, broken chair was packed beside the cart with an explanation that it was customary to always pack something in a load that was not wanted as a practical joke. The semi was full and doors were secured.

A Woman's Perspective

Erma, Abe's wife, greeted me and gave me an assignment. She asked me to drive her to an English neighbor's house across the road where she was to pick up passengers and hot food. The food would be served to workers at the new farm. The passengers were two Amish mothers and their three young children. Once loaded, we drove past the old farm, and Erma said: "There it goes. I'll never see that place again." She saw the mailbox still in place along the road and stated that it was probably forgotten and being left behind. She is very observant and does not miss anything. As we drove to the new home, she spoke of the presidential voting fiasco in Florida that she found humorous. She seemed to camouflage her sadness about leaving, but was also excited about the new place. The 5-year-old boy proudly counted to ten for me in English. His sisters slept much of the way.

Arrival to New Comforts and Conveniences

When we arrived, we toured the house. A furnace thermostat was set for 68 degrees and the lights were on. Electric baseboard heaters gave off columns of warm air. The previous owners were English with all the comforts of "civilized" people. Our group enjoyed the novelty of just turning lights off and on, as did the boys in the barn. I gave Erma woolen blankets, hand towels, washcloths, and dishtowels from my mother's living estate sale. The towels came in handy when the men washed up for the noon meal.

The heating stove for the kitchen was brought in, but the stovepipe was too short. Someone said a hardware store was just down the road. I offered to drive if someone else would join me and do the shopping. Chris Hershberger from Wautoma volunteered and we got in my car heading for Tru-Value in Manawa. During the ride, we struck up a conversation. He explained to me that he was raised in Arthur,

Illinois, a large settlement of 4,000 Amish and on my list of places to see. (See Part II, Chapter 3). He asked if I had ever been to an Amish church service, which I had not. I had been invited to a Mennonite service in Nova Scotia, but declined because German was used exclusively and I did not know the language. He began telling me a story of an English man he had invited to an Amish service. The English man said he did not understand the words, but he knew what was going on.

I had been fortunate, following my Nova Scotia trip, to be invited to an English-speaking Mennonite service in Lancaster with Mennonite friends. When I said services could be emotional for me, especially with my mother's slow death from Alzheimer's, he empathetically sympathized, as several in his family recently died including a brother who suffered from the same disease. He was such a warm, sensitive and kind man that I felt I had found a new friend. His sense of humor was evident at the hardware store when he kidded with the clerk. His hands were strong and calloused as he used a shears to cut the stovepipe to size. On the way back he told me one last story of how as a retirement project he built toy Conestoga wagons that sold at auction for $60 each. He said it gave him something to do in the winter and brought in a little spending money.

HUSBAND AND FATHER
The man of the house, Abe, deserves description. He is tall, medium build, (I've yet to see an obese Amish man), with large calloused hands and dark wavy hair. His eyes are dark and focused and he is a soft-spoken man. I never heard his voice above a conversational level. He is thoughtful and uses a minimum of words to express himself. When he corrects his young son at the kitchen table at mealtime, he uses the German dialect and nearly whispers. Other descriptors include versatile, physically strong, patient, humble, and

almost stern or stoic in demeanor. He is kind, sensitive, very observant, and dedicated to his faith and family. Singing "Das Lob Sang" is not his strong suit, as I witnessed. ("Das Lob Sang" is a traditional Anabaptist song sung at church service.) He is friendly and generous. These are the virtues extolled in every pulpit on Sunday mornings in English churches.

THE MEAL

The noon meal was interesting. Before we ate, the men stood around the kitchen walls and everyone in the entire house was silent, heads bowed, hands clasped and arms hanging as the traditional silent meal prayer was offered. How everyone knew the time to start was bewildering to me. There was no leader or verbal command.

A Coleman camp stove was used to heat up the casserole we had brought, as well as a pot of noodles. Perked coffee warmed the innards and hamburger patties (which may have been venison) were tasty and fit nicely in the store bought buns. We piled our Styrofoam plates with a flavorful cold pasta salad that contained peas and celery and mayo, which gave us energy to unload the semi. Red Jello with cherries capped a good meal. The men sat on the floor in the front room braced against the walls with their legs crossed exactly alike. We chatted about fishing and hunting, some of us telling tales of bending the rules. I asked naïve questions about deer and the meat you can glean from a dressed-out carcass. Their responses were informative and cordial, and made me feel like "one of the boys" again. These men were not much different from the men at my church once I mingled and exchanged stories with them

FARM ANIMALS AND PROPERTY

It had warmed up to 10 degrees. The young heifers that I had seen at the old farm were housed in an open lean-to shed and were huddled together for warmth. They had doubled in size since I saw them three months before. One of the sons said they stay outdoors all winter. I asked him where their property ended to the east, and he offered to show me if I would drive my car. Several other boys asked to go along and we saw the creek at the end of their land. One boy tested the frozen creek and eventually it cracked. I warned everyone that if anybody got soaked, they would have to walk home. The boys laughed. Once again, I became the novelty for them.

The original barn had burned down. Spontaneous hay fires often killed entire herds of cattle and livestock. This replacement had a firewall ceiling made of concrete slabs that spanned the width of the barn. There was room for 60 cows, but now housed only about 20 with four Belgian workhorses, two Standardbred buggy horses, a pony (used in pulling a golf course lawn mower), and a neighbor's mid-sized horse. It was 20 to 30 degrees warmer in the barn than outside with the heat being generated by the beasts.

UNLOADING

The crisscrossing of the men bringing boxes and furniture into the house from the semi was like termites carrying egg casks from a damaged nest to safety. The house was vintage 1860s, and the basement was a catacomb of walls and halls all lighted with electric light bulbs. I could only imagine what it was going to be like once the new owners cut the circuit to the main switch and there was darkness throughout. Men carried in a half dozen each of 100-pound sacks of potatoes and flour with smaller sacks of sugar to the basement. Each cardboard box had been carefully sealed with the ever-present duct tape by the woman of the house.

The unloading of the semi-truck ended late afternoon. I was exhausted, and my drive would take another two or three hours as it was beginning to sleet. I said farewell and best wishes to my Amish friends and headed for home.

We corresponded by letter in spring and arranged for me to visit them when the farm plowing began. On April 19th, I received a letter that their son was plowing with a six-horse team; I was invited to stay overnight on May 4th on my way to the Bonduel settlement. There I would stay with a preacher's family overnight and ride to church with them the next morning in the family surrey. It occurred to me I was beginning to visit just as the Amish so frequently do. Was their culture beginning to seep into my veins? And what if it did? Who would I become then?

PART I   *Wisconsin Settlements*

Chapter 4

MARION REVISITED

FRIENDSHIP AND TRUST

I had been invited to return to visit and stay overnight with the family I helped move from Amherst to the Marion settlement. It was May 4th, a warm, clear-weather day for Wisconsin. When I arrived, the woman of the house, Erma, was in the garage stirring a kettle on the floor. There was strong camphor odor, for which she apologized. Actually, it was rather refreshing and cleared out my sinuses. It was to be a poultice, a recipe of her mother's. Later she poured the soupy mixture into small, half-pint jars. Her husband did not like the smell, she said.

After some greetings with her young Amish daughter, Katie, Erma returned to her quilting project. She worked in a small bright room off the kitchen that had a large picture window. It provided generous light on the shaded side of the house. I watched her skillful hands push the needle through the material along faint pencil guidelines. One hand was below the material that was scrolled up on the rack. It pushed the needlepoint back up through the material, and the top hand pushed it back down. This was done quickly for five or six stitches, and then the thread was pulled through. I left her to her work, and went outside to photograph the farm.

PHOTOGRAPHING ISSUES

During the move in December, Erma had asked me in a letter not to bring my camera. Later that day, she would tell me why. It was because a camera would have caused concern and skepticism among her new neighbors as to who I was and what I was up to. "Later," she said, "they will learn to trust you as we do." She thought I may not have understood her request, but I did. Exodus 20:4, "You shall not make for yourself an idol" is well imbedded in the hearts and souls of Amish people.

The photographing on this day was for use in my classes. It included the barn, home, and Red Holstein cows in the concrete barnyard and Belgian and Standardbred horses in the field. According to World Book Encyclopedia, "Standardbred, also called the American Trotting Horse, is considered the best horse for harness racing. Owners train these horses as fast trotters or as pacers. Breeders developed the Standardbred by crossing Thoroughbreds with other types." Photographs also captured Red Holstein calves and one-year-olds in their outdoor pen, a Standardbred stallion, a plow in the field, and equipment in a large storage shed. One piece was a modified tractor complete with rubber tractor tires bolted to the steel wheel rims, and an Italian air-cooled diesel engine. Other pieces included a two-bottom plow, several wagons, seed drillers, hay rake, and silo filler. This was not your father's Oldsmobile. This was heavy-duty farm mechanization, including a threshing machine.

MECHANIZED FARM EQUIPMENT

The father, Abe, and two of his boys, Jacob and Andy, arrived with a wagon filled with stove wood and a corn picker in tow. They unloaded the wood into the garage for use in the cooking/heating stove in the kitchen. Then an older son, Ray, hooked up the tractor's power takeoff to the corn picker to check out the mechanical operation of the picker. Abe stopped him almost immediately when he heard a safety clutch clacking. Something was binding; it was old corn stalks jammed in the conveyer.

Farmers need to be mechanics, and Amish farmers need to know about old equipment and how to repair it. This picker had been stored indoors and was purchased for a good price. Abe planned to add a gasoline engine to replace the power takeoff and a horse hitch. Most Amish do not use tractors in the field to pull machinery. The tractors would pack down the ground and have higher costs due to the higher initial expense plus fuel and repairs.

Three inches of rain the previous week caused some flooding in the house basement. Cows and horses were painted with earth-brown ooze. The soil here was not as sandy and absorbent as at their former farm. Consequently, plowing and planting had to be delayed. Many settlements are founded in the north-central part of Wisconsin because the sandy soil enables the Amish horse-drawn equipment to get into the fields early in spring and shortly after it rains.

CHORES AND CHORES

Chores were dealt out to the boys after breakfast. Ray and Jacob removed the previous owner's useless 8-year-old moldy-baled hay from the mow. The team of horses and wagon evacuated about a ton of hay in two days. A burning permit was secured from a ranger in nearby Symco, and the first pile was lit at 6 a.m. It burned for six hours. The youngest son, Andy, hitched up the pony to a golf course reel mower and cut the lawn. Indoor chores were left to the daughter, Katie.

Milking began at 4 p.m. About 18 cows were still fresh, and three had dried up. The entire family milked by hand, small hands on little teats, big hands on big teats. Abe witnessed the young bull doing his chores in the pasture that day carrying out its job by impregnating cows. This arduous task provides new stock, an economic necessity. More cows means more milk, and a bigger check from the creamery. Jacob was responsible for doling out special supplements to certain cows and grain to all. Milk was poured into a large bulk tank in the milk house. It was cooled and refrigerated with the help of a gas, 4-cycle engine. A commercial cream-ery picks up the milk about five times each week. Electricity was still supplied to this Amish barn, because the seller was English who used fluorescent ceiling lights. They would probably be shut off later to comply with the settlement's rules, the Ordnung.

Horses were enticed into their stalls by the feed placed in their manger. There were 21 horses to care for. Another team of Belgians was being worked for a neighbor to keep them exercised. One team was getting old and worked only half the time. The stud was kept outside the barn to prevent his eagerness from upsetting the rest. One of the three ponies was only a boarder here, another was used to pull a mower and cut grass and one was used for riding and fetch-ing frozen ice cream at the non-Amish Kemp farm nearby. Farms are identified by their owner's name, a matter of pride and ownership.

MEALS AND AFTER

Katie prepared most of our meals. For lunch, we had gravy and potato soup mixed with bread and cracker crumbs. The meat dish was canned beef (not Spam) that had been put up in Ball jars the old fashioned way. It was home-slaughtered beef, and it was delicious. Water and home-made spearmint tea were the choices for beverage. For dessert, homemade rhubarb pie a la mode. For supper our menu included meat, kernel corn with breadcrumbs, "coffee soup," applesauce, and pie. Hardy work demands hearty meals.

At night we visited. Abe was fascinated with a book I had purchased in Bonduel, *Our Heritage, Hope and Faith*. It contained German/English translations for Amish hymns, prayers and confessions. He said he had always wanted a book with these translations. We bartered it for the night's lodging and board. The parents and young boys read my draft of this chapter for this book documenting their move to this farm.

SATURDAY, MAY 5

Most of the farming family was up by 4:30 a.m. for chores and making breakfast. Some of us lingered longer in bed. The breakfast menu was sausage, fried eggs, bread, and garden tea (spearmint). Erma wanted me to take her to a farm auction. She had surveyed the Wisconsin Gazetteer I had given them and knew the back roads. Her goal was to purchase a treadle sewing machine. Once at the auction site, she negotiated with the auctioneers to have the sewing machine put up early in the bidding. She got her way, but the bidding was higher than she was willing to go, and she dropped out. However, she did get some feather tick pillows to remake with quilt-like patterns on the cover to sell at other auctions.

I was invited to stay for lunch. Canned meat was on the menu—-the family knew how much I had enjoyed it the last time it was served. Some light-hearted teasing ended another stay.

SEPTEMBER 11, 2001

Shortly after the terrorist attack in New York, Erma sent me a postcard. She was hopeful that "more people will turn to God after the huge happenings in large cities." It was the first time I ever heard her make a religious remark in her letters or in conversation. My conclusion is that she was deeply moved by the tragedy. She filled me in on some of the projects being tackled by the men in the family, such as building a silo house and pump house. She was doing her fall house cleaning, going to weddings, and attending quilt auctions.

ANOTHER MARION VISIT

On a windy day, May 11, 2002, I set sails for my Amish friends in the Marion settlement. To insure they were home I called their neighbors, the Kemps, to see if they could see anybody working in the fields. They could. With all my cargo stowed away in the trunk of my Honda, I shoved off. As I approached the farm, I could see Andy's pet pony pulling a golf course mower to cut grass along the road. He had built a two-wheeled cart for himself and attached the mower behind and pony in front.

"What are you doing out here?" I asked.

"What are you doing here?" he replied in a surprised voice now deeper than it was the last time I visited. I was to find out later that he had graduated from 8th grade and was finished with his schooling. He was entering manhood through the rites of passage by graduating.

Andy's father, Abe, came out of the barn to greet me. His smiling and friendly face was very different from the first time I met him at his Amherst home three years ago. Then he was cautious, stern, and business-like. But after a few hours of sizing me up, his good-natured self broke through and has remained ever since, as sure as day turns into night. He invited me to go into the house and greet Erma and Katie while he finished his work. His two other sons, Ray and Jacob, were in the south field disking and dragging a five-acre field in preparation for seeding to be done that day.

Erma and Katie were both quilting in a bright room off the kitchen. The six-foot wide picture window on the north side of the house provided soft indirect sun light for the tedious needlework. The quilt rack had wound up all but the last 18 inches of this consignment project. Erma's eight stitches per inch were accomplished with deftness, while apprentice Katie needed more time for hers. She was now 20 years old and according to her mother would become a candidate for marriage in a year or two. She prepared most of the meals for the family and other household tasks to prepare her for the role of wife in the Amish culture. Without her contribution in a marriage, a husband could not be a good provider. Each needed the other. Neither was subservient to the other. Decisions would be made jointly.

Erma was her good-natured self, smiling and chuckling at my teasing comments. Katie looked at me and smiled as if to see if I showed any sign of seriousness in my comments. She seldom added to the conversation, tending to her needlework. However, she announced with excitement that a ruby-throated hummingbird hovered over the feeder outside the kitchen window as she worked at the sink. Erma had put an orange peel on a fencepost nearby to attract the tiny creature. Even the boys found interest in the bird's antics as they helped themselves to the Kringle Danish pastry I brought for a treat. Such opportunities are afforded country folks who value the gifts of nature that they immerse themselves in every day on the farm. Their free-running dog, Rex, would probably become neurotic in a city environment where it would be tied up in a confining yard or house all day.

Even the horses seemed content to work and discipline themselves to the needs of their masters. Ray provided periodical rest stops for them while doing fieldwork. Harnessed horses left unattended while being hitched to machinery stood patiently wherever the farmer left them. Even Andy's pony hitched to the lawn mower would stand wherever he was stopped even though his driver was somewhere else. This master and servant relationship was not an imposition, but an accepted relationship. These animals were well cared for at this farm and they knew it. They knew their place in the order of things. These massive one-ton harnessed Belgian horses unhitched after work in the field walked through the barn unattended without knocking over milk pails in the alleyway on their way to their own stalls. There was order to the slow rhythm of the day.

EVENING RITUALS

The evening was spent in the living room. Abe sat in his reserved chair and looked at a travel book on Germany I had brought along. Andy and I sat in bent hickory rocking chairs while Jacob showed me scrapbooks of his schoolwork that his mother had put together in a three-ring binder. Ray and Katie had retired early upstairs as they had done on my other visits. Erma bustled about organizing for another day. After I retired to the guest bedroom, I could hear Abe read out loud from the Christenpflicht book's evening prayer. It established the boundary between the day's work and rest, just as silent prayers at mealtime delineate one activity from another. Such is the order in an Amish home.

"There is a time for everything and a season for every activity under heaven: a time to be born and a time to die, a time to plant and a time to uproot, a time to kill and a time to heal, a time to tear down and a time to build, a time to weep and a time to laugh, a time to mourn and a time to dance, a time to scatter stones and a time to gather them, a time to embrace and a time to refrain, a time to search and a time to give up, a time to keep and a time to throw away, a time to tear and a time to mend, a time to be silent and a time to speak, a time to love and a time to hate, a time for war and a time for peace." (Ecclesiastes 3:1-8.)

Early the next morning I could hear Abe trudge upstairs to wake the "milk hands." The next thing I heard was a knock on my door. It was time for breakfast and I had slept through the milking time. Everyone was in the living room outside my door as I made my entrance. After pancakes and home made mint tea, I bade farewell and drove off to the Bonduel settlement and the Amish quilt and furniture auction.

PART I   Wisconsin Settlements

Chapter 5
ALBANY
AUCTION HAVEN

The settlement at Albany is north of Brodhead in Rock County. It can be reached from Janesville on Hwy 11, or from Beloit on Hwy 81 and then four more miles north of Brodhead on Hwy 104. A prominent land feature that identifies an Amish settlement are the buildings on the Lester Detweiler farm at N5055 Hwy 104, and the new schoolhouse. For years a consignment auction was held on his farm to include draft horses (Halflinger), horse machinery, furniture, harness equipment and supplies, and quilts. The fall auction was held at the Amish school immediately north of Lester's farm. The newly constructed schoolhouse served as the kitchen and concession, selling meals made by the Amish.

A large circus-type tent seated about 200 people and was the site for the quilt and small furniture auction. Several hundred quilts and wall hangings brought prices from $40 to $1,200. Some equipment and household items are pre-owned, but bring money to the settlement for medical expenses or to maintain the school operation. The fall sale is normally in September and the summer sale in July. As of 2001, only the July auction is held. A small bulk food store with health food supplement products is operated in a front room of the Detweiler home and run by Lester's wife.

Stereotypes Revised
All this information may seem contrary to what you imagined about the Amish way of living. My observations of the auction over the past three years leads me to believe

that this is probably the most liberal settlement I have seen so far. Lester sells the Halflinger workhorses from his herd of about 50. These majestic animals are about the size of the more recognizable Belgian workhorses. This is only the second Amish farm that I have seen that sells such a large number of horses. Only in St. Anna did I observe another horse herd half the size of Lester's herd used as a business to supplement the farm income. Other anomalies about the farm include the rubber tires on hay wagons and carts as well as on modern, ten speed Trek brand bicycles and a Bobcat front-end loader. Lester's son drove the Bobcat in the field to load newly purchased equipment onto flatbeds to be hauled away. Further, Lester's wife used an electric calculator in her "store," but electricity is generated only by a solar panel on the roof of the house. Finally, the visible name and phone number of Lester Detweiler on the auction flyer bears witness to the changes taking place in some settlements.

Two other Amish businesses are on Atkinson Road west of the Detweiler home. One is a small bulk and packaged food store selling mostly slightly damaged goods. The other is the Detweiler-Kauffman furniture store. It advertises "quality and service you can depend on" on a small refrigerator magnet which also includes the address and phone number on it. In Lancaster, Pennsylvania, a 220-page directory of Amish businesses is published which includes phone numbers.

I know the labors of farming having worked summers on two farms as a young boy 12, 13 and 14 years old. I rode a horse on the hayfork, hung an entire tobacco shed of tobacco, and did all the related fieldwork. I mowed hay in the hay loft, shocked grain at night in the cool light of a harvest moon, gathered, washed, and sorted eggs, and drove International Farmall "A," "M," and "H" tractors as well as John Deere, Minneapolis Moline, and Ferguson tractors. I felt at home on a farm as a kid, and now as an adult on Amish farms felt as though I was with kinfolks.

JULY 2001 AUCTION

The last Saturday in July, I attended my fourth Albany auction. This time I was a bidder on furniture. The two items sought were a small nightstand and a bookcase. I got them both. The lady I brought along, Mrs. Arndt, who was experiencing her first Amish quilt auction, also bought two quilt items. She is a quilt maker herself, and now plans to attend the next two auctions in Amherst. The economic climate seems to influence the market for quilts; the buying climate inside the large tent seemed to be dampened by the hazy fog and drizzle outside. This year prices were low and bargains were numerous. Even the auctioneer commented that the bids were some of the lowest he had witnessed. A corner cabinet is a case in point; the cabinetmaker himself was bidding on his item to keep the bidding going. Had he won the bid, he would have paid only the commission to the auctioneer, and then returned the item to his shop with a higher price tag.

Young Amish are becoming entrepreneurs. Two young boys were giving wagon rides around the farm for $2.00. A shorter ride brought 50 cents. Amish and non-Amish alike were steady customers all day long. The wagons had recycled white-walled, rubber automobile tires on them, as did other farm wagons and equipment. This is a sign of the progressiveness of this settlement. Strict Old Order Amish would have steel rim wheels on their wagons. Other boys were keeping canned soda and water bottles cold in a large cattle water tank filled with blocks of ice, readying them for sale.

BAKERY
Another tent housed the bakery goods for sale. It also

provided homemade ice cream being made with a twin-bucket unit powered by an old "hit-and-miss" portable engine. Many customers added a scoop on their pie selection. Cookies and breads were also sold. These donated items raise money for the school operation, teacher's salary, supplies, fuel, and maintenance.

CLOTHING

Amish clothing styles continue to change. The plain people at this auction are brightening up. Men's shirts were shades of maroon, lime green, peach, and mauve. Suspenders were all over both shoulders and two button fasteners in back. Trousers were sporting a side pocket on the pant leg for pliers, other tools, or pens. Straw hats were in a variety of shapes, typical of the wide variety of settlements from which these men came. Each congregation adopts one style of straw hat for adult males and another for male children, usually made of black, lacquered straw. Many did not wear any hat.

Women's styles are changing, too. Black moccasin-toed shoes are now bought in Wal-Mart and other discount local stores. They are the Bass-brand style shoes. Bonnets were seldom seen. Many dresses were void of the typical "bertha," or cape, or v-shaped shawl that is dropped over the head and draped across the shoulders. They are tucked in the waist in back and front. Many old European costumes used these, and as one writer of that day said, their purpose was "not to show a woman's advantage." Pastel colors were the predominant material worn. Fewer straight pins and more stitching from sewing machines were evident.

A unique front dress cover enabled the woman who sat down next to me to nurse discreetly while we "visited." Instead of a bertha, two strips of material criss-crossed her bosom. This enabled her to reach into the left side and provide a covered breast for the child on her right side. When that side was sucked dry, she reversed the process to the left side. The young lady was from the Kingston settlement, so I was able to "catch up" on the medical condition of folks I know who are living there. Auctions provide for the Amish a time to visit relatives from other settlements who bring goods to sell or help in a variety of ways.

PART I   Wisconsin Settlements

Chapter 6

CASHTON, WILTON, CHASEBURG
WISCONSIN'S LARGEST AMISH SETTLEMENT

In the record hot summer of 1995, I spent a month at Brush Creek Campground in the heart of Amish country between Cashton and Ontario, Wisconsin. My comfortable thirty-four foot long Avion travel trailer served as base camp. I was to learn that the campground also served as the sales platform for the local Amish pastries and bakery. It was the place for the Amish families to get ice cream cones and dishes, chocolate shakes, and malts. The owner, Bud, was friendly with many of the 246 or more Amish families comprising the largest Amish settlement in the state of Wisconsin. Within a few days, I had explained to him my purpose in staying in the area, to which he offered his help and advice in my effort to learn more about the Amish culture.

VITAL FIRST CONTACT
Another valued English resource person was Kathy Kuderer. Her husband's father sold his family farm to one of the first Amish families in the area in the 1960s. Her own family still worked a small farm east of Cashton on state Hwy 33. She owned a building built by the Amish to sell their wares on consignment, such as bent hickory rocking chairs, quilts, wall hangings, furniture, and knickknacks. She calls it "Down a Country Road Gift Shop." Kathy had begun a tour service through the settlement for curiosity seekers and serious observers, like me. Her tour was interesting and served to assist me in finding my way around the winding country roads. She introduced me to Amish folks she knew who would be able to answer my questions. As the

summer went by, she questioned me about what I heard from the Amish about her reputation as a tour guide through the settlement. I heard no negative comments, as many Amish had sales in their homes, and she brought business. There were 13 church districts in Cashton at that time, according to my field notes. With about 25 families in a church district, this would amount to 325 families, or 1,959 persons. A state publication puts their population at over 2,000. The document was part of a long project on the Kickapoo River Watershed that bisects the Amish settlement titled, "Soil Conservation Education for Amish Farmers in Southwest Wisconsin."

TAXI DRIVER

The cheese factory provided a communal bulletin board. It was here that I posted my availability as a driver for Amish folks. Soon I was driving Clemens, an Amish man who did carpentry, to the local hardware store for nails and other supplies. Then his wife, Amanda, requested a ride to Viroqua some eight miles away, to a Wal-Mart store. She wore her black dress and bonnet, and came out of the store with several bundles of commercial diapers clasped under her arms. It appeared incongruous. One other trip was to a reflexologist, or "foot therapist," that massaged the foot to cure ills in other parts of the body. Clemens had back problems and this was his cure. We stopped at a restaurant in Viroqua where he sat quietly and ate, belched a few times in a European good-will gesture, and paid for his own meal as well as a stipend to me as the driver. As we reached the settlement, I noticed the friendly hand waving by the Amish in their buggies along the highway. It reminded me of the same tradition on Washington Island, Wisconsin, a large Icelandic ethnic community off the tip of Door County that juts off into Lake Michigan north of Green Bay.

QUILT REPAIR

One rainy spell in Cashton, I brought a quilt that my mother had made years ago to an Amish woman for repairs. I knocked on the back door, and Elizabeth greeted me. When I told her the story of the quilt, what I needed, and that she was recommended, she invited me in. The entrance-way was void of anything except what I later learned was a water heater. It was a large iron kettle about three feet in diameter, surrounded with steel sheeting, and under the kettle was a grate for a wood or coal fire. Inside the kitchen, it was warm and dry from the heat of a large cast iron stove. She examined the quilt, saw the border threads unraveling, and said she could repair it. I told her there was no rush, but that I would return in a few days in case there were any questions she would need to ask me. When I did, I found that the quilt had been repaired at the behest of her husband to tend to it immediately. When I asked her what the charge was, she spoke so softly I thought I heard $50. I repeated it to be sure, and she corrected me. It was $15! I was dumbfounded, and begged her to take $20, which she humbly accepted. I was grateful and inspired by her caring and friendliness.

INTRUSIVENESS AND MYTHS

The Amish Cheese Factory was a "message center" for the Amish. The bulletin board mentioned before was in the outer hallway that was not locked and therefore enabled Amish folks to access it, as well as a pay phone after hours. Notices of local frolics (work projects) and items for sale were tacked up. I bought farmers' cheese there. One day I observed two Amish boys looking at postcards for sale. The cards captured Amish scenes by John M. Zielinski's camera, as well as Amish folks. The boys were excited looking at the cards and exclaimed that they knew some of the Amish folks in the postcards. Adult Amish are not pleased with Mr. Zielinski's intrusive photos.

Another illustration of Amish dislike of intrusion from the outside world occurred when the Amish filed a petition with 573 signatures. Such active political participation is unusual. But they were complaining that a military flight-training plan would result in low-flying jets from Volk Field at Camp Douglas, flying over the settlement at 410 to 615 mph. It would startle cattle as well as horses that pulled the buggies on the roads and highways and would be a safety hazard. The Amish quiet life was threatened. I have heard nothing more about the case.

There are myths about the window curtains in Amish homes. One story I heard was that the blue curtain pulled to one side indicated that there was a young female living in the house, eligible for marriage. Such story was never confirmed, but if it is true, there are plenty of Amish women ready to marry in every household. With six to eight children in most families, the odds are good that all children will eventually marry. In other state settlements, the color of the curtains and how they are hung may vary. One other Pennsylvania Dutch myth from Lancaster was that a blue gate in front of a house indicates the marriage eligibility of a woman in the house. Courtship is done in secret, or at least in the pretence of secrecy. According to John E. Sharp, "In a Gemeinschaft, all are acquainted; every boy knows exactly which girls have reached the dating age."

JULY 4, 1995

It was on Independence Day in Ontario that I observed my first Amish buggy and occupants closely. It was late, and the skies were dark enough to begin the fireworks at the city center where I had parked. An Amish couple was preparing to leave in their buggy, while a child sat patiently on the front seat with a pacifier in his mouth. Someone nearby, a prankster, set off a firecracker. Although the horse flinched, it never moved its feet or spooked. The red triangle slow moving vehicle (SMV) sign was hung on the left rear of the buggy, and battery powered lights hung on both sides with a red lens facing to the rear and a white lens facing forward. The family seemed to be in a hurry to leave before the fireworks started.

As I arrived back at the campground, the Lambright Amish folks whose property straddled the campground driveway were still in the fields cultivating corn by horse and by hoe. The children waved as I passed, recognizing my bright red Suburban. I had purchased some maple syrup from them and watched several hummingbirds feast on the plastic bird feeder that was hanging from their porch. They also sold firewood and rabbits. Later I found out the husband had been in the "lot," or drawing, to become a preacher for the congregation. This was an awesome responsibility. Every able-bodied male must accept it if the "lot" falls to him. Mr. Lambright was not chosen, and the next year the family moved to another settlement. Perhaps the odds were too great that on the next drawing he would become the preacher. Religious leaders are chosen for life with no formal education, so all had better be ready to serve when called.

JULY 5, 1995

Buggies on the highway are a hazard. On this day, I traveled on Hwy 27 between Cashton and Westby, eight miles away. Many Amish buggies were holding up traffic as they traveled in convoy, probably to a funeral. This was a Wednesday, not a church day and probably not a wedding, as weddings are usually in the fall of the year when the harvesting is finished.

Later in the day, I bought strawberries at the Stutzman farm. The farm was for sale and the family was moving to northern Kentucky where his children lived. I saw my first barn raising in progress. I counted 47 men working together both on the ground and swarming over the framework of the barn. Eager to photograph, I naively inquired of two Amish men busily sawing lumber for the project if I could photograph the barn. They looked at each other for what seemed like minutes to me, and then one said to the other, "What do you think?" After a long pause, the second man replied, "Better ask the owner," and then directed me to the owner for his opinion. When I found him, he was busily measuring lumber, so busy that I began to feel uncomfortable and embarrassed for my intrusion. I walked away without a word spoken, and drove away. Had I never inquired and just photographed from my car on the road, I would have captured my first photo of a barn raising.

JULY 6, 1995

Drizzle cancelled my tour of the settlement with Kathy Kuderer, so we visited. She told me that about two acres of their 100-acre farm was in tobacco, used as a cash crop, and harvested for cigar leaf wrappers. None of the Amish here raise tobacco as they do in Lancaster County, Pennsylvania. Although Amish do not generally smoke, the Lancaster Amish do use tobacco as a cash crop, engaging the family in cooperative work, and leave the smoking controversy to others to wrangle over.

Kathy was the one who told me Clemens needed a ride to his reflexologist. I contacted him in his woodshop, and we set a date for his appointment. I invited his wife Amanda to come along and stop at my mother's apartment where we were having a living estate sale. Amanda was eager, and ended up buying a wicker clothes hamper that she said she had always wanted, a canning tub, a bathroom scale and other household goods. When she saw the family heirlooms, such as cake pedestals, set aside in the kitchen cabinets, her eyes beamed in recognition of their vintage, and she quickly asked their prices. She was disappointed when I told her they were not for sale.

JULY 7, 1995

I find information by getting lost. Driving through the settlement, I spotted several Amish men herding two buggy horses to pasture. Pulling the car over to the side, I got out and walked toward the young men for directions to the cheese factory. Although I knew where it was, asking was an easy and innocent way to initially engage the plain people. The elder man, probably the father, began to give some instructions, but was surprisingly interrupted by one of the young men who countered the elder's directions. This was the third time I had witnessed younger people upstaging elders.

Back at base camp, I asked Bud, camp owner, what monetary pay the Amish give for driving them. Bud suggested $7.00 for driving and waiting time, otherwise "they take advantage of you." In the background could be heard a horse drawn cycle mower cutting alfalfa and the strong, almost angry voice commanding, "back, back, whoa."

Later, on Hwy 27 between Cashton and Westby, I saw two very well dressed Amish women walking along the road. Each wore the same "costume" of black shaded bonnet, long dark green dress and black apron. In Westby at a drug store, I saw two young Amish girls wearing green dresses of the same shade, wearing sneakers and looking at lipsticks with great alacrity and giggling.

July 8, 1995

On Norwegian Road, I observed a horse drawn wagon carrying English folks, but driven by what appeared to be an Amish man. Perhaps this was another tour, but I was surprised to see the Amish driver. Perhaps this was a side job.

JULY 10, 1995

I started out the day to find a buggy builder. I thought the place was just off Hwy 33 and north on 16th Court Road, but what I thought was the right place, was the wrong family. Last names are not enough in Amish country. You need to know the first and middle initial as well. For men, the middle initial is the first letter of the father's first name. For example, John A. Schrock's middle initial would be the first letter of the father's first name, such as Amos. In other settlements, the middle initial is the initial of their mother's maiden name. In others there seems to be no uniform practice.

SAWMILL AND HORSES

A young boy who was with a woman picking green beans gave me directions to the wheelwright, or buggy maker. He was a close relative to the boy, which was no surprise to me. But a "slab lumber for sale" sign sidetracked me. I drove into the farmyard and up to an Amish sawmill. The Amish man who ran it greeted me. After I disclosed my interest in Anabaptists and in the noise coming from a metal shed, he led me into the sawmill. A recycled Cummins diesel engine powered all the mill equipment. The owner had created a unique starter for the diesel engine. Instead of the conventional battery and starter motor, there was a shaft inserted in the starter motor housing, which was connected to a 5 HP gasoline two-cycle engine. To start the diesel you started the gas motor, which in turn started the diesel.

He showed me his project, a square-log cabin. It measured 12 feet by 20 feet and was on a skid to enable it to be towed to the purchaser's property location. He gave me a sheet of promotional material and a business card and asked that I might help him let others know about his product, which cost $9,000. The man also worked with two realtors to promote the cabins.

I asked if I might photograph his Belgian horses that were standing near a fence in a nearby pasture. The man was hesitant because another person had asked the same a year ago and the colt that was photographed died shortly after. Superstition is alive in the minds of the Amish. But he let me take the photograph. I then asked about a cinder block building near the white clapboard sided house, and he said it was an icehouse. This was July and the ice blocks inside had been cut last December and would last until this December. One-inch Styrofoam sheets lined the interior walls and ceiling. The man's two boys were running the sawmill as I drove out the long gravel driveway and on to the wheelwright.

WHEELWRIGHT AND TOUR

The carriage shop was south of St. Mary, a small settlement northeast of Cashton. The owner was in his shop and showed me the buggy he was working on. He permitted me to photograph the workbench and wheels he was building and apologized for its messiness, but I needed the photograph. Outside I photographed a horse that was in training to pull a buggy, and a windmill water pump that provided pressure enough to send water to the house and barn. Inside the house, I purchased a quart of maple syrup and a tub of apple butter. Then it was time to return to Kathy Kuderer for my tour of the settlement.

On the tour, an Amish woman rode along to be taxied to her sister's farm. We talked about death, funerals, and cemeteries. A local funeral director picks up the bodies for embalming, and an Amish man builds a wooden casket inlaid with white cloth. Wakes are held in homes followed by a procession of buggies to the cemetery. A simple stone marker is erected later. Cremation is never used.

When we arrived at the sister's farm, I was invited inside where I photographed the cooking stove fired by kerosene. I was presented with a home-baked loaf of white bread, which quickly molded after I had it back to my trailer a few days. How we English rely on preservatives! Another topic of conversation was about baptisms, which occur at 17 or 18 years of age, and about one male who left the settlement shortly after baptism and was shunned.

Next Kathy took me to the farm of a former teacher. He was just arriving himself by buggy, which I photographed from our car. He unhitched the Standardbred horse, and it proceeded without leading to a barn and disappeared. Its grain allotment and water in the barn explained its eagerness to get there without supervision. The teacher, a tall trim cheerful elderly man, was very talkative and asked if I was from a newspaper, noticing the camera hanging around my neck. When I denied any affiliation, my answer cleared the way for him to talk more freely about teacher recruitment and the annual seminars held to train them. He was humorous and affectionate to his one and two-year-old granddaughters who had come out of the house to greet him.

Our final stop for the day was a trout farm on Hwy 33 run by an Amish family for supplemental income. A natural spring fed the bubbling brook that cascaded over rocks and into a pen that held dozens of speckled trout for sale. A young boy sprinkled food pellets into the pen, causing a stirring like that of an Amazon River piranha feasting on a piglet. Then he returned to his chore of cutting the grass. He pushed an "antique" reel lawn mower and his brother assisted by pulling it with a long length of binder-twine clutched over his shoulder.

The complete tour was a two-hour trek on a hot 89-degree day, and I appreciated the cold beer I had waiting in the refrigerator at my base camp trailer. How grateful I was for the conveniences of "our" inventions and comforts. It was a magnificent day.

JULY 11, 1995

Today was equestrian day. I set out to get lost, using that ploy to ask for directions and engage in conversation with Amish "strangers." My first inquiry was at Clemens' brother Joseph's farm. In the barn, I spotted a team of horses that were unusual for Amish. They were Buckskins, distinguished by a black narrow stripe extending from the mane to the tail. The rest of the horse was a sandy color, and smaller than a Standardbred or Belgian. Before I entered the barn, the man of the house directed his son to shovel away the fresh droppings with its pungent odor (spurred on by the 90 degree heat), so I could get a closer look at the beasts. Not only did the boy shovel, he swept! A homemade two-wheeled training cart was in the barnyard. The father explained that it was built to train young horses to pull and respond to rein commands in preparation for their buggy duty.

As I drove back to base camp, I was conscious of the horses in pastures, in fields doing yeoman duty, and all the other reminders that horses are a mainstay in the Amish culture. I recalled the comment of Menno Froese, Beloit College sociology professor and a Mennonite, that without the horse, the Amish culture was doomed. Donald B. Kraybill, author of *The Riddle of Amish Culture*, has observed that one of the most effective boundary markers is the preservation of a horse culture. In his words, a horse is "a striking symbol of nonconformity, [as it] separates the Amish from the modern world and anchors them in another one…Safeguarding the horse culture is one sure way of preserving the continuity of tradition."

JULY 12, 1995

A lazy, eerie fog hung over the base camp at 5 a.m. as I set off to Eau Claire. A sign on the highway advertised furniture at The Wood Shed in Augusta. I knew there was an

Amish settlement there and decided to investigate. As I entered the town, a large sign with bold letters said "Augusta," surrounded by a dozen "coats of arms" of all the service and fraternal organizations in the town and their meeting times. I was struck by the absence of any notice of the Amish. Didn't the town appreciate them? Or did the Amish not want to be noticed?

On Main Street in Augusta, I came to the red brick, two story building, The Wood Shed. The parking lot in the back displayed two artifacts, apparently symbols of Amish handiwork. One was an Amish buggy, and the second was an outhouse. I am not sure the second is complimentary to the lifestyle of the Amish, although it is certainly functional, or whether they would want to be characterized by it as a symbol of their culture.

Inside, the Wood Shed was wall-to-wall furniture, mostly Borkholder brand from Nappanee, Indiana. I engaged a clerk to get permission to photograph some of the furniture, but was refused. Then I asked her about the buggies parked in the parking lot, and she said they belonged to Old Order Amish who had moved away from their previous settlement in order to "preserve the traditions." They had told her there was too much progress where they came from, and that there were no shops at their farms to sell goods. Yet, she showed me a small 10 by 12 foot room in the extreme rear of the building where the "local" Amish furniture was displayed. It included a bent hickory rocking chair, and a few other wood items. From my perspective, this was a sham and a shame. For example, the advertising motto, "Made the Amish Way," is not the same as "Amish Made." We English who do not have a depth of understanding about the Amish culture are taken in everyday by marginally deceiving or deceitful entrepreneurs in our free market economy. Buyers beware.

BUD'S TOUR

Back at base camp, Bud offered to take me with him on a visit to an Amish machine shop. This large metal building was located near the entrance to the farm. Inside were drill presses and new and rebuilt small engines that the Amish use for a variety of farm and home use. Some power generators while others turn circular saws and washing machines. It was 90 degrees outside, but these creative Amish men had designed a blower in the building that kept the inside a comfortable temperature. They were friendly, perhaps because of Bud's familiar presence, and they allowed me to photograph the parts bins and new two-cycle engines stacked up on large shelves. This was an efficient and organized operation! An office desk had service manuals for the engines, neatly arranged, and behind it was a large bulletin board with hundreds of business cards neatly arranged. Bud said later that the local Bishop had told the enterprising men not to expand their business any more as it would distract from their Amish ways of traditional farm work.

Bud's next stop was at another machine shop to order something from the Amish machinist. The day before I had photographed a newborn colt with the machinist's permission. Now the son asked me if he could have a photo of the colt, and months later I was able to send him one. Bud said there was indoor plumbing in the house of the grandfather and son. I marked their farm location on a topographical map of Clinton Township at the intersection of Cary Road and Hilltop Drive. Then we headed back home.

SCHOOL ISSUE

The Amish owned half of the Clinton township land parcels in Cashton in 1995. They began settling here in 1965 because of its remoteness and increased their emigration here after the school case Wisconsin vs. Yoder was settled by the United States Supreme Court allowing all Amish communities to set up their own parochial school system with 8th grade tops. This decision drew the attention of other Amish settlements that were having difficulty with their state and local school boards pressing Amish to attend public schools through the high school grades. Ohio's Supreme Court had settled this issue in 1961.

OBSERVING THE AMISH

By 7 p.m., the campground was quiet. Then the sound of the gravel in the driveway crunched by buggy wheels caught my attention. An Amish buggy pulled up to the campground store and the Borntreger family exited. Dressed in their Sunday best black clothing, family members entered the store. Eager to learn the reason for their visit, I followed them. They had come to have an ice cream and Tombstone pizza treat for their children. They sat at the counter and so did I, to observe. They spoke in the Amish German dialect among themselves.

When they had finished their pizza, the mother, Amanda, acknowledged my presence, as I had been to their farm several times by now. She was vibrant and talkative, and wanted to try the "bar game" I was playing. The tasks was to drop a coin into a large glass jar filled with water and have it fall into a shot glass at the bottom of the jar. If you are successful with a nickel, you get a free single dip ice cream cone. If you use a dime, you get a double dip cone. Amanda got her double dip cone on the first try and was jubilant. Then their oldest daughter tried, but was unsuccessful. Their treat finished, they loaded up the buggy and headed for home, crunching the gravel on the road with their buggy wheels.

JULY 13, 1995

Fog settled over the valley at the campground this morning. Amanda was ready for our second shopping trip wearing her Sunday best, a dark green dress and large black bonnet. The boys wore dark blue pants and shirts with narrow suspenders. Clemens's suspenders had a pocket to hold a pen or pencil. Clemens had asked me to take him to Bud, a burg near Viroqua, to have his second reflexologist treatment. He had trouble with his back and sought the relief provided by foot massage. Amanda told me of a new Old Order settlement in Chaseburg via Hwy 56 and then to County Road O. I set out to find it after dropping off Amanda at Wal-Mart to shop.

PUNXSUTAWNEY AMISH

Along County Road Y, I met an Amish man walking along the road. I asked him where the settlement was, and he replied, "Right here." He was carrying a dozen eggs to a neighbor, John M. Yoder. I offered him a ride in my air-conditioned van, which he quickly accepted as it was a sizzling 94-degree humid day. Surprisingly, I was invited to sit under a huge tree in the yard and "visit" along with sons and a dog, Sparky, which reminded me of a hyena. He had white eyes, and its coat was a gray and silver that gave off an unwashed odor. The family had moved here in October of 1994 from Punxsutawney, Pennsylvania, the town where a ground hog is observed to "scientifically" predict how much of winter is left as of February 2nd each year. But I had not known such trivia, and when I acknowledged my ignorance, John laughed and said, "You live in this country and you don't know about Punxsutawney?" His sons and I all began to laugh and that broke the ice in conversation. John was an engaging man, full of humor and teasing. His sons seemed to enjoy the "theater" of it all and sat contentedly on the lawn while a light cool breeze circulated under the oaks and 100 year old pines. Clemens's wife had told me a saying of the Amish: "Don't let the shade go to waste."

When I introduced myself, John thoughtfully said,

"That's a good English name." Richard is not a name often chosen by the Amish. So, his observation was accurate. We talked about Lancaster, Pennsylvania, and he affirmed that it had superior earth for farming. This is attributed to the care the Amish have given it over the generations and to the natural limestone in the soil, which provides the nutrients and porosity for drainage. He said that Clemens Borntreger was related to them somehow. I talked about my interest in the Amish way of living, photographed the garden and barns for my slide collection to show to my classes, and then we parted. Later, I found out they had moved back to Pennsylvania.

SHOPPING

After picking up Clemens, we stopped at Wal-Mart for Amanda. She carried out two huge bundles of Huggies diapers and cornflakes. After her shopping, she looked over the estate items again at my mother's apartment in Viroqua. This time she bought drinking glasses and a canning cooker that she said she had always wanted. I was glad to see it had found a good home. Her husband held the baby and shared an ice cream cone with him while their two other girls and two other boys sat quietly observing everything in the room. She knew old kitchenware and antiques and they filled her cupboards in her home.

When we arrived at their farm, Amanda gave me money for the trip based on the standard fare for time and distance. I photographed Clemens's wood shop, and then he invited me inside their house. They allowed me to photograph whatever I wanted in the house, insuring that none of the children or they were in the photos. Clemens had made the cabinetry, and colorful and antique dishes lined the shelves of the glass door cabinet. Seemingly contradictory to their austerity, colorful dishes are an appreciation of old and nostalgic items from the past, a symbol of hospitality and not pridefulness. I bought an Amish straw hat for $2.50 from their small craft and quilt store, (a small room off the dining room), and thanked them without much fanfare. The Amish understand simple, brief accolades rather than typical English pomposity and overindulgence. The Amish in their "prideless" ways understand that kind deeds are done as a matter of course and do not require special attention or acknowledgement. Humility would not allow such attention.

JULY 17, 1995

Clemens waved me down on the road. He wanted to schedule another trip to the reflexologist. That done, I went across the road to Clemens's brother and father's farm to get some fresh eggs. His brother handled the transaction in the basement of the house, where he had his room. He apologized for the mess on the floor as it was washday, and there was water on the floor from a converted wringer-washer powered by a Briggs-Stratton gasoline engine. Outside there were many plastic toys strewn about the yard. Plastic balls and bats and a wagon all had evidence of dog chewing—or little hungry Amish children. A small arboretum, or hothouse, was attached to the front of the house where tomato plants were started for their 15' by 30' garden in the front lawn. It was obvious the house needed paint, and the outhouse needed propping up, as it leaned precipitously toward the barn. I reflected that the buildings in this settlement were not as pristine as those in Lancaster where multiple generations pampered their estates. But it may say something else about the English folks who sold the Cashton farms to the Amish in a rather poorly kept and run down condition.

JULY 18, 1995

Today I set out in my bright red Suburban to get lost

again. Along 14th Drive, I photographed several old farm implements—corn picker, hay rake, and baler. An Amish man was walking with a very young child hand-in-hand toward the barn. I could imagine the bonding that was cementing these two and the socialization process that was affected by a teaching father and learning son.

In Dell, the junction of County Road P, Dell Church Road, and Weister Creek Road, I hailed a passing Amish buggy to find out where I was. The Amish man was on his way to Bloomingdale, a small burg to the east, to help repair a metal-sided building for an elderly man who had had a heart attack. He was English and had befriended the Amish in the settlement in words and deeds. His generosity was being returned in kind with a second buggy heading down the road to Bloomingdale. So, I followed County Road P and logged a Yoder farm on my topographic map, and another Borntreger farm at the intersection of S, and another Amish farm just before Bloomingdale. By the end of the month, I would have 47 Amish farms and businesses marked on the map and began to appreciate the size of the settlement. It was a beautiful day to get lost.

July 19, 1995

It was another quiet morning with a thin fog settled in the low areas of the valley. The fog was appropriate for the day as an Amish funeral was being held for a three-month-old baby. The hole in his heart could not be repaired at the hospital in LaCrosse twenty-eight miles away along the Mississippi River. Thirty to forty buggies were parked at farms on both sides of the road, and the horses, still in their harnesses but unhooked from the buggies, fed on the hay in flatbed wagons that were brought into the pasture. Everyone was inside the farmhouse for the service, so I used a tele-photo long-range lens and photographed the horses and buggies from the settlement. The community gathers in times of grief to console the family. Such support is to be counted on.

JULY 21, 1995

Clemens had scheduled today for some driving. We started out at 2:30 p.m. to the chiropractor in Viroqua for his back problems, but the doctor was not in. Then we trekked to Nelson's Agri-center in town for a solution to a radiator leak on a motor. Next, it was off to the reflexologist for another "treatment" on his feet for his back problem. Some Amish seek remedies from non-traditional practitioners. They use less technical equipment and procedures that are simply understood and are in keeping with the Ordnung of simplicity.

We passed through the Chaseburg settlement and Clemens looked at two properties for sale. He jokingly asked if I had any extra money I could loan him. (Two years later, I learned that he had purchased a small parcel and built his own house on it. Then I read in the *Budget* newspaper that Amanda and Clemens became scribes for the *Budget* and were living in the Reedstown settlement near Richland Center.)

Our next stop was the bank and grocery store in Chaseburg. Then it was on to Westby and the lumberyard for cabinet making supplies, but it was closed. Then we tried the lumberyard in Cashton, but it too was closed. Such are the inconveniences of not being able to let your fingers do the walking through the yellow pages! Clemens did get dowels from the hardware store in Cashton that he would use for his cabinet project. Finally he went to a realtor who was also an auctioneer and farmer on Hwy 33 east of Cashton. Clemens was doing his homework for the upcoming move.

JULY 24, 1995

Bud, the campground owner, informed me that a "neighbor" in the next trailer was a psychologist. It turned out that he was an itinerant counselor for the Amish in the Westby area and now in the Cashton and Ontario settlements. I was not able to meet him to find out more about his experiences. I saw my first "courting" buggy on the road this day. They have no cover, seats for only two persons, and are used for courting. The two occupants only were covered to the waist with a "throw" made of buggy canvas material to keep off the misty drizzle that enveloped the couple.

JULY 26, 1995

My brother, Alan Dawley challenged me to answer the question, "What keeps the community alive among the Amish?" My answer included the following:

-Religious fervor, highlighted by a history of martyrdom
-Commonality in clothes, occupation as farmer, geography, and language
-Blood relations, maintained in family genealogy
-Humility, sharing, kindness
-Communication, *Budget* newspaper, the *Diary*
-Farming and quilting
-Fellowship, personal contact, gatherings
-Non-competitiveness

Our culture is constantly confronted with the encroachment of technology into our lives at a pace that can be overwhelming. A series on PBS, the "Lehrer News Hour," once discussed the impact of cyberspace on society. An author on the program was investigating how culture is changed by technology. He was worried about the trend to "anonymity" and the lack of "co-presence" with other human beings, and the boundary deterioration that enables us in cyberspace to "be anyone you want to be" without the reflection of who you really are.

Neil Postman authored *The Surrender of Culture to Technology*, in which he asks, "Where is community?" And Emiti Etzioni, revered sociologist, in his book *The Communitarian Movement*, pleads with people to renew their connection to groups and community both in spirit and deed. Maybe the Amish have it right.

JULY 27, 1995

Today will be my last day with the Amish in this settlement. Two Amish women came to my mother's living estate sale in Viroqua having read about it in a local shopper newspaper. They lived in the Cashton settlement on Irish Ridge Road and were driven to the sale by a hired driver. They bought a kitchen stool, assorted knickknacks, and linens. The older woman recently had knee surgery and was in town to see the doctor for a follow-up. She reminded me that I had failed to charge for an item she bought, and I thanked her for her honesty. After a month with the Amish, I felt comfortable with them. They were no longer a strange group, although different. I understood more about their traditions and personally experienced their friendship, limited as it was, especially with Clemens and Amanda. Little did I know then that six years later I would be writing this book to share my experience with others.

A FOOTNOTE

Heinous crimes are committed against the Amish folks. One example occurred in November of 1995. Michael J. Vieth, a local carpenter from Elroy, stopped in for a few beers at a Wilton tavern, five miles northeast of the Cashton settlement. On his drive home, he came upon an Amish horse and buggy on the road. Recalling how he had to swerve to miss an Amish buggy some time previous and had ended up in the ditch, he became angry. He retaliated by stopping his pickup, removing a 22-caliber rifle from the cab, and firing seven shots at the horse and buggy. He hit the horse five times and shattered the Plexiglas windshield, injuring the passengers. He then proceeded down the road in his pickup and abducted and raped an Amish girl who was walking along the road. He was apprehended and tried under hate crimes law, found guilty, and sentenced to 60 years.

On February 1, 2001, Governor Tommy Thompson resigned to become President George W. Bush's Secretary of Health and Human Services. It was reported by the media that the Governor's wife visited Vieth in jail on two occasions, as they were acquainted because both Vieth's and the Governor's residence were in Elroy. Furthermore, the Governor on his last day had a long list of pardon requests. Michael J. Vieth's name was on it. Fortunately, the Pardon Advisory Board recommended denial, and the Governor concurred without a pardon. The Amish involved in the case sought litigation as a remedy for their misfortune.

PART I Wisconsin Settlements

Chapter 7

ST. ANNA/ELKHART LAKE

A FORGOTTEN SETTLEMENT

In our modern, technological, and sophisticated world, everything eventually becomes obsolete. It is called "planned obsolescence" and fills our garbage dumps with its fruit. Computer programs now satisfy the same marketing strategy by requiring version upgrades. The uniqueness of the Amish is that they are already "obsolete" and need no upgrades except as decided by the community and then at their own pace. Perhaps the only upgrade they have is the exclusive weekly newspaper that brings them up to date with the news of other settlements and their friends and relatives.

The newspaper is the *Budget*, and is published in Sugar Creek, Ohio. Its front-page feature is an index of the settlements, colonies, and Mennonite communities from around the world. Each of these has a scribe, a person who writes a letter to the publisher telling the world of readers what is going on in their part of the world.

One Amish settlement that has not been included in the *Budget* for some time is the St. Anna settlement, sometimes called Elkhart Lake settlement. The name of a settlement is usually the nearest town or landmark. A student in my Amish Culture class told me about the settlement. Her aunt lived in the area and knew of their presence. I decided to visit the settlement after two years of procrastination and asked a lady friend to accompany me. Amish women will defer questions asked by a male outsider to their husbands. However, with a female friend present, I would be able to ask questions with impunity.

BAKERY

A sign on the road advertised the bakery with the days it was closed: "No sales on Sunday, Fresh Bakery Fri and Sat". We were there Monday. The Amish woman who greeted us with a wave was working in a garden. It was the Eli Gingerich farm. The restaurant owner in St. Anna, Mr. Schwartz, gave us directions to the farm and said Eli was the deacon for the settlement. It was two miles west on County Road Q that we found the bakery. The sole schoolhouse for the settlement was on their property, and there were several Amish men at work there getting it ready for school opening. It was not opened on schedule due to a large wedding that had delayed the needed repairs and preparation, especially to the outhouses for boys and girls. A sign over the door of the schoolhouse proclaimed, "St. Anna Parochial School."

Another Amish woman greeted us in the bakery. She freely answered most of my questions about the "herd" of Belgian horses in the field, which were for sale to supplement their income. However, she remained silent to questions that bordered on compromises of traditions and gender roles. Milk prices were low, $10 per hundredweight, and dairy farmers across the country were protesting the low subsidy by dumping thousands of gallons the past few days. She lamented the struggle paying for feed for their herd of 40 Holstein cows, the ones with the black and white patches. She said families were moving to the Livingston settlement because land prices were better. Six families had left already of the 12 that once were part of the community of Amish here. Barefooted and dressed in a lime-green dress without the traditional cape, she sold us one cherry pie, one pecan pie, molasses cookies, and a loaf of bread at half price because it was day old bakery.

The bakery was housed in what appeared to be a new structure. The bakery show room occupied a quarter of the first floor. The second floor appeared to be living quarters. The exterior had typical white clapboard siding, with non-typical red brick, waist high along the bottom perimeter. Windows were the typical same-size across the whole building. A larger house was set farther back and a dilapidated old mobile home was beside it. The mobile home was apparently the previous owner's, probably English.

ANOTHER FARM

The Schlabach farm was the only other farm we saw. It was located south of St. Anna on County Road H. A large sign on the front yard appeared to indicate that cheese was sold there. As we drove in the yard, an Amish woman appeared from the house and explained that the sign belonged to the previous owners, and that no cheese was for sale. The Schneider Creamery from Waldo was the cooperative that picked up milk from their bulk milk tank and that was the name on the sign. The bulk tank surprised me, as I had not found any in the Kingston, Albany, or Cashton Amish settlements. Both of the St. Anna farms had bulk milk tanks. This is "progress" for the Amish done at their own pace. It means higher income as this milk is now marketed as Grade A, because it is cooled by refrigeration. To supplement their income, the husband did carpentry work in the local area.

ST. ANNA REVISITED

In late spring 2001, I revisited the Gingerich Home Bakery in the settlement. The same Amish woman who served me before was behind the counter again. Now they had a small 3x6 inch printed card on the table with their address, location, directions to their bakery, hours of operation, and a hand-drawn cartoon of a chicken stirring something in a bowl with a cookbook in its wing. The caption below read, "We make our bakery from scratch."

CORN PLANTER AND POWER WAGON

After my purchase of donuts and blackcurrant jam, I visited with the young unmarried Amish man, probably one of Eli's four brothers, working on a corn planter. He had just come out of the field and his team of four Belgian horses was dripping with sweat. He was converting the seed feeding mechanism to handle soybeans, which he was going to plant with the corn as an experiment. The soy plant once fully-grown covers the roots of the corn and retains moisture as well as provides nutrients in the fodder. He was socially engaging and personable, and permitted me to photograph a portable power wagon nearby. From other sources, I learned that this wagon might have caused concern on the part of some members of the congregation for being too technical, especially for the Bishop. I had seen these power wagons before in Bonduel. Its four used automobile rubber tires held a frame of about 5x5 feet. On it was a diesel engine with a power takeoff. It was used in the field to power mechanized farm implements, such as hay balers. Horses pulled the power wagon, hay baler, and wagon to catch the catapulted bales. He then gave us directions to another Amish family six miles away and the settlement's harness maker.

HARNESS MAKER AND POTENTIAL SCRIBE

Ivan was located on Hwy 57 about a quarter mile north of New Holstein. A small tent in the yard sheltered an assortment of bakery that his wife made. He was a happy and personable young father, and offered to show us his harness shop. It was in a new commercial metal building filled with sewing machines and leather stock. He knew the harness maker in the Bonduel settlement when I mentioned his name. He said he made a good living with his harness work, enough to support a family and horse and buggy on his six acres of land. Ivan was a recent arrival to the settlement that had grown from six to eight families since last year. He said his wife might be the *Budget* scribe when the baby was a little older. There had been no scribe willing to write the local news for the *Budget* newspaper for some time. He was surprised that I subscribed to it.

There are no other businesses in the settlement's seven other farming families. The traditional farming practice of many generations is perpetuated. It provides the tight cohesive family that works together, so children learn the role they will play as adults.

PART I   Wisconsin Settlements

Chapter 8

BONDUEL
PROGRESSIVE AND FRIENDLY

A compass heading of 320 degrees by air from Green Bay would get you to the city of Bonduel. It is 21 miles northwest of Green Bay on Hwy 29. The city of Marion, where there is another Amish settlement, is located 20 miles to the southwest.

In the *Budget* newspaper, the scribe of Bonduel, Arlene, recorded the names of Amish visitors to this remote area from Shipshewana, IN, Kalona, IA, Lancaster, MO, Wautoma, Milladore, Spenser, Athens, Kingston, Loganville, Marion, Hillsboro, and Mondovi, WI, Flat Rock, IL, and Apple Creek, OH, all in a matter of five weeks. The Amish in Bonduel are remote but accessible; visiting is important for the Amish.

The locations of shops within the area are difficult to find. One student in my class pointed out the general location of Amish homes on a Wisconsin map south of Bonduel along Hwy 47. He was incorrect, but networking helps. At these businesses, I can easily meet local Amish and get information about the settlement. Women run most bakeries, but furniture shops usually have a male available to answer questions. Young, aspiring offspring often help as needed, including serving at the checkout. What better way to put together the teachings in the classroom with the worldly settings of family businesses? Just do not get too worldly. Chambers of Commerce and visitor's bureaus are also helpful. But on this trip, I was not sure what I would find.

Sandy my friend had assisted on the expedition to St. Anna and would accompany me on this trip. English women relate better than English men with Amish women because they speak a common kitchen and domestic vocabulary unknown to most males. Her very presence with me provided a more auspicious beginning for our meeting. Buying something in the shop cinches the bond and opens the guarded conversation to more topics. Allowing the interviewed to know your purpose for asking questions establishes your degree of understanding and experience with Amish folks and will help remove doubts in the minds of the understandably cautious, plain people. Jews remember the Holocaust and incorporate its lesson in their daily transactions. Anabaptists remember years of defenseless persecution in the sixteenth and seventeenth centuries and incorporate those memories in their lifestyle. According to John E. Sharp, "When the Amish emerged in 1693, there was persecution in Switzerland for several more decades; what they experienced mainly in the Alsace and the Palatine was limitations on ownership of land, heavy taxation, etc." What is past is prologue.

This voyage was in late March. It was a Friday afternoon. Little farming activity in the fields has started in Wisconsin that early. The season lends itself to a more relaxed time for Amish and, therefore, more time for visiting. Weddings are usually in the fall, therefore not in conflict with our visit.

MAKING CONTACT

Our first stop was at the "Wood Shed," a furniture store advertising Amish-made goods. Two other stores owned by the same person are in Cambridge and Augusta. After some conversation, the store manager gave us directions to some Amish homes north of Bonduel along Hwy 117. We located a sign on the road indicating furniture and crafts, which was our invitation to drive in. We knocked on the shop door and an average height, friendly smiling woman, Treva

Yoder, greeted us in a gray dress, rubber barn boots, and white head cover. Although the shop was closed until April 14, she granted my request to photograph the buggy in the yard and its hydraulic brake apparatus. She invited us into the garage where she showed us her twin boys' brand new buggies built in Shipshewana, Indiana. The nearest wheelwright is in Marion about 25 miles southwest. Buggy design changes with settlements, but this one has an eclectic design, i.e., a little bit from everywhere. She said she was proud of them and showed us the battery-powered headlights, directional signals, and electric control panel in the cab. The spokes of the wheels glistened with its multi-layered black paint and lacquer. Parts of the upper structure were plastic composite material. The newest buggy had the hydraulic brakes installed on the rear wheels at an Indiana wheelwright's shop. The buggy purchased last year did not. This hydraulic brake system is new to older Amish in this state. It is an example of the creeping invasion of technology from eastern settlements. She also told us of her brother who owned the Lark Country Store, a bulk food store, and gave us a direction sheet to find it.

Her husband, Owen, arrived in a pickup truck as a passenger, and I asked him again if I could photograph his farm machinery the next day. As head of the family, he makes the final decision. He consented quickly and warmly. Then a collie dog greeted us with wagging tail and promptly laid on its back to have its belly rubbed. This friendly, polite behavior is characteristic of most of the Amish animals.

Viewing an Amish Farm

Saturday morning we returned to photograph. Owen greeted us and showed us his furniture shop filled with solid oak pieces built and finished by his brother. A monstrous roll top desk was in the corner. The outbuilding was heated by a kerosene-fueled stove, which gave a homey feel for the shoppers from a dozen cars that drove in. Two Bobcats, rubber-tired, front-end loaders, were in the farmyard. Other equipment included a corn picker, hay loader, grain elevator, and others not identifiable by this city dwelling author. A small four-wheeled rubber-tired vehicle with a power-take-off (a shaft to drive or power machinery) similar to the St. Anna vehicle we saw was used to run these machines. One was powered with a Duetz diesel engine. A vintage Case rubber-wheeled tractor was also photographed, as well as a nearby dead Holstein calf that had been naturally aborted before term by its sick mother. One of the twin Amish sons showed us the seven Belgian workhorses in the barnyard. To pull their three bladed plow, they borrowed a neighbor's Belgian to complete the eight horses required. I photographed a large 25 square foot wooden box in the garage, which was used as a refrigerator. A small Japanese gasoline engine powered a compressor. Large white plastic bags filled with silage stretched 100 yards along a fence line. They took the place of silos. Three girls were on a large 8-foot diameter trampoline in the front yard as we left. Folks inside the house waved at a window as we drove onto the highway.

The Lee and Orpha Yoder farm was along Porter Road, as were several other Amish farms, (including Floyd E. Yoder's) and Ed's bicycle shop. (Ed and Lizzie Ann had two boys and two girls under eight years old.) Lee and Orpha's yard was filled with old machinery, plows, wagons, (one I recalled from a Kingston auction) bicycles and assorted artifacts. Orpha said, "They [items for auction] weren't moving. He just buys too much at auctions and needs to sell it to make space." Two ten-speed or more Trek bicycles leaned against the house. The settlement was filled with bikes, much like Albany. She said there is one school (Deer View on Valley Road), two deacons, and three ministers (one being owner of the Lark Country Store) in the settlement.

A yellow county school bus provides service for some Amish children in the settlement, and was the only one I have seen in Wisconsin. Then it was off to the races, the harness shop.

Harness Shop

Valley Harness Shop is owned and operated by Dennis Bontrager. Horse collars lined the walls near the ceiling. Black leather harnesses hung from hangers in the ceiling. One hanger held a large, egg shaped basket filled with leather harnesses that had been dipped in oil to preserve them. He said this should be done once every three years. Several commercial sewing machines, clamps, and presses were in the back of the store, away from the distraction of visitors and tourists. Hardware buckles, clamps, and snaffle hooks glistened in the sunlight in their pigeon-holed upright boxes in the middle aisle of the shop near the door, and synthetic lines and reins decorated the walls in spiral wheels like hubcaps in a junk yard.

I was welcome to photograph as much as I wanted, and took 24 frames. Dennis asked me if I would photograph a few harnesses that he would like to show to prospective buyers. He was surprised to see me get in close (with my 18mm lens), until I gave him the camera to see for himself. He was surprised to be able to see so much so close. He was running out of business cards so I offered to have some printed in Greenfield at a better price than he was paying. It was gratifying to be able to return a favor. While I photographed, Sandy chatted with Dennis's wife, Mary, and their special handicapped child of eight years in their home that abuts the entire length of the shop wall. Next on our agenda was a visit to Mary's father's bulk food store.

Bulk Food Store

Melvin Miller owns the Miller Crafts and Food Store.

It carries groceries, bulk food, spices, organic whole grains, whole wheat, bread flour, LP tank refills, homemade hickory furniture, quilts, and crafts according to his business card. We learned much more in the two hours we spent there with him. He is a short man with black hair somewhat short and wore a black knit watchman's cap. A toothpick was parked on the right side of his mouth while he talked. Cautious at first, he soon fed me a *Sports Illustrated* magazine article (March 5, 2001, pg 46-60) about Amish boys playing basketball coached by the only black coach in Holmes County, Ohio. Melvin grew up in this area. He knew I was writing a book and showed us another *Budget* newspaper, a local edition for Sugar Creek, Ohio, with another newspaper article about a relative of his. Then the *Wisconsin, Minnesota and Montana Amish Directory* was presented. It listed all the settlements as of 1996, with a history of each as well as religious leaders and residents. I had seen it only once before in Kingston at Pleasant View bakery. Seeing my delight, he loaned it to me. It had hand-drawn maps of each settlement with locations marked where each family lived. This was a key to finding the settlements.

Then there was the *Green Bay Press Gazette* from August 20, 2000. Melvin showed us a full-page article on Bonduel that quoted him and pictured his shop, "Katie's Kupboard." I asked him if he read much of the *Martyrs Mirror*. (This is a 1,100-page recording of 17 centuries of Christian martyrdom). He said yes, and asked Mary, his daughter, if she had. She replied no. A 6,500-watt generator running in the garage next door kept a 60-watt bulb glowing near the electric powered cash register. As darkness fell, Melvin lit the three gas mantle light fixtures suspended from the ceiling. I had obtained his permission to photograph the house and store and proceeded to do so. Sandy noticed a solar cell panel on the roof that trickle-charged batteries. We then left to go to Lark County Store, run by a preacher.

LARK COUNTRY STORE

We found this store through Treva Yoder, the preacher's sister. She and Owen are on the farm on Hwy 117 described above. She gave us a single sheet of paper showing their merchandise and some hand-rendered items and profile of the store, as well as address and phone number. The store was 80 feet long and about 40 feet wide and was made of white sheet-metal horizontal siding with narrow rectangular windows under the eaves and across the length of the new building. There was a full bathroom at the west end of the building for customers and perhaps family and worshipers at church. It also had a tub, shower, hot water, and catalytic space wall heater. The store was the family's primary income source. The preacher, Chris, also did carpentry and said he missed working outdoors and farming. The grounds were impeccably clean and organized. Inside the store, the same meticulous attention to detail stood out. Shelves were in order and nicely spaced. The clerestory windows flooded sunlight onto the gleaming interior white plasterboard walls. As I talked with the preacher, Sandy meandered through the aisles, keeping a keen ear to the conversation in order to corroborate what we each heard.

Intuitively, I knew he was a preacher, despite his young appearance. I had spoken only with two other religious leaders. He brought out his "Luther Bible" with cross-references in the passages. It was in High German. He gave his sermons as he was moved to do so, but with a plan in mind and scripture to carry his lesson for the day. I asked if they had the *Ausbund*, the longest continuously used hymnal in the Christian faith. He did, and his wife fetched it from the shelves. It was an artifact to show to my classes, so I bought it. He knew my purpose for coming to Bonduel, and asked if I had read *One Way Street* by Elmo Stoll (former editor of Family Life Newsletter). I had not. He suggested I do so; therefore, I bought it, as well.

Then the miracle of miracles happened. He had a paperback book containing all the scribes for the *Budget* newspaper. Titled *Who is Who* it is published by the *Budget*. Each scribe had written something about themselves and their family archival information, including their home mailing address and phone if they had one. What a gold mine of vital statistics! Maps of each state pinpointed the location of each Amish settlement and Mennonite congregation in the continental United States. It easily and quickly provided the contacts I would need to write this book.

Now his wife, Emma, brought us a slice of her homemade rhubarb pie. We talked about the bent hickory rocking chairs he had for sale for $175. His supplier is from Michigan and uses screws instead of nails in his rockers. He asked me what I thought kept the Amish together, and I said, "Your faith and family." Later as we left, he came out to the parking lot to ask me if I thought the language and clothing also held them together. I agreed. Watching his three well-mannered children around us all this time taking in every detail proved my point.

Chris had a sizeable investment in inventory. Except for Sundays, he is open all year round. When he is traveling to other settlements or doing carpenter work, he has another person fill in for him. Many regular customers come from Green Bay for special items. We discussed the possibility of hearing him preach some Sunday morning and staying with them in their home. When it came time to check out, I did not have enough money or my checkbook. They do not take plastic money. He totaled up my bill, gave me a copy and said to send him a check for $26.48 in the mail. Seeing this enterprising young father gave me a positive and optimistic outlook for the Amish in this settlement.

DEER VIEW SCHOOL
Experience is the name we give to our mistakes.
(Anonymous saying for the day written on the front board)

The Deer View parochial schoolhouse was off Potter Road at Valley Road. The relatively new one story building, about 80 feet long, looked bright and plain. We knocked on the door without success, so we entered what was the basement and called out if anyone was there. Two young Amish women greeted us. I told them my mission and they escorted us upstairs. They had been cleaning the classroom that was already spotless. The single open classroom had matching desks for 30 scholars from first to eighth grade. Reading material and workbooks lined the windowsills in neat stacks. The only heat came from a grate in the floor, below which was the coal burning stove, (coal supplied by Lark Country Store) and a propane stove. The two women lived in an old cream brick square house a football field away from the school. Its windows were winterized and covered with clear plastic and new shingles covered the roof. A small metal pole building protected their buggy. Their horse was in a neighbor's pasture next door.

VISITING THE CLASSROOM IN SESSION
When I arrived at the school on a warm October day, "playground" was in full swing. Scholars were playing baseball during midday recess following lunch. One group was comprised of older scholars, while a second group was younger. A third group, made up of the youngest children, was playing kickball. Altogether, I counted 47 children. Lila, the teacher, and Rose, the substitute teacher, were also involved in the games, not as umpires or rule implementers, but as players and respected equals. A rotation system moved players from the outfield through third base, shortstop, second base, and first base, and then on to pitcher and

catcher before batting. They all knew the system, including how many bases to take on an overthrow error to first base. One overweight seventh grade boy was the only challenger of the routines. Other players, however, politely advised him of his errors, and he obliged by complying quietly. One ring of the steeple bell ended the recess, and everyone promptly ran to the school's back door.

Their demeanor changed from ball player to scholars the moment they entered the room. Each sat quietly until all had taken their seats. Then Lila began to read *Summer of the Monkeys* by Wilson Rawls to the class. This is a classic story read to many Amish generations. An eighth grade girl fiddled with hair at the nape of her neck, sticking it under her white starched cap. A first grade boy opened a window next to his desk for cool air. Many turned around to look at me, curious as to what an English man was doing sitting in the back of the room.

No other words were spoken during the teacher's 20 minute reading. Scholars behaved respectfully and responsibly with self-discipline. Humor did elicit soft chuckles. Then Lila stopped reading. She stood up and pulled a green sheer curtain along a wire suspended a foot below the glossy white ceiling, separating the two teacher groups. Scholars immediately opened their desks by lifting their desktop, removing books or materials, and proceeded with the work written on the front blackboard.

Scholars raised their hands for help. Teachers moved about the room to answer questions and give direction or clarification with pleasant smiles and soft voices. This was the second year teaching in Bonduel for Lila, and the second time this year for Rose. The regular teacher was attending the funeral of a relative. They wore white caps; Lila wore a colorful blue dress, and the substitute wore a purple dress without an apron. Their black stockings were evident as they ran the bases at recess. Their dresses appeared to be one piece without the use of straight pins except to secure the bosom. Some call the triangular cloth piece that drapes front and back from the shoulder a bertha, or cape. It appeared to be an integral part of the garment, but is usually a separate piece pinned on. This was the contemporary fashion worn by these two young women.

Younger scholars were seated in the front of the classroom, older ones in the back. Groups were summoned to the front of the room for short lessons with the teacher. Flash cards were used for phonetic sound drills. Workbooks for math and English were checked and reviewed. Reading groups read short selections out loud. Other groups covered the apostrophe mark in singular and plural possessive forms, noun and verb recognition, and spelling. First graders were using scissors to cut out a monkey related to the storybook reading. Classroom management and organization were impressive, the like of which I have not seen in many public school settings.

Six young Amish women entered the back of the classroom and sat on the bench provided for visitors. One woman carried a baby who was adopted. Its cooing sounds attracted the attention of several scholars, but the lessons went on unhampered. I asked one of them, "Do you have a child in class?" to which she replied, "No, we have nieces and nephews in the class." All signed in the Guest Book on the bench including me. I had nothing but praise and high marks for the teachers and scholars.

Becoming restless, I now turned my attention to the cloakrooms. The girls' side had a framed inscription from Numbers 32:23: "Be sure your sin will be found out." Estelle, a fourth grader, asked me about its meaning the evening I stayed at her parents' house. I answered that it was better to admit your sin than to feel guilty. She accepted my response. The boys' cloakroom had scripture from Philippians 2:14: "Do all things without murmurings and disputing."

One songbook had this inscription: "It does not take a great mind to be a Christian, but it takes all the mind a man has." On a shelf were a pile of songbooks written in German, *Das Neue kinder Lieder* and *Mir Lessen und Sprechen Deutsch*, and a dozen well-used and tattered copies of *Cassell's German and English Dictionary*. I found Estelle's brother's math book that showed good scores and I informed his parents that night. He was humble but proud of his accomplishment. A set of *History of the Patriarchs for the Young* and *World Book Encyclopedia* adorned the back shelf. In the field outside, I noticed an Amish girl instructing another girl how to ride a horse using a Western saddle. Then the silence was cut with one ding on the teacher's desk bell, and scholars immediately became physically and verbally active.

This was Friday—the day to clean out the trash from the desks and put it on the floor to be swept up, and to clean the room thoroughly. Buckets of water and mops along with brooms and dust cloths appeared with a brigade of workers swarming over the room. They began washing the blackboard and sweeping the floor. And I got out of the way. Now the presence of a guest was totally ignored. It was time for me to leave. I thanked Lila and praised her work and dedication.

IMPRESSIONS

This was my first experience in a working Amish school, and I was impressed. In these three hours, I had witnessed the forging of the Amish adults-to-be: disciplined, obedient, quiet, respectful, humble, kind, honest, and sincere. School is part of a continuum from home to church. Children see a consistency of lifestyle between all three institutions of Amish society. There is security in its certainty that fosters confidence in the youth. There is a rhythm and predictability of life; seasons come and go with planting and harvesting beating out the meter. The routines in school create an atmosphere of familiarity and repetition rather than challenge and competition. Mistakes are experience, not failure.

As I read the book, *The Amish School*, by Sara E. Fisher and Rachel K. Stahl, I realized that the routine is so consistent in other states that moving to another settlement is not traumatic for the child. One example is the hot lunches prepared by parents on a rotating basis and brought to school on an organized schedule. Such is the case in Bonduel, according to Estelle's mother, Emma. Parents are involved in their school, and their cherubs know it and feel secure in that awareness.

TOO WORLDLY?

I enjoyed visiting with Estelle's parents and her brothers. Yet, I began to question how friendly I should be. Were they becoming too exposed to worldliness with my visits? It was time to ask the parents that question before my presence intruded too much in their lifestyle. I had asked the question in a letter I wrote to them the week before, and I needed to follow up. I called and talked with their father, Chris, in the store. He said he and Emma had started to discuss the issue. He deferred any decision until we could discuss it in person. He assured me that I was not the only person that was often visiting with the children.

Although my visits were enjoyable and provided insight into the Amish culture in this settlement, I felt a responsibility not to violate their values and principles. It was a relief to raise the question with Chris. But it raised other questions as well. What are the parental guidelines for raising their children? Are they derived from scripture? Are there admonishments from the church leaders? Are standards set by the interchange of families in the settlement on church days, weddings, and funerals? To what extent should Amish folks befriend English folks? Where is the dividing line between friendship and enterprise? As for my visits, how often is too often?

I needed answers to all these questions to discipline my behavior and stay in the good graces of these generous people. The more I learned, the more I questioned.

Meeting a Scribe

Then it was on to the next appointment with the settlement scribe for the *Budget*. Arlene had approved my request the day before to visit at 3:00 p.m. A college student was also scheduled to meet at the same time with her for an interview, but never appeared. The Bontrager home was attached to her daughter's home, and Grandma was caring for their daughter. It is a universal arrangement to have the two generations living side by side, called the Gross Dawdy Haus (grandfather house). Their home was still under construction with insulation and aluminum siding being applied. The large open living room was appointed with two overstuffed davenports, two desks (one for her income tax service business), rockers, and a large frame with a quilt in the making. Several non-flowering plants framed the picture window.

Arlene was short and full-figured, in her mid-50s (my guess), and was just finishing her hair as we arrived. She wore the traditional white bonnet and a dark maroon dress without a bertha (a triangular cape worn over the shoulders, tucked into the waist in front and back). She held a sick granddaughter in her lap (their adopted son's who now owns the farm) and rocked gently in a bent hickory rocker as we talked. She said getting all the news for the *Budget* was not easy, but has done it for 20 years. A good source for gathering news was at church and lunch afterwards. She remembers most of it, hand writes it, and ships it off to Sugar Creek, Ohio, where it is published weekly with other scribes' articles from around the world. This family lived in Evansville before moving to Bonduel in November of 1989. Both her husband Ivan and she taught school, teaching 12 years. She verified that Amish often travel to Mexico for medical attention because of lower cost and alternative remedies for cancer.

Ivan told of a young Frenchman who saw the movie

Witness and wanted to become Amish because he admired their steadfast faith. He also took pride in the fact that Bonduel Amish young people are not into "rumspringa," or running around. In some settlements, it is common for youth to "sew their wild oats" before committing their lives to the faith in communion. They may secretly smoke (as Ivan did!) or even buy cars in this last taste of "civilized" culture in order to make an informed and total commitment to the congregation. He said there is an Ordnung (unwritten rules of the congregation) Conference semi-annually in which there is a review of current rules and consideration of new ones.

After the visit, Ivan wanted to show us his horses. Ivan is a short, medium build man with dark hair and eyes, and a salt and pepper wavy beard. His conversation is engaging to the point of demanding your attention. He pleasantly rambles and at one point Arlene needed to bring him back on track. Liberalizing traditions is a concern of his, and he described the schism that took place in the settlement when the conservative faction opposed the use of tractors in the fields. From my observations in the settlement, it is already liberal. One observation by a bed and breakfast owner in nearby Shawano was that people in the area had viewed the Amish as a closed community. But within the last five years, that perception has changed greatly as people became familiar with each other through the quilt auctions and other business enterprises the Amish operate, including a business that now offers tours to various farms and businesses in the area.

The massive Belgian and trim Standardbred horses were in a water soaked pasture. Ivan called to them in some German dialect and they all immediately came to him. Belgians are huge animals, their shaggy winter coats making them appear even larger. The imprint of their hoofs was as large as dinner plates. They are not shod because they work in fields, not roads where the footing is less secure. Horseshoes are needed on the Standardbred horses and are changed about every six weeks. The shoe is literally nailed to the hoof. It was time for us to leave after a busy and gratifying visit with the Bontragers and the Bonduel settlement Amish people.

AUCTIONS

It was a warm, sunny Saturday in late April when two of my students from the Amish class at UW-Waukesha joined me in Bonduel for an auction. Gavin Donaldson, a photographer, is from New Zealand. Mary was raised near Augusta and is familiar with the Amish settlement near there. Neither had ever attended an Amish auction.

We saw some familiar faces as we walked up the drive to the main event. Ivan Bontreger and his wife, Arlene, the settlement's scribe, arrived at the drive at the same time and we greeted each other. It is a good feeling to be recognized as a friend by the Amish you have met. Later I recognized Abe (from Marion settlement) in the crowd and introduced my two "scholars" to him. They were delighted to be able to carry on a normal conversation with him having learned some background in class and in their reading. He was full of humor, relaxed, and enjoyed the visit. He was there to buy a single bottom plow for his farm.

YODER AUCTION

The auction was at Lee and Orpha Yoder's farm. Lee had gone to many other auctions and picked up bargains and put them all together at this auction in hopes of increasing their worth and his supplemental income. A large poster was headlined with the Yoder's name in red with horse and black buggy silhouettes at the top. Hundreds of farm implements were listed, some as antiques and collectibles. A few

Haflinger colts and horses were listed to go on the "block." Lightning rods with round colored glass balls sold for $20 apiece. Milk cans, a sausage stuffer, horseshoes, broad ax, copper boiler, and oxen yoke were sold, the last for $90. Perhaps it will hang above somebody's mantel symbolizing "teamwork." Andy Rooney would have fun with this one.

A large lettered part of the poster said: "Lunch served by the Amish." It was sold inside a metal building with a few tables and church benches to accommodate the hungry. A dozen women worked in the makeshift kitchen to prepare hot dogs, hamburgers with chips, and washtubs filled with ice and canned soda. A variety of homemade pies invited our attention, with a la mode as an option for only $1.50.

The majority of buyers were non-Amish. Their cars and pickup trucks lined Porter Road west of Bonduel. Only a few Amish buggies were parked on the front lawn of the farmhouse. Perhaps there was something special about an auction. It drew the two cultures together for a while, and maybe longer. Perhaps it would keep them compatible, if not downright friendly, for the next generation as well.

Bonduel Quilt Auction

On May 12, Mary and I returned to Bonduel. Along the way, we picked up two Amish women from Marion. One had two quilts in the sale and the other wanted to shop at the Lark Country Store for supplies. The store is owned and operated by an Amish preacher in the settlement. A large circus type tent was set up in a field on Porter Road as it has been for several years.

Mader and Mader Auctioneer Service took charge, but Amish men and women worked also. Several men hung up the quilts and wall hangings on a large display board on a flatbed trailer where the auctioneer sat. Several were in the audience of over 200 "hawking" bids and shouting out when somebody bid in order to alert the auctioneer. Women were in the racks of 300 quilts bringing them forward to the flatbed in sequence. Lee Yoder was in the field with a portable bullhorn auctioning off furniture. He has attended many auctions to collect the massive number of items for his own auction described above. He even sounded like an auctioneer. I have seen licensed Amish auctioneers at other auctions.

Farm machinery was auctioned off in a pasture. One 15 feet long and 7 feet high corn husker sold for $7.50. The general economy seemed to keep people from spending very much. Quilts sold for $125, exceptionally low return for a lot of work donated by the settlement's Amish women. An Amish man bought a portable 1000kw generator for $300. One wonders what his application for it will be.

Amish children were omnipresent. A team of four pulled a rubber-tired wagon filled with kids around the gravel roadways in the yard. Another half dozen played with a dozen baby domestic and wild bunnies corralled inside a wire fence. Some squeezed them tightly and then dropped them from one or two feet. It seemed they had never held animals or pets before. I asked the spectator older girls to have them be gentler, but they did not respond to my plea. An Amish mother came by and witnessed this behavior, but did nothing to correct the situation. An older Amish boy chased several younger boys away from a large pond in the pasture. It reminded me of Mishler's son who drowned in a situation like this. Three boys were riding bicycles and scooters in the yard next door when a pregnant Amish woman came out of the house and scolded them in German. They left the yard, and she turned to us and said she was concerned and surprised that parents were not supervising them more carefully.

The harness maker, Dennis, was also working in the tent. He needed business cards reprinted, so I had some made and delivered them to him. He also wanted a copy of a photograph I had taken weeks before of a complete harness in his shop. He would use it for advertising. His wife recognized and greeted me while working in the kitchen and carrying her child on her hip. She told of another auction at Melvin Schmucker's farm in Sugar Grove, Wisconsin, the first Saturday in June.

Ivan Bontreger was sitting in a folding chair outside the tent. I knew his 95-year-old father was not well and had not been eating or drinking. Ivan said he had died and asked if I was coming to the funeral tomorrow. I felt honored to be asked, but had just gone through the death of my mother who was 94 years, and felt I would appear to be too much of a spectator at this solemn time. Ivan was upset after seeing his father in the hospital with tubes in him.

Earlier I had driven the two Amish passengers to the house where the corpse lay in state in a wood coffin. A 40' by 60' farm shed had benches arranged inside for the service. An Amish graveside prayer in a documentary video ("The Amish: A People of Preservation," narrated by John L. Ruth) leaves this message:

"Here man, discover what you are
Learn here what your existence is
How swiftly flees your span of life
From time into eternity."

Even Ivan's wife was put to work at the auction. She was on the flatbed trailer where the auctioneer was. Her job was to maintain the documents with bids and buyers' numbers. As bids were final, she recorded the dollar amount and the bidder's number on a card issued at registration. This card was forwarded to the cashier in a nearby shed. Just before we left, we saw the preacher doing the same recording at another corner of the house where household goods were being auctioned off.

This community of Amish comes together at auction

time to raise needed money for medical expenses and school operation or for any other emergency that a family sustains. They are a *Gemeinschaft* society, as sociologist Ferdinand Tonnies used the term, where there is an "intimate community," and everyone knows everyone else, where people closely identify with one another, and where there are shared values. These societies are slow moving, with little stress on advanced education, where the elderly are cared for at home, and morals are seen in absolute terms. The opposite is called a *Gesellschaft* society where there are short-term relationships stressing individualism and self-interests. I believe the Amish have it right.

CHURCH SERVICE

The overnight with my Marion Amish friends was joyful. Now it was on to Bonduel and another overnight with the preacher's family I had visited before. The next morning I was promised a buggy ride to the church service. Chris and his young wife Emma ran the Lark County Store at W5431 Lark Road (open 9 to 5 except Sunday) and had a business phone in their new bulk food store.

His three young children were in the store to run errands and do small tasks. The 10-year-old girl, Rhoda, was sent to shut down the refrigeration on the large communal freezer. It was a 48-foot long semi-truck trailer and used the diesel refrigeration unit mounted at the front of the trailer. Special insulation covered the interior walls, and large shelves held food of individual family stores.

I bought another book, *Our Heritage, Hope and Faith*, to replace the one I gave to the Marion Amish family. It contained translations of songs, prayers, and hymns used in the service the next morning. A few potential customers came into the store but purchased little. They were more curious than serious about buying. Because it was not busy,

Preacher Chris announced we could visit. Amish like to visit. I must have established a trust with the preacher, as he shared how he sold a farm in Indiana to move here. The leaders did not approve a farm practice that he assumed would be. Reluctantly, he turned to a business, the bulk food store. There was already a smaller, older store in the settlement, Melvin Miller's, but I never saw Amish trade there.

After the evening meal, the propane floor lamps were lit and the children huddled around to show me a picture reading book. The youngest boy, Harold, turned the pages and made a running commentary about the persons and objects on the page. The middle boy, Paul, translated whatever I did not understand. The daughter, Rhoda, quietly observed the event, content to watch her brothers politely and without interference. This was Harold's time. Then I was ready to retire for the evening to prepare for a long, three-hour church service in the morning.

Buggy Ride and Church Service

Chris brought the buggy horse out of the barn and hitched it up to the surrey. No horse collar was used. Collars collect salt and dirt and embed in the leather to create a sandpaper-like surface. This in turn can scrape the hair off the skin. Instead, a cushioned wide leather band stretched across the chest of the horse. It was against this that the pulling power was generated. Hydraulic brakes scraped and ground on the hills. Such brakes are rare in Wisconsin-made buggies, but seen on buggies from Ohio. (See *Plain Buggies* by Stephen Scott, Good Books). The ride was pleasant at eight miles per hour as the preacher put the 14-year-old horse through trot, pace, and gallops with a jiggle of the reins. Mother and children sat silently in the rear seat for the entire trip, perhaps enjoying my excited conversation and the scenery. Soon we arrived at the farm where the service would be held.

Chris led his horse into a barn at the host's farm. As I
followed inside, a dozen men had formed a semicircle to
greet newcomers. They seemed friendly and the man next to
me immediately engaged me in small talk that lessened my
nervousness. Then I witnessed what the preacher told me
about the night before, the holy kiss. (See Rom 16:16; I Cor
16:20; II Cor 13:12; I Thes 5:26) Each newcomer embraced
each Amish man, cocked his head to the right, and quickly
pecked a kiss on the lips of his brother. I saw no lingering
or puckering, except perhaps to cushion the collision. It was
the first time I had seen such a greeting.

Ezra, brother to Ivan and brother-in-law to Arlene, (settlement scribe to the *Budget*), escorted me into the house for
the service. He offered me a seat on the long benches in the
front row. I recognized the religious leaders sitting there and
politely declined the seat saying, "I don't belong up there."
Ivan answered, "We're all the same," as he had when I interviewed him and his wife in their home weeks before. I sat
in the second row next to Ivan who pointed out the place in
the *Ausbund* as they sang hymns from the longest used hymnal in Christian history from the sixteenth century. Many
were written in dungeons in Passau, Germany, which I visited in 1999. The order of service is listed in Kraybill's *The
Riddle of Amish Culture*:

Fellowship upon arrival
Silence in worship areas
Congregational singing
Leaders meet in separate room
Opening sermon
Silent kneeling prayer
Scripture reading by deacon
Main sermon
Affirmations from ordained leaders
Kneeling prayer, which is read
Benediction

Closing hymn
Members' meeting
Meal
Fellowship

"The Amish have no organ, offering, church school, ushers, professional pastors, printed liturgy, pulpit, cross, candles, steeples, robes, flowers, choirs, hand bells, altar." (p.102). A lead singer started by singing the first word or syllable of each line of the hymn in the *Ausbund.* There are no notes or staff to refer to. The second song of every service is number 131, page 770, the "Lob Song." Scripture reading was from John 3:16. Two other prayers were given while the people knelt in the following unusual manner. The men suddenly crouched between the benches, thrust their legs under the bench in front of them pivoting at the same time, and pressed their chest down on the bench where they were sitting. I sat. I would have caused a disruption trying to perform this movement. The benediction was given as they stood. I sat, not disrespectfully, but in deference to the solemnity of the moment.

Although the entire service was in "Pennsylvania Deutsch", the guest Bishop spoke a few words in English: "We all fall short of the glory of God." I thought the message might have been only for me, as I neither read nor speak German. He repeated it and I knew it was for me if I had not gotten it the first time. Later he used English to proclaim: "The Lord gets more important as I get less important." This he also repeated. I mentally retraced my steps since my arrival and could not think of any action that would have called for such reprisal. I was later reassured the message was for everyone. When we are in a foreign culture, people speculate about us, and they are the spectators.

There were 25 families in this settlement. Nearly 125

persons attended this service. The home was a two-level ranch style house built in the 1970s. Women sat on chairs and benches on the upper level kitchen and faced the center of the house. The preachers stood at the bottom of the steps leading down from the kitchen. A bathroom, designated for women's use, was to his left. Throughout the service, young girls and older women walked past the preacher to that facility without interruption or comment to use the room. On the main floor, which was the living room, men and boys sat on narrow wooden benches facing the preachers and the stoic looking women "on stage" in the kitchen. Behind the men were younger women and mothers with their babies. A bed was used to change diapers or settle tired babies on it with naps. A removable partition may have separated the two rooms before church service.

LUNCH

Following the service, the living room was rearranged to serve lunch. Two benches were placed together and an extension added to their legs to make a table. Glossy white paper was rolled out and clamped down. There were no napkins or plates and only a knife and fork at each place.

Women servers placed stacks of homemade white and dark bread at intervals directly on the tables. A soup dish was filled with peanut butter and laced with a light corn syrup. Another soup dish was filled with bread-and-butter pickles, another with sliced pickled beets. There were no salt or peppershakers on the table.

Following this first course, servers came with plates of cheese and bologna for sandwiches. Some of us placed them on the table, cut them into bite sizes, and ate them with our fingers or forks. Finally, women servers offered milk, coffee, and homemade garden tea (spearmint). A short silent prayer ended the meal.

VISITING

Visiting followed. Young teens went outside for volleyball in the front yard; about 20 participated. Another band of young men gathered in a barn and yard. Younger children played in a sandbox. Two coaster wagons were hitched together and filled with riders. A team of four boys served as horses for the wagons and they circled the yard on the gravel driveway.

Women did housework. Men clustered together in the house on benches in small groups of six or eight. They would often eavesdrop on conversations in nearby groups. Ivan offered to instruct me on the German words in the *Ausbund*. After a few lessons on the letters, "v, "w", "f" and "b", we moved on to the topic of "rumspringa" which brought smiles to the faces of the young unmarried men gathered. It means "running around." It is adolescent time when some young "sow their wild oats" before deciding to join or not join the congregation and become baptized. Only then are they truly Amish.

Suddenly there was a call for silent prayer said in German. This was the beginning of the second meal serving at the tables. Everyone stopped talking and moving, bowed their heads, and remained silent for about one minute. There was no announced end to the prayer, but people gradually began to talk and move about.

Lee Yoder, who had held a large auction at his farm the week before, told me about the process of shunning and banning (excommunicating) of church members. Those who have not joined the church are not shunned or banned because they have not come under the rules of the Ordnung. In the case of adultery by members, excommunication is almost automatic. Smoking, if not curbed after repeated counsel and pleas by church leaders, may be grounds for shunning. These are attempts to return the wayward sheep to the flock, not to punish. That is God's business.

SUNDAY NIGHT SINGING

Several weeks later, the preacher invited me to a Sunday night singing at his farm. In order to accommodate everyone in the metal pole shed, only about half of the settlement was invited. As I drove in, a group of about 20 young Amish were playing volleyball in the front yard. They all turned and scrutinized my entrance. Young boys were playing in groups of four or six. Women were preparing the meal in the home and shed. Men were sitting on the lawn and visiting near a grape arbor, where I headed. I recognized and greeted several of them with a handshake and their first names.

MEALTIME

Ezra escorted me into the shed for our meal. When all the families were inside, the preacher called for a silent prayer. A large church bench table held a dozen large salad bowls with an assortment of foods. They included rice, garden lettuce, tomato sections, cheese curds, melted American cheese, applesauce, broken pieces of potato chips, and more. I copied the man in front of me who took a sample from every bowl, but I took only half the amount. The ingredients were stacked on top of each layer, and it was called a "haystack" meal. I had never heard of it nor read of this typical Indiana concoction.

Desserts filled another table and included cherry and apple pie, puddings, Jello cubes, and something with marshmallows and whipped cream. Plastic water glasses on the tables were filled with cool well water and filled often by the preacher on this hot, muggy night. As folks finished, they moved outside to enable the women to clear the tables for the singing.

Standing near the doorway, men watched a group of

young six to 12 year old boys playing outside. The preacher's youngest son, Tyler, recognized me and waved. It was a small gesture, but it made me feel welcome. They used a rubber-tired coaster wagon to ride down a steep incline from a ramp to the hayloft barn door. Some lost control but managed to prevent tipping over. Others over-steered and managed to balance precariously on two wheels. Then two would ride together, each trip bringing thrills to the boys and delight and laughter to the fathers watching, including me.

Singing Time

Then the singing began. Ten girls sat on one side of the bench-long table and ten boys on the other side. Someone would start a song from the songbook (not to be confused with the *Ausbund* hymnbook), followed by the rest of the group. Soon the adults filed into the shed and joined in the singing. Ivan began his favorite song, which it was said he did at every sing he attended. The last 30 minutes were used to sing from a Baptist songbook in English. I joined in, and with a few other deep voices, added a bit of harmony. Although harmony is never allowed in church, it is done in limited amounts at the sing. Children began to fall asleep on their parents' and grandparents' laps. There was very little movement during the 90 minutes of singing, and the mood was solemn, but friendly and social. Darkness had fallen by 10 p.m.; the preacher called for a closing silent prayer.

Women packed up the food and offspring. The preacher's wife Emma and eldest son Tim and I picked up the songbooks and packed them in wooden carrying boxes. Men hitched up horses to buggies, and their lights made the yard look like a firefly convention. One wayward horse created some trouble but soon trotted out the drive followed by a stream of other buggies. I wondered how they were able to see the ditch and roadbed with such small, faint white headlights. Soon it was quiet, the crackling and crunching of steel wagon wheels on the gravel only a memory. The preacher's three children headed for bed. Emma, Chris, and I sat up until 11 p.m. and discussed the ban as well as other Amish traditions. The breakfast menu was established, and, after my warm shower, I retired for the evening. A cool breeze blew over my bed offsetting the blistering heat of the day. I reviewed the day's events and felt grateful to be accepted by these "plain and peculiar" people who are tied tightly to their faith, their family, and their community.

CHRISTMAS

This was the first time I ever received a Christmas card from an Amish person. It came from the Kingston settlement. The card itself was personalized with embossed gold letters on the cover and a scripture passage inside from I John 4:9: "This is how God showed His love among us: He sent His one and only son into the world that we might live through Him." A sprig of holly and berries adorned the cover that replicated a family Bible. The senders' first names were also embossed in gold letters. It was commercially produced in Colorado Springs, Colorado.

The day before Christmas, I phoned Chris at the Bonduel settlement to place an order. His family had been to a Christmas program at school, which surprised me. It seemed too worldly and I thought religion was not part of school activity. But learning new things is always a surprise. "We sang songs and scholars recited memorized Bible verses. We don't go overboard so we don't lose the meaning of Christmas," he said.

PART I *Wisconsin Settlements*
Chapter 9
BLAIR

SCHISM

Discovering settlement locations requires some luck, patience, and openness. Being open to other people in conversation often exposes their experience with Amish. Being patient for suitable weather to travel to settlements listed in the *Budget* newspaper's Index can be trying. Finally, with a little luck, a connection with someone who knows someone leads to a new settlement. That is how I discovered the Blair settlement.

I had found a bed and breakfast in Wisconsin's Directory of B&B's listing for Manawa. My plans were to visit the Amish family I had helped move here from Amherst and I needed a place to stay. Innkeeper Judith Burkhart of the Lindsey House in Manawa accommodated my reservation questions and led me to her father, Frank Watland, who lived near Blair, for more information on the Amish settlement there. Frank offered to introduce me to Raymond Schrock, a "falling away" former Amish bishop from the settlement. Frank said Ray would tell me enough to fill my book. He offered to let me park my VW camper at his mobile home for a few days while I researched the area. I had the lead I needed to plan my first spring excursion.

THE WENGERDS OF BLAIR
A star student in my Amish class, Mary, agreed to accompany me to visit the Amish in northwest Wisconsin. She provided a woman's perspective and insight in the interview with Linda Wengerd of the Blair settlement. I had

written to Lydia Mae, her mother and scribe for the *Budget* newspaper, to arrange the meeting for Friday morning, October 18th. However, when we arrived at their house on Snake Coulee Road, mother and father were on their way to the Whitehall hospital five miles away by buggy with Moses, their 18-year-old son. He had fallen fourteen feet from a scaffold that morning and appeared to have broken something in the right leg or ankle. However, Linda was home and knew about our interview plan and invited us into the house.

The afternoon was planned to take their autistic son, Willie, to the chiropractor. He was 22 years old and had just toppled a "slop bucket" in the kitchen that Linda was trying to clean up when we arrived. He had a seizure that morning and tripped over the bucket. Willie sat patiently at the edge of a quilt rack and stared out the living room window. Mary engaged Linda with questions about the family while I logged notes in my field notebook.

Linda, an outspoken young lady, was one of nine girls in a family of twelve children. All had left the house except Moses and Linda. Willie lived with and was taken care of by a sister that lived in the smaller house on the property with her husband and children. One sister left the Amish several years ago. Their father Andrew, who was called Andy, was chairman of the school board for the two schools in the settlement—-Pine Hill and Fly Creek. He was also involved in the quilt auctions held the last Saturday in July each year where 200 quilts are sold. Linda said they were stored in their house and took up every inch of space in the living and dining room. Andy was negotiating to buy a one-acre property to construct a building to house the auction.

Linda said they had two church congregations of twenty-two families each or forty-four families. They had one bishop, four preachers, and one deacon, but she was not sure of the latter's title. She enjoyed the Christian book by

Gilbert Morris, *Heavenly Fugitive*, as well as books by Lori Wick and Janet Obe.

Mary asked her, "Have you read anything by Beverly Lewis?" Lewis had written several fiction books about Amish life such as *The Shunning*.

"No, but our parents used to read her books to us girls," she said.

"Would you like to have some of her books?" Mary asked.

"Yes, I would very much," she excitedly answered.

"I'll mail some to you that I was going to give to our church. I'm through with them and you can have them."

MIDWIFERY AND A NEAR DEATH EXPERIENCE

Linda said her father had delivered her at home. The sudden onset of birthing was a surprise and was the only thing to do. After that, Lydia Mae took midwifery classes from a professional midwife. The nearest hospitals for child delivery are Black River Falls, Eau Claire, and La Crosse, all beyond buggy distance. Linda also disclosed to Mary that Moses seemed to be accident-prone. Not only did he fall that morning, but had once nearly drowned.

Nobody in the family knows how to swim, but they wade in a river in Blair. One day last year, Moses took off his life jacket and waded out into the green scum covered water only to find a drop-off and disappeared under the water. He bobbed and came to the surface three times and then vanished. An English man nearby heard the cries for help and dove under the murky water and luckily grabbed onto Moses' leg and brought him to shore where resuscitation brought life back to Moses. A sister was present and had taken training in CPR as a first responder to an accident. She had left the Amish but returned by some quirk of fate or providence to save Moses' life. He had no pulse and was not breathing, Linda said. He could not see for a short period after he regained consciousness, but he fully recovered. He told the family that he sunk to the bottom of the river and held his breath as long as he could and walked along the bottom hoping to reach shallow water before he passed out. Linda said Moses could dog paddle and swam three times to the island near the boat dock. She also said he was "low on iron" that may have accounted for his tiredness.

Each of the girls in the family received a chest of drawers and china cabinet if they married after their twenty-first birthday. Perhaps this incentive might have provided more help around the house. One of Linda's sisters lived in Rexford, Montana, near the Canadian border. They had eight children and sent photographs of them back home.

Linda admitted to some depression during her adolescent years due to the stress within the family. With the help of a counselor and medications, she was able to overcome the depression.

Soon the parents returned home with Moses who had only sustained a severely sprained ankle. Mary provided a plastic milk bottle with ice in it that she had used in our cooler and applied it to his ankle to reduce swelling.

Lydia Mae emptied a rocking chair filled with clean laundry and sat down to talk with me. I asked about the bishop that had left the Amish to become preacher for an "Outreach Ministry" outside of Blair on the way to Pigeon Falls. Bishop Ray Schrock was a charismatic and persuasive speaker and drew a following from the Blair Amish settlement. Several converts eventually returned to the settlement and were received by the congregation. When I phoned his Outreach church, a recording said the phone was disconnected or no longer is service. When I called his home, nobody answered.

RUGGED INDIVIDUALISM
Frank Watland lived at the end of a dead end road. He

said it was an appropriate place for him. He had survived five heart bypasses and two marriages and now lived alone with old rugged buildings, ATVs, tractors and a few pickups in varying degrees of serviceability. His very old Marshfield mobile home, covered with a peaked roof to squelch the rain leaks, was filled with memorabilia of a lifetime, including a petrified ivory elephant tusk he received from an Eskimo. He had no public electricity service, but generated his own for his power tools and light. He knew Ray Schrock as a friend for many years. It seems somewhat incongruous that a reclusive 20th century English would befriend a progressive falling-away Amish bishop. His stories were endless and enchanting. He seemed to want to hold our attention forever, and served cheese and crackers and slivers of roast beef that had been cooking on top of a kerosene portable heater for the entire time we toured his buildings and property. He invited us to stay for the night in his loft. He seemed disenchanted with Amish folks who argue over using hooks and eyes in their coats and other "rule making" to the detriment of their faith. Frank said that that was what drew Ray away from the Amish congregation. I want to know more about this unusual schism and will have to return to find out. It pointed up the vulnerability of people when a charismatic person weaves his magic. Such schisms are part of the long history of Anabaptism and other religious groups—charismatic speakers wielding their powers over like-minded or weak-minded folks. Dr. Martin Luther King, Jr. was a positive model.

PART I   Wisconsin Settlements
Chapter 10

VIROQUA, SUGAR GROVE, AND SYLVAN

OLD ORDER AMISH AND SWARTZENTRUBER

As my brother Alan and I drove into the town, an Amish buggy in a parking lot off to the left caught my eye. I had seen one there several times before on my visits to our mother who lived in Viroqua for 20 years. It belonged to an Amish family that sold baked goods on Saturday mornings. I drove into the lot and parked near the buggy.

The first thing I noted was that the buggy had no shaft in front. The shafts are the long, usually hickory pole-like piece of wood that holds the horse in line with the buggy. This buggy had a "double tree," which is a single pole with hitches for two horses. The reason became clear as Alan and I drove through hilly glacial "driftless" country to the Amish settlement. It is called driftless because the last glacier in Wisconsin 10,000 years ago did not shear off these hills and ridges. More horse power was required to negotiate this terrain.

Two Amish women were selling quilted wall hangings and baskets. One appeared pregnant under her heavy, black and plain calf-length cape tied at the neck. The other, a grandmother of the two young children at her side, was wrapped in a black plain buggy blanket. It was a cold and windy 42-degree day in western Wisconsin. An Amish man joined the group after having checked on the horses that were out of sight.

I asked about the basket construction. The man made the plywood base and covers and the women did the weaving.

One of the women said the flat, half-inch weaving reed came from Japan. It was soaked in linseed oil and gave off a pleasant scent. She gave Alan a sheet of paper with a list of all the baskets available through mail order. It was organized in typed columns in what looked like a computer database. Their address was at the top—Daniel Gingerich Basket Shop, E6084 County Rd. NN, Viroqua, WI 54665. The other basket shop was in nearby Liberty Pole: Dan E. Swartzentruber, S6459 Thompson Rd, Viroqua, WI 54665. Ironically, Alan's wife had purchased a small basket on this site in May to carry the "cremains" of our mother to the cemetery. Alan bought a basket as well as a small quilt for his first granddaughter. It had a blue border and a green, maroon, and blue square-block pattern. It was marked down from $75 to $50.

Another small quilt hanging on a clothesline caught my eye. It had a black border and rectangular "scrap-piece" pattern in the center. I asked what it would cost if I commissioned a queen sized quilt with that pattern. I suggested $400. "We can do it for $350," the woman replied. She said she had a wide enough quilt frame to handle king size. I said I would be back, perhaps to visit, as I was writing a book about the Amish in Wisconsin. She said a man was laid up with a dislocated shoulder, not able to work. He would be able to visit with me. I asked if he was a preacher. She answered, "Yes, and Eli is a good talker and could tell you a lot." When I asked if they could put me up, she said, "You could sleep on the couch." Then I asked if I could work off the cost of the quilt on their farm. That was answered by laughter from all present. It was joyful to feel comfortable jesting and cajoling with plain folks. They seemed to enjoy it also, as they parried well.

SUGAR GROVE

On our way home on Hwy 14, about 20 miles southeast of Viroqua, I turned off at Sugar Grove, County Road X to find the Schwartz Cabinet Shop. Alan needed new cabinets in his home. Since it was Sunday, no business would be transacted, but we wanted to know where the shop was. In a front yard of another Amish farm, I asked two Amish boys on a trampoline if they knew where the quilt auction would be held. One pointed to a red shed on their property and said it would be held there the first Saturday in June. I photographed their silo filler and portable power unit on a wagon and we continued on our way.

HILL CREST LOG CABINS

Ervin Schumucker had been at the same Amish quilt auction at LaValle on May 4, 2002 that I had. Unfortunately, neither one of us knew that. I could have given him a ride home, because I ended up at his house and sawmill. I was looking for Clemens and Amanda Borntrager down the road from Schumucker's house, but they had moved to Stratford. I was their taxi driver in July of 1995 when they lived in Cashton. There is variation in the spelling of names, such as Borntrager, Bontrager, Borntreger, and Bontreger. Yoder (allegedly the first family to set foot in Pennsylvania from Europe was Barbara Yoder, widowed while at sea, and with nine children) and Gingerich are plentiful.

The new, white aluminum-sided house sat atop a knoll on Hwy 14, 15 miles west of Richland Center. A small Amish settlement had started here 12 years ago close to Sylvan Amish settlement. The new red metal-sided barn was nestled in a small dip north of the house, its roof top level with the house basement. To the north was Ervin's sawmill; a neatly organized stack of logs was waiting to be "quartered." The building was as big as the house, which seemed to be as big as the barn.

I drove up the newly laid gravel circular driveway to the house. A short, young full-bodied Amish woman, dressed in a light blue dress without apron, was straightening up the yard picking up rakes and shovels and storing them in a basement closet. Two young preschool children were playing in the yard.

"Hello. How are you this fine day?" I greeted her, as she stood on the porch ready to retreat into her house if needed. "I've noticed your new house before while driving to visit my mother in Viroqua just up the road." She began to smile. "Is that your sawmill?" I asked pointing north.

"Yes it is, but he's at an auction in LaValle today."

"What a coincidence. I just came from there. I could have given him a ride home," I said as I stood at the foot of the stairs leading up to the new rough-sawn wood and unpainted porch.

"Would you like a brochure for the sawmill?" she asked with a now friendly smile as she waved me in. "Come on in while I get one for you."

The inside of the house was neat and clean. Hardwood oak floors glistened with the light from windows all the way around. The rooms were large enough to accommodate church services. A bent hickory rocking chair with an Amish braided multicolored rug draped over it sat near the middle of the living room. She handed me a trifold multicolored brochure. At the top of the front page, "Hill Crest Log Cabins" was imposed upon a blazing sun rising from a green hillside. "Standard Cabin Fully Assembled Only $15,500, 24'x30.' Our Model is Open 24 Hours" was in bold black print. She confirmed that the cabin at the top of the hill on Hwy 14 was the model.

I complimented her on the attractive home and building and in jest asked if she had rooms for rent like a bed and breakfast. They did not, she answered, but that it might be something to try. I said I would be ready to stay and visit for a week. She laughed goodheartedly. As I left, I said I would like to see the sawmill in operation some time. "Come any time," she said as I turned and let myself out the door. The two children, playing with a lawn roller, saw me and waved with beaming smiles. This family was intact, prosperous, productive, and healthy. All God's children.

AUCTION

In the middle of the Readstown settlement are the remnants of a small burg on Hwy 14 called Sugar Grove. The eastern border is Sylvan, hardly noticeable on a map. To the west is Viroqua. Thirty-six families comprise one church congregation, and the steel rimmed buggy-wheel marks on the highway attest to much travel to get to the service every other Sunday. The 90-degree heat on this June 1, 2002 auction day made ruts instead of marks in the softening asphalt and tar.

I signed in on a yellow-lined pad of paper to get my bidder's number and took a robin's egg blue business card with flat-black print and a map to Sugar Grove on the back. I asked the Amish man who gave me number 140 at 11:00 a.m. if he ever had a bidder not pay his bill. He said only once, and that man finally did.

Next, I photographed. Unusual buggies near the house were my first targets. One was what is called a "pickup or cab wagon." The back is an open wagon with a covered single seat for driver and passenger. It could have been used for transporting milk cans, hardware, or sacks of grain. The other was a newer two-bench seat open buggy with a rubberized canvas over the front bench. Another nice group photo was of folks bidding on lawn items—steel wheels from an old manure spreader, a doghouse and puppy, seven-foot high windmill yard ornament, a three-pot kerosene stove without the oven, and a newer wood chest. Larger farm machinery had been sold earlier in the morning.

DANIEL SCHWARTZ OF SUGAR GROVE

I began a conversation with Daniel Schwartz, an Amish man from the settlement. As we talked, he realized I had met him a year ago in front of his home near the Amish school. He was also a brother to my friend in the Marion settlement. In the Amish community, these coincidences are not rare. The cohesiveness of Amish society is built on connections with friends and relatives. Daniel gave me his business card for "Country Carriages" on Kokamonjo Road off Hwy 14. The card has a black and white horse and buggy, address, and "custom built and rebuilt buggies, sleighs, carts and carriages" and "buggy parts, quality work and upholstery work" written across the front. On the back is a novel commercial: "For Serious or Joy Rides We've Got You Covered!" He is three and a half miles west of the town of Boaz. I asked if I might be able to photograph his shop some day, and he promptly said I could go there whenever I was ready. I gave assurances I would not photograph his family in keeping with his Ordnung.

When I left the auction, I went to his buggy shop. Six of his children and a friend were home and came out of a metal shed together as I drove into the yard. I wondered what the attraction was in the shed. A slender eight-year-old girl with photo-gray prescription glasses and a brown sack-dress did the talking. I gained her confidence and she became the delightful spokesperson for the group that hovered around her like the Pied Piper of Hamlin. Only a taller girl joined to answer my questions or offer comments.

A buggy was under construction inside the shop. Wheels and frame were awaiting the superstructure. It looked like a single bench, traditional Indiana style. The disciplined children, aged three to eight or nine, cleared away from the wagon as I raised my camera. Outside again, I asked the leader if she could fill my water bottle at the wellhead. She offered to fill it inside with filtered water. "Some people say it doesn't taste good, but some people say it does," she said with patronizing care.

"I'll take it either way," I reassured her. I took a long drink to ward off the heat of the day. It was cold and delicious. I waved goodbye as I drove out the drive. They waved back, my "Gunga Din" (water boy) with a big smile.

JOE C. BORNTRAGER OF CASHTON, WISCONSIN

Back at the auction, another older Amish man had been standing next to Daniel and me. He wore a more formal hook and eye black coat and pants and greenish/turquoise pullover shirt with three buttons at the top and a Nehru collar. His hair was graying and speech slowing. I asked about the windmill in the west yard of the house.

"It runs on wind power and pumps water up the hill to fill a cistern on the other side of the road. Then it uses gravity to bring it down to the house and barn. You put a motor on it when there's no wind," he said. His words were carefully chosen and deliberately delivered. Was he a writer, I thought?

"Do you get the *Plain Interests* newspaper?" I asked. He said he was from the Cashton settlement and did get it.

"There is an Amish man, a Borntrager, who writes something in every issue—nitrogen in the soil, tapping a spring to push water up hill. He's a good writer. I drove his son Clemens and wife Amanda around when I stayed in the settlement in 1995."

"That's my son," he said softly. Joe lived on a farm across the street from Clemens. Then he gave me a ball point pen from his inside coat pocket with a white finger grip and glitzy iridescent blue barrel with his name, address, and "Custom Quilting and Chair Caning" on it. I gave him my "Amish Insight" card. It was another "small world" incident. "Come and visit me sometime," he said. Later, I saw him sitting on yard furniture with his wife observing the auction action in the "Thinker" statue pose. What was he planning next?

THE DINING ROOM

Half of the 40 by 100 foot metal and pole building held the eating and serving area. At the beginning of the serving line were ice cream, then cherry, blueberry, apple, and pecan pie slices in clear plastic triangular shaped containers to keep flies off. The main course items were hot dogs, barbeque beef, and hamburgers. When I asked how many families were in the settlement, heads and eyes of nearby Amish women servers turned in my direction. I suspect it was because not many tourists ask that kind of question. The cashier at the end of the serving line told me 36 families lived in the settlement and one church district. A one-year-old Amish child sat on the concrete floor under the cashier's end of the table. The child was still there when I bought ice cream, seemingly never moving from the spot. When I went back for another barbeque beef sandwich, the pastor of my late mother's church in Viroqua was in line behind me. Pastor Thompson officiated at her memorial service, as well. Short white hair and five day beard and mustache stubble made him easy to recognize. His wife was a quilt enthusiast. We reminisced at one of the three tables set up for diners in Amish style, sparse but adequate.

QUILT AND FURNITURE AUCTION STORAGE

In the other half of the building, 100 quilts and wall hangings were on racks and furniture items were readied to bring to the auction tent. All the typical bent hickory rocking chairs, bedroom sets, bookcases, and bric-a-brac were here. Several Amish men carried items out to the tent and back to await the buyer's collection. Payment for goods was done where the bidder's number was obtained.

AUCTION TENT AND EXTENSIONS

A smaller than usual all-white circus style tent was erected at the rear of the dining and storage building. Two large 10 x 10 foot canvasses, one on either side of the main tent, were attached to handle the overflow crowd. To the right of the auctioneer's platform a recycled bulk milk tank cooled soda that was for sale. Two adolescent Amish girls plunged their hands in the icy waters to retrieve the cans. They also collected the money. I heard someone call my name. It was a student in my Amish class who sold her quilts at these auctions.

SYLVAN

My last side trip was off Hwy 14 in Richland County, past another Amish farm near Sylvan, north of Bosstown. A small girl was pulling a coaster wagon in the yard. I had been here before on Sunday when church let out. About 12 buggies were parked, giving some indication of the size of the settlement. An English creamery was nearby, perhaps servicing the Amish farms. I would have to make another trip to fully explore this settlement.

PART I Wisconsin Settlements
Chapter 11
WAUTOMA, COLOMA, AND HANCOCK

The warm early morning air on this late October day was inviting. The week before it had rained with winds up to fifty miles per hour. This day was a blessing. The Wautoma settlement is in the central part of Wisconsin off Interstate 39 at State Hwy 21. Its mailing addresses include Coloma and Hancock, small towns just off I-39. My friend, Sandy, who helped on the St. Anna trip, and I found ten of the estimated forty-seven family homes and farms. Amish women find it is easier to talk with another woman, especially about domestic topics.

One of the Amish residents of the settlement answered my letter in which I asked for directions to a bulk food store in the settlement. A store is an easy public place to find out more about the area. My letter was mailed to Fannie, a scribe for the *Budget* newspaper. Her address was in a publication of 500 scribes called *Who is Who* in the *Budget*. She had returned my self addressed stamped envelope with "Greetings in Jesus' Name." Fannie gave directions to the settlement's bulk food store, which just happened to be run by her son-in-law and daughter, Millie. It was only an eighth of a mile away. Fannie works there a few days each week.

Bulk Food Store

The T & M Country Market is off Hwy 21 on County Road II. A quarter mile south is Cumberland Road, and the store is a hundred yards west. Millie, the "M" in the name of the store, was near the door as we walked in. A short narrow checkout counter hugged the north wall. I introduced myself as the person writing to her mother researching the Amish in Wisconsin. Her caution vanished and was replaced by engaging conversation. She said there were three church districts with nineteen, sixteen, and thirteen families in the settlement, and four schools. She herself had been a teacher in Iowa, and coincidentally she had taught my preacher friend from Bonduel when he was in the 8th grade in Milton, Iowa. She liked the climate in Wisconsin better, though, as it is not as "bone chilling cold in winter."

The aisles in the store were claustrophobic. I overheard Millie tell another customer that they were planning to expand the size of the building. A large 20x20 foot multi-colored tent with long tables was near the store, attesting to the need for expansion. Fresh vegetables were sold here in summer. Inside the store, large brown paper bags of salt, sugar, and flour were stacked in a corner. Red McIntosh and Delicious apples were displayed next to them. The white-wall paneling had listings and prices written in colored marker for each kind of apple and other products around the store. The classic spices and clear plastic bags filled with baking needs crammed the shelves. Brooms, sticky fly-catching spiral paper and fly swatters, bottles of laundry bluing, straight pins, and other not-so-often-seen products lined the shelves. All the while, a quiet hiss of the pressurized gas lamp was a reminder that we were in Amish country.

A building next to the store looked familiar to me. I had seen one like it in the Arthur, Illinois settlement. It was rectangular at the base, 5x6 feet and about 15 feet high with a pitched roof. It housed a water storage tank, providing a "water head" of pressure to push water to the house and barn for cattle. The water well was beneath it and an engine and pump were enclosed to suck the water up and push it up into the reservoir.

Outside, men were splitting logs for winter firewood.

Kittens and cats roamed the yard. Toby, the "T" in T&M, strolled toward the house, coffee cup in hand, as we left. Wearing his brown quilted vest, he looked like a deer hunter. But his wide rimmed black hat, untrimmed beard, and dark blue pants gave him away. It was deer season, and we saw two Amish men on the road dressed in their bright orange overalls. The house was modern looking, uncharacteristic for the Amish, a one-story ranch with white clapboard aluminum siding, and a few petunias sprinkled across the front border. Perhaps they had brought this style house when they migrated from Milton, Iowa.

Another familiar structure in their yard was a 60-foot semi-truck wagon parked next to the store on the blind side from the road. I had seen one other in Bonduel at the Lark Country Store. A gas engine at the front provided power for the refrigeration unit on the wagon. This is the same kind of unit found on other domestic wagons carrying produce, frozen foods, or beer. Here it served to keep food products frozen or home cooked food preserved. It was cleverly recycled from the non-Amish, fast moving, and technologically correct culture. However, the business was ending. By August 2002, they were closing. "It takes too much time away from the family responsibilities," Millie said. They had evaluated their priorities; family came ahead of economics.

CANVAS SHOP

Turning west out of the store on Cumberland Road, we headed for a canvas shop. Next to the sign by the road advertising "Miller's Canvas Shop" and "Repairs and Custom Work" was a pontoon boat waiting to be covered. As we turned in to the drive, two young boys were hitching a horse to a buggy. Their father, Sam Miller, sized me up as I walked toward him. He was tall and slim with black hair under a black felt hat. He wore a new looking denim coat with snaps closing the front.

Assuring Sam I would not hold him up long, I asked to have a brief look at his shop. He seemed hesitant, but obliged. Inside the large garage-like building was another pontoon boat awaiting a cover. Large tables provided working space for the large pieces of rubberized canvas-like material. A commercial sewing machine stood at one edge of the tables. Sam demonstrated a unique homemade clutch mechanism that engaged the sewing machine gently. I asked if I could photograph it for use in my Amish classes, and he agreed without hesitation. He also showed me the shoe and boot repair equipment that he operated for the settlement. We exchanged business cards. I asked to photograph the house, to which he agreed providing no person was included. Then he added, "Take a picture of the windmill to show your class how we get water." Sam got into his all-black buggy and drove away.

LEATHER REPAIR AND HARNESS SHOP

Along Hwy 21 a few miles east of Coloma is the David Borntreger Leather Repair Shop. Its large "sentinel" blue A.O. Smith glass-lined silos help recognize the 125-acre farm on the south side of the road. A large sign near the road solicits business. Work is done in a garage-sized, metal-sided building. David appeared as we got out of the car. He is a young man, slight build, with piercing-blue eyes. We entered his shop for a look.

Several black leather harnesses hanging from meat hooks reflected the dark interior. They had been dipped in a large barrel of preserving oil and were drip-drying over a sloping trough to collect the oil for reuse. Recycling is not a new concept for the Amish. Frugality drives the practice. It reminds me of the same practice I saw in Alaska's boondocks where isolation drives people to save every broken device from which to scavenge parts. Yards are often littered with "junk" in our eyes, but it is survival in theirs. A table on the south wall was piled with scraps of leather of varying thickness and color. The north wall sported brightly colored horse collar pads and tear-shaped horse collars along with saddle pads. Tall racks of horseshoes and bridles and other tack loomed in the center of the shed. A western style saddle sat on a floor prop awaiting stirrup replacement, a task David said would be time consuming. He would need to remove several layers and fixtures to customize the English customer's saddle. I had taken enough of his time and thanked him before he went off to the barn to finish winterizing it.

A LITTLE LUCK HELPS

Farther south, we turned west on Cree Avenue. Within a few miles of twist-and-turn road, we came to a pleasant looking farmhouse, barn, and other outbuildings. Soaring pine trees bordered the road and two sentinel cedar trees guarded the gravel drive into the yard. I began to photograph, and shortly an Amish man strolled from the house toward me. He was rotund, wearing a weathered straw hat, a sawdust-coated denim coat, and boots with a hole on the side of the left one. His head was down as he approached me never responding to my repeated greetings. Standing in the ditch next to the road I made one final greeting, his head came up and he said, "Hello. What are you doing here?"

I explained my purpose for photographing Amish homes and farms and that I was from Milwaukee and taught several classes about the Amish. I explained that I had written to scribes in the Coloma and Hancock settlements to visit. He said he got a letter but never responded. What a coincidence! As it turned out the address was given to me by two of the women in my class who had visited with them. We both laughed over the coincidence, and by now we were both standing in the ditch, literally on equal footing.

It seemed symbolic to be at the same level. There was equality and humility not being higher or more important than another.

Emmon invited us to see his woodshop. He had covered an old wood-sided tool shed with vertically corrugated metal. His bushy gray eyebrows raised slightly, proud of his accomplishment. A large square, flat-topped steel-plated stove in the middle of the shop provided heat. Two "line shafts" powered all the machines, one down the center and the other along the west wall. He pointed to the north wall and said the engine for turning the shafts was outside. A homemade clutch on the line shaft engaged each machine independently. A modified school bus front door opener engaged one clutch. Planks of wood were stored from the ceiling in a homemade 14-foot long pipe rack. They provided some of the oak for the custom hutch Emmon was building. He apologized for the messy shop, as did his wife, Edna, as she came in the doorway.

Her full-bodied figure was enclosed by a pale blue calf-length dress without the bertha or cape. Her silver-gray hair was uncovered, and she joined in the conversation after several minutes of cautious observing. She casually leaned against the band saw and planer as we visited. They had lived in LaGrange and Shipshewana, Indiana as well as Iowa and Amherst, Wisconsin over 25 years. They knew my Amish friends who had lived in Amherst. Edna said they were now living in the Marion settlement. I said, "Yes, I know. I helped them move on a 5 degree below zero day in December last year."

As we left the shop, Edna went to the house and Emmon told us about the old 24-year-old horse standing beside the white barn. He did not know what to do with her. She had been a faithful worker for him all these years. He could not sell her or put her down for the fox farm. So, he let her graze as she wished with the rest of the horses. He told us about the history of the white barn, promising the seller when he bought it that he would put on new shingles to preserve the building. Emmon pointed to the dilapidated storage shed with its vertical weathered planks and wondered out-loud what to do with it. It seemed he was reviewing his life story with us, sharing it, perhaps hoping to preserve it in our care or memory. As we walked toward my car, I thought this was the most sentimentality I had heard from an Amish person in my ten years of research. Perhaps in some way to approve our visit, in a final gesture, he pointed to a metal ring that encircled and was embedded in the base of the two sentinel cedar trees that guarded the gravel driveway into their yard. In his soft and slow voice he said, "Do you think if I try to take those rings off it will kill the tree?" His horse and tree bordered on death, and perhaps his concern for them was a projection of concern for his own.

WAUTOMA'S FIRST SETTLEMENT FAMILY

Fannie Hershberger and her husband Chris set foot on this new settlement on December 29, 1983. Their farm is off Hwy 21 at County Road II. The original house has a red brick base with shingles above and a sloping roof to the front and back. Their quarters are in the attachment to the north, with an addition being added to it. Six or seven buildings are visible from the drive, and one was being repaired. It was the white, horizontally slatted wood corncrib. Sandy, the lady who helped in St. Anna, went to photograph the Belgian horse team standing in harness near the crib. Chris was bent over a gas-powered chain saw trimming the butt end of the corner joists of the tilting crib. His son wore a leather tool pouch held up with a WWII web belt around his waist. His two children were nearby observing the work. Chris shooed away one that was edging too close to the corner, ignored me standing nearby, and continued working. When he finished his part of the job, he pointed to a rotted 4x4 beam off to the side and exclaimed, "That's what was causing the problem." A few more shims and he asked his son to hitch up the team and pull out the 30-foot-long "I" beam that had been holding up the side of the crib. Then he greeted me.

After introductions, he said Fannie was looking for me the day before. He was right. It was what I had written in the letter. I was embarrassed. Dates and times are critical to Amish folks who need to plan and are not prone to whimsical, extemporaneous, or spur-of-the-moment trips or gatherings.

Chris escorted us to the back door of their Gross Daudy Haus. Woven scrap throw rugs were under our feet as we stepped onto the porch and again in the large living room, dining room, and kitchen. Fannie was cooking in modern stainless steel cookware on the black steel plate stove. It was an Airtight brand wood-burning cook stove. The refrigerator used kerosene. A soft light drifted into the 30x30 foot room filtered by the fluttering leaves on the silver maple tree outside.

Somebody was sleeping on the overstuffed davenport. "Don't worry about him," Chris said. "He's our retarded son. He won't bother you." He told us about their daughter and son-in-law operating the bulk food store on Cumberland Road, 600 yards away. Fran works there several days a week. He told us about the overwhelming crowd that attended the first auction held at their farm in 1985. The farmyard was filled with quilts, Amish furniture, and junk for sale. Randy Stockwell was the auctioneer.

Chris said I might be interested in knowing that several Wisconsin settlements came directly from Pennsylvania. He mentioned Livingston, Loyal, Athens, Dorchester and Fennimore. (Others are Owen, Unity, and Wulff Valley).

Then he gave directions to Aaron Beechy who had a cabinet shop on 11th Drive off Hwy 21. Yoder's Quilt Shop on Hwy 21 about four miles west of Wautoma had rugs, crafts, wall hangings, and quilts made to order. Yoder's woodworking shop was on County Road T off Hwy 21 about five miles west of Wautoma. His son lived on the next farm to the south on land subdivided from Hershberger. He ran a portable sawmill that we saw later in a field across from Chris's place and near the school. The rubber-tired band saw was identical to the one I had seen at the Dueck Mennonite farm in Nova Scotia.

AUCTION

The hot day of Saturday, June 29, 2002 drew a crowd of nearly 500 eager bidders to the Schmucker farm on 11th Avenue west of Wautoma. The gigantic yellow and white striped circus-type tent held the auctioneer for the furniture and quilts. The auctioneer was R. J. Stockwell of Dorchester, Wisconsin. A second smaller tent held the furniture for pre-auction viewing, as did a third tent with quilts and wall hangings. A fourth tent held the homemade ice cream maker, soda sales, and tables for customers to eat and get protection from the searing sun. A Wick metal and pole building housed the kitchen where greaseless and tasty bratwurst were served, as well as cherry, rhubarb, boysenberry, and pecan pie slices in plastic containers for 75 cents. There were other sundry menu items with coffee and milk. Finally, an empty farm implement shed housed bakery for sale, including donuts, pies, breads, cookies, muffins, and the inimitable Amish cookbooks. Another auctioneer performing his chanting warble sold garden and farm tools and implements, sewing machines, Coleman lanterns, goats, rabbits, and a plethora of human artifacts.

Authentic Amish-made Furniture
I began photographing inside the furniture tent and saw a lady in need. She was from England, unaccustomed to auctions, and trying to find the maker of a piece of furniture. I retrieved a map of the Kingston Amish settlement and showed her how to find the Schlabach shop. Mr. Schlabach was in the auctioneer's tent and I told him where to find the lady to cinch a sale. Eli Yoder, another woodworker, overheard our conversation, and I asked him about a store in Milwaukee, "P.M. Bedroom Gallery," that sold Amish and Mennonite-made furniture. He knew about it and directed me to Monroe Miller, who furnished the furniture for that store. From Monroe's answers to my questions, the TV and radio ads were legitimate. It changed my perspective and I arranged to meet with the storeowner to learn more about his operation with Amish craftsmen. Now curious about who the woodworkers were that made the items at this auction, I asked Aaron Beachy, another furniture maker, if he had a list of them. He did and said he would write it out and send me a copy for my Amish class students. But he never did. Aaron had recognized me as somebody he had seen before and my acquaintance or friendship was now becoming functional, not just inquisitive as a tourist or ethnographer.

Children, Children Everywhere
Amish children were evident everywhere. Their bright green, blue, maroon, and mauve shirts stood out in the crowd. Their bare feet did too, as did their mothers' and older sisters' in some cases. One Amish lady in a faded green sack-dress said, "It is cooler without shoes on days like this." Two four- or five-year-old Amish children wore atypical beige-colored straw hats compared with the usual black. I sat next to an adolescent Amish baby-sitter with a 16-month-old boy whose right leg and foot were swollen, resembling elephantitis. She said it was a birth defect and

would be surgically modified when he was 12 years old. An elastic stocking was wet in places where blisters had burst. His toes wiggled with normal action and he could walk on his foot, the sitter explained. Later in the day, I heard from the child's uncle that there were only 175 cases in the country similar to this boy's defect.

Four pre-teen boys devouring ice cream strolled through the folks sitting under a shade tree and dropped their empty Styrofoam cups and plastic spoons on the ground, one boy crushing them underfoot with a resounding crunch. I admonished them that they had dropped something. They ignored my comment, as did the two Amish women sitting under the tree. "Boys will be boys," a non-Amish lady exclaimed as she picked up the debris. Another Tom Sawyer-like young adolescent Amish boy in an untidy shirt, rumpled hair, and no hat politely and subtly tried to "extort" money from me, using his Amish image to flatter or exude trust. He said he wanted to buy something but did not have any money. I asked, "Is your father here?"

"Well, yes, but I don't know where he is," he said.

"I'd feel a little out of place if I gave you money without your father knowing about it," I said.

"Well, maybe I can find him." He never asked for money again, but I saw him several times throughout the day and he exchanged a pleasant smile when we passed each other. The next time I engaged him was when I purchased a soda. He was the money-taker and dipped his hand in the ice-cube cooled tank of soda cans to retrieve my can of Squirt with the enthusiasm of a reprieved sinner. When I gave him my dollar for the 50-cent can of soda, he said, "Do you want the change?"

"Yes, I think I'd better have it," I said as seriously as possible. Now he reminded me of David Copperfield, crafty in his work. I changed my perspective from the stereotypical always well-behaved Amish children.

BECOMING RECOGNIZABLE

My perception was better, too. I recognized the casket maker from Kingston and Emmon from Wautoma. Judy Wisniewski was there from one of my Amish classes and we chatted. The ice cream maker recognized me from the LaValle, Sugar Grove and Bonduel auctions and we chatted as he retrieved a one gallon bucket of ice cream being cooled in a freezer salvaged from a truck with a King refrigerator on the front and powered by a one horsepower gasoline motor with pulley and belt. Sarah Hershberger from the Sugar Grove Candy Shop recognized me as the guy who teased her husband about the price of their peanut and cashew brittle.

CLEANUP

One last scene caught my eye. It was outside the kitchen where the food had been served. Along the south wall was a pile of pots, pans, rolling pins, cookie sheets, and utensils. The stainless steel bowls used for mixing dough for the donuts were stacked a dozen or more high by size. How they were kept separate by owner puzzled me, so I asked the Amish woman who had just finished cleaning them and organizing them how it was done. Dressed in a dark brown dress, she showed me the painted initials on the outside edge of the pans. Her task was to get them together by family for easy retrieval at the end of the day when such searching could be exasperating.

I asked her, "Could I photograph the pile? It's an interesting collection."

"As long as I'm not in the picture," she admonished somewhat sternly and swiftly backed away from the area. Then the sternness turned to an invitation to see the wash rack and the huge four-foot diameter steel kettle filled with steaming hot water used for washing the cooking utensils. The kettle was in a cradle holding it four feet off the ground with room beneath to kindle a fire and heat the water. A sheet metal shroud surrounded the kettle and cradle to contain the fire and heat efficiently. A smoke stack ran up the wall to dissipate the smoke with less efficiency, as wisps leaked out between kettle and shroud. How quickly this Amish woman sized me up. Once done, her friendliness was infectious. She also knew the family I knew, the Schwartz's, and had seen and talked with the wife and daughter who were here. It was good to be with honest, straightforward folks who enjoyed what they did and the way they lived. They were not detached from the world around them, but were committed to their way.

BUGGIES, BUGGIES, AND MORE BUGGIES

Before I headed for home, I photographed several clusters of buggies. A lady was packing one up that she said was from Kentucky. Her husband, Monroe, came by and qualified that by saying it was made in Delaware with its distinctive style. Called a Dover (Delaware) surrey, the doors on both sides slid on tracks outside the buggy and were curved inward toward the bottom. From the roof, a rigid and immovable awning hung eight inches out over the front window. The red/orange triangular sign was affixed to the back of the buggy. A hinged-from-the-top wooden window with a smaller glass window in it was open on the walk-in back door. Stephen Scott's book, *Plain Buggies*, shows this style on page 68. The brake drum on the back wheels was operated by cable rather than hydraulic fluid. Wheel rims were steel, not rubber. The distinctiveness of local or state buggy styles, however, is being lost. I met Menno Mullet, the part-time buggy maker for the Wautoma settlement. With the mobility of Amish to other settlements, their buggy adds to a conglomeration of mixed styles. Will buggy and clothing styles merge into a non-distinct identity?

SPRING LAKE MENNONITE BULK FOOD STORE

The shopkeeper for the Vintage Shoppe in Wautoma on Hwy 21 east of town told us about Spring Lake Country Store. Just east of the Shoppe is Hwy 73. Going south on 73 around Silver Lake, we came to County Road F to the left and followed it for about five miles to Spring Lake at County Road Z intersection. The large long black building dead ahead was the store. The mailing address is Neshkoro. A large sign on the road identified it, as well as a vegetable garden, now littered with rotting tomatoes and squash.

It was Sunday and the store was closed, but their phone numbers were displayed in the thermal pane windows in front, 920-566-0272. A second number was that of Mattie's Kitchen Delight, which provides bakery for the store. Mattie is not related to the storeowner, Luke Ebersole. My phone call to him revealed that his Mennonite congregation was conducting a religious service at the Milwaukee Rescue Mission the night I had called. Luke said they do the same at a state prison.

What we could see inside replicated all the other bulk food stores I had seen in Amish settlements. A small modest wooden desk in the front was neatly stacked with file baskets and desk paraphernalia.

On December 6, 2001, I received a letter from Luke with an insert that listed the Mennonite churches in Wisconsin. They were in Athens, Augusta, Beloit, Redgranite, Tony, Thorp, and Unity. He wrote, "All Mennonites have church houses, even the horse and buggy Mennonites." Luke's handwritten note closed with an invitation to join them in a church service sometime.

PART I *Wisconsin Settlements*
Chapter 12
LAVALLE

ANOTHER AUCTION & CASHEW CRUNCH

Urius Borntrager hosted a quilt and farm equipment auction on a sunny, 60 degrees Saturday, May 4, 2002 at his farm on County Road G off Hwy 58. A large crowd had gathered by the time I got there. One group was in the pasture north of the barn to bid on farm machinery, tools, and other consignment items from English folks. Another group was in the newly built barn that replaced one that had burned down, looking at horses that would soon go on the block. A third group was on the front lawn pawing through the household items left over from garage and estate sales. Lines of people were forming at the small building where buyers got their bidding numbers from the Tracy Jennings auction representative. Another line was drawn to the doorway of the house by the aroma of freshly baked pecan pies, breads, and glazed donuts. The Amish cashier lady calculated my purchases on a spiral notebook page with ballpoint pen. Two hotdogs, coffee, homemade chicken noodle soup, and a glazed donut came to $4.00. An Amish man saw my dilemma of trying to find a place to sit down and opened the nearby church bench wagon doors and took out two benches and set them up. His awareness, concern, and decisiveness were impressive and spoke of hospitality and caring for other people. It is one of the hallmarks of Amish people.

PHOTOGRAPHING
With my hunger pangs relieved, I retrieved my 35-millimeter camera from my car and began to document what I

saw. With a 28-millimeter wide-angle lens, I was able to capture the entire front yard and century old pine tree. Armand Hamburg strolled by and admonished me not to photograph the Amish folks. His wife added specifically not to take their faces. I agreed, and that started a conversation with Armand. He was a retired farmer in the area having suffered ill health and had also lost most of his front teeth. His well-worn baseball cap sported a hybrid corn logo above the bill. His handshake revealed swollen and callused fingers, gnarled knuckles, and a muscular grip. He was anxious to talk. At my request, he agreed to mail me a handmade map of the area showing where the Amish lived and gave me his address if I had other questions. He said there were 30 or 40 Amish families and five schools in the settlement. Later I found out there were also three church districts, listed as "Ironton" in the *New American Almanac*, which I had purchased in Pennsylvania. In this issue, the bishops, deacons, and preachers and their addresses were listed for all the church districts in the US. This kind of communication network keeps people informed and tied together.

As far as I could see, I was the only person with a camera in the crowd. Was this a rule local people followed, or was it a lack of interest in documenting these events and the Amish culture? Despite Armand's warning, I was never questioned or admonished by any Amish during my visit. But I never photographed individual Amish and photographed groups of Amish only when their backs were toward me. That was true in my next excursion to the pasture and the farm equipment sale. The auctioneer's pickup truck with a cap on the back and a speaker system for him and an accountant drove through the aisles of wringer washing machines, steel wagon wheels, double trees, plows, cultivators, and generators. Two-dozen frugal Amish men gathered here to get a bargain. I took one photograph and left.

HORSE SENSE

Two Standardbred buggy horses with their harness still on were tied to a hay feeder near the pasture entrance. Looking for a possible photo, I stood still three feet away from one, curious as to what it would do. Within a few minutes, its head hanging down, the horse slowly inched forward toward me, and then stopped. Its nose was almost on the camera resting on my belly. A clot of dried mud stuck to the side of its head an inch below its sad eye. Slowly, I reached up and deliberately scratched it off with my fingernail. The horse stood motionless, content, and trusting. Was this a friendly greeting or a bored horse? Amish animals seem to have a demure manner about them, mirroring that of their humble masters.

CASHEW CRUNCH

I returned to the house and the baked goods. Cashew Crunch Candy in clear plastic boxes lined a shelf near the pecan pies. Mose Hershberger made it in his Sugar Grove Candy Shop in LaValle. I had met him a year ago at the Amherst Quilt Auction where he was hawking his candy wares like a barker at a circus. Today he wore a turquoise long sleeve shirt, sleeveless down-filled vest, and reflecting sunglasses. Not your typical Amish male attire.

While I was deciding between a pound or half-pound box of Cashew Crunch, an English man, Don, standing next to me raved about the candy and sounded like a spokesperson for Mose. Sure enough, he said he brought this candy to sell in Milwaukee. His wife, Gayle Hooper, was in one of my Amish classes at University of Wisconsin-Waukesha and was here at this auction. All this coincidental conversation went on with the Amish audience enjoying the humor of it all.

I found Gayle and Mose standing in line to buy homemade ice cream. Jacob Mast, an Amish man from Wautoma was working an old-fashioned ice cream maker a few feet away. A thirty inch high wooden bucket with an aluminum bucket inside it held the ingredients of ice cream. It was cooled to below 32 degrees with crushed ice and salt. An antique and refurbished John Deere hit-and-miss engine furnished churning power. It looked brand new. Several Amish and English men surrounded the apparatus while I photographed close-ups of the engine. I sampled a $1.00 cup of the creamy white stuff. It was delicious.

An Inside Look

Quilts were on display inside the house. Very few people viewed them before they were sold. Urius's wife was cutting out donuts on a tabletop using a tin can lubricated with vegetable oil and a small glass for the donut hole. One of her four daughters was pouring glaze over donuts strung on a dowel. Other daughters tended to the oven. One special daughter played a harmonica as she strolled through the house. Urius's wife and I talked about her way of life that she hoped would be perpetuated. Living in this out-of-the-way valley was one way to do that, she said. Depending on one another was important to glue the community together. She said past generations gave up too much and suffered so that the Amish way of life would survive. For this generation to give it up would be a discredit to their heritage. She was content in her work, family, and community and, it seemed to me, her faith. What more could you ask for to live out your life?

An Outside Look

Outside, an Amish man was carrying tack and a horse-collar pad to a shed. Curious, I asked him about the pad. He explained that workhorses lose weight as the summer wears on and their collars become loose. The pad absorbs the difference. He was a Yoder and I asked if he was a bishop. He said no, but that there was a Yoder bishop in the settlement. I told him I taught classes about the Anabaptists and come to these auctions to visit, learn, and photograph in order to show and tell what the Amish are really like. I said I was upset by the buggy burnings, torching of buildings, shootings, and rapes committed against Wisconsin Amish and hoped my teaching would reduce anti-Amish sentiments. I asked if he thought my mission would be helpful. He said anything that enables all persons to live together would be helpful. I apologized for taking up his time, but thanked him and wished him a good day. Dark, threatening rain clouds painted the sky to the west. I had two other stops to make and decided to leave.

OTHER OBSERVATIONS

One was at what appeared to be a woodworking shop along Hwy 58 south of LaValle. No signs were on the road to tell me that, but the house configuration and shop construction did. Inside, two bearded Amish men were building a cabinet to order. I asked if they built cabinets for auctions, and they said they were behind in their order work already and had a year's backlog of orders. The noise was deafening, so I left quickly.

When I returned home I remembered an article in the Wisconsin State Journal about the David Borntrager incident in LaValle. High school and older boys tried to steal David's buggy and in the melee drove over him with their car. It took from January to August for David to recuperate and be able to walk. His farm work had to be done by other Amish folks. The article warranted front-page status: "An Amish family's slow comeback." I had donated to the fund set up, according to the article, at St. Paul's Lutheran Church in Hillpoint. His thankful letter was published in the Journal. My next visit to LaValle will be to visit David.

PART I Wisconsin Settlements
Chapter 13
MILLADORE

A NEW SETTLEMENT

IRA BORNTRAGER

Along Hwy 10 west of Stevens Point is the small town of Milladore. At the IGA store, I asked where the Amish live in the area and got directions from a customer who overheard my request to the clerk. Ira Borntrager was on County Road N one mile to the east. What luck! I was at the right place at the right time.

A black top Amish buggy parked by the shed near the road was the clue that this was the place. A modern, red brick house adorned the front lawn. Large French windows lined the south exposure of the house. The gray cinderblock newer model barn was behind the house and 75 yards long. I parked my car in the driveway and greeted a young 12-year-old boy with a team of four Percheron horses. Three were dapple-gray. Not the usual choice for Amish work horses, they were hitched to a seed driller. The boy directed me to his father who was around the end of the metal shed. I heard a motor running as I approached. It stopped and a pickup truck with a fertilizing sprayer on it backed out of the shed. The driver, a tall heavy-set English man, strolled toward Ira. I listened to the conversation along with Ira's two sons.

Ira was short of six feet. His denim jacket fit tightly and was fastened with the middle three snaps. Three garments with buttons were visible underneath. He wore a black knit watchman's cap and prescription sunglasses. Leaning against the metal shed, he told me where to find the other two families in the settlement, Gingerich and Yoder. He said he hoped this would be a permanent settlement. No congregation had formed, so Ira's family went to Wautoma to attend Sunday services. It was an hour's drive in a taxi that cost $90 round trip. The driver was a local man who often drove the Amish in his van.

Ira's short and cheerful wife and two other teenage boys joined us. I jotted some notes in my small spiral notebook about him milking 60 cows by machine and said I was writing a book about the Amish in our state. Ira joked when I forgot some of the names he rattled off of relatives that lived in settlements I had visited. "How are you going to write a book when you forget information?" he quipped. Then he said Thomas Gerleman had also interviewed him for a book he was writing, and that I had better hurry up with mine.

In jest, I said I would help on his farm this summer as I had worked on farms as a kid. Ira retorted, "Bring money!"

As I left, I said, "Pretty nice modern house you have." Ira's wife laughed. "It was here when we bought it one year ago." Just as the Amish are a novelty to me, I may be a novelty to them and a break in their ordinary daily living.

ELI GINGERICH

My next stop was at the Eli Gingerich farm on Robin Road off Hwy 34. Giant fir trees hid the dilapidated old red brick house with a metal roof. A young boy with an anxious expression on his face sat on the back steps as I drove up. A husky looking brown shorthaired dog with head bowed slowly walked up to my backside. I quickly asked the boy if the dog was friendly. He said he was, and I dropped my hand down behind me to let him sniff it. Feeling no bite, I turned and cautiously petted it. The lad disappeared into the house to get his father.

Eli came out on the steps dressed in denim that was covered with sawdust or ground feed. He wore a black watchman's knit cap and several layers of clothing under his snap-buttoned coat. His two attractive, rosy-cheeked adolescent daughters, dressed in spotless robin's egg blue long dresses, peered at the doorway. They chuckled and smiled during the whole conversation, but said nothing at all, typical of Amish children when adults are speaking. I was hoping Eli would invite me in, but he sat down on the step to talk. He said the owner of the property (Eli was only renting) had an airstrip next to the field that Ira had plowed. The owner had taken away a single engine, two-passenger airplane from one of the sheds recently. Eli described the two rudders on the vertical stabilizer and I knew it was an Aircoupe. His keen observation led me to believe he might have fantasized about flying in one, which is not allowed in the Ordnung of most, if not all, Amish congregations.

Eli said he needed to go to the Livingston settlement. Since I was going to the Amish quilt auction the next week, I offered him and his wife a ride if they could take a Greyhound bus as far as Milwaukee. He made no comment except to say he needed to drill oat seed in his field before nightfall. It was a hint for my departure. He never took me up on the offer.

PART I *Wisconsin Settlements*
Chapter 14
LIVINGSTON

MORE AUCTIONS

The early morning drive between Cassville and Livingston across ridges and through valleys was inspiring. A long, light rain had fallen during the night and the contoured fields were sprouting two-inch high corn. Lush green grass between corn strips would provide a bountiful crop of hay in weeks.

A bright yellow flyer directed me to the Henry Nisley farm three miles west of Livingston on County Road E. The ground was muddy from the rain with the temperature in the 50s, but it was warm and dry in the metal pole shed where two auctioneers were barking. One was selling bric-a-brac and the other handled quilts and furniture. Boysenberry, cherry, rhubarb, and apple pies were set out for lunch along with hot dogs, hamburgers, barbeque, donuts, coffee, and ice cream. Amish kerosene stoves kept meats warm in eight-quart stainless-steel kettles. A 92x108 quilt hung from the side wall and was raffled off at noon. My $1.00 ticket and 30 others were never counted, as the Amish woman selling a large batch failed to separate the tickets to put one in the barrel from which the lucky number would be drawn.

Next to me, an Amish man holding his one-year-old daughter laughed as the child stared at my red cherry pie with ice cream. The color red drew the child's attention, he said, as it did with toys at home. A cheerful and attractive Old Order Mennonite woman nearby laughed, too. She wore a puffed-up black nylon jacket over a print dress and light blue scarf on her head. Her daughters wore long pigtails

162 Amish in Wisconsin

under their scarves. A baby wore a robin's egg blue and white checked bonnet. Her husband, a handsome 30-year-old, was clean-shaven. He wore commercial blue jeans and jacket and a dark gray chapeau. It appeared to be made of a woven plastic material with a dented crown and narrow brim. The Lark Country Store in Bonduel has similar hats for sale in their Amish settlement. Amish men wear them during the week in winter instead of the customary black felt, wide-brimmed hat.

The husband, whose name was Jake Zimmerman, informed me that he and 17 other Old Order Mennonite families lived in the Livingston settlement. Most were from Lancaster, Pennsylvania, except one from Indiana and one from New York. They still belong to the Lancaster Conference on Mennonite churches and use a Lancaster hymnal in English instead of the *Ausbund*. They speak "Pennsylvania Dutch" with a mixture of other dialects.

Jake estimated 200 Old Order Mennonite families live in Wisconsin in the settlements of Thorp, Stanley, Colby, and Withee all along Hwy 29 in the northwestern part of the state. The immigration began in the 1970s.

Jake had a cell phone and commercial electricity in his home and barn. He milked 65 cows with a milking machine and used a refrigerated bulk tank.

Giving Jake my business card, I jested that I could be a hired hand during the summer for room and board. This idea made him chuckle. Then it was time for chores, and he left with his wife and family. Our conversation, amid the chatter of the auctioneers and buyers, was interesting and informative.

Meeting folks like this makes going to auctions worthwhile.

QUILT AND FURNITURE STORE

Dan and Iva Helmuth, Jr. own and operate an Amish

store in a new two-story split-level wood-sided building located five miles west of Livingston on County Road E. The lower level is their home. The ground level is the store. They are also scribes for the *Budget*. Dan was in the store when I went in to find out where the auction was held. He said it was just down the road. He is related to my Amish friends from Marion, who stopped here on our way to an Amish wedding last winter. I was their driver. Here I was back again like it was family.

Dan is a tall, well-built man. He bears a friendly smile and delivers a quick, to the point answer to questions. He has a good sense of humor and ready wit. Polite and businesslike, he makes positive impressions on his customers. His wife's notices in the *Budget* are crisp and compassionate. In the May 22, 2002 issue, another scribe wrote about a five-year-old Amish boy, Wayne Schwartz, who broke both bones in his leg. "He was with his dad planting corn and his pant leg got caught very tight and had to give, so it broke both of his bones right through." The scribe asked readers to look in the "Showers" section of the paper for the address to send cards and probably money to offset the hospital bill.

The store is perched on the side of a steep incline from the ridge road. A deep valley continues beyond their store and home. His buggy horses feed on the pasture to the west, and a white sheet metal closet-sized building is tucked against a telephone pole next to the road. It may be a community telephone for emergencies. Enterprising and change-minded Amish are paving the way to new and modified lifestyles. Where it will be in 100 years is anybody's guess.

DRIVING THE AMISH

A WEDDING

I offered to drive my Amish friends from Marion, Wisconsin to a wedding without monetary payment. My only payoff was being with these folks to answer my questions and enjoy some humor and teasing. My last trip was late January 2002 to a wedding near Beetown, Wisconsin. The first night our accommodation was in a relative's home. With seven children in the family, some had to give up their beds for us as guests. We shared a dinner and breakfast and an evening of conversation in English and German (I understood very little despite my recent Conversational German class.) The youth were in the living room and we sat in the kitchen under the hissing bright propane lamp hanging from the ceiling.

My Honda Accord plowed its way through a snow blizzard and unplowed gravel country roads the evening of the wedding to another relative host's home for the night. Again, eight-year-old and six-year-old daughters gave up their warm bed for me. Where these displaced daughters found refuge to sleep I will never know, but they were alert and cheery at breakfast before going off to school in a contracted eight-passenger custom Chevy van the next morning.

The visit gave me an opportunity to observe the 5 a.m. milking of 34 Holstein cows. Husband and wife and two older children helped in the chores. The milking machine was a modern electric powered DeLaval model draining four cows at a time. Milk was conveyed through stainless steel pipes to a 1,000-gallon bulk milk tank. Electric powered machinery was possible and allowed by the church/community Ordnung because this farm was rented from English folks and not owned by the Amish. Had the Amish family owned the farm, electricity would not have been allowed.

Freddie J. Simpson

One of the other eight drivers at the wedding was Freddie, also an auctioneer. He drove the Amish to fill his time and distract him from the sadness of his son's accidental death. His custom GMC van was equipped with cell phone, weather radio, and portable television, all valuable on this blizzard night. His late return trip to Kentucky after the wedding with his Amish passengers was questionable as sleet, wind, and drifting were along his route. I left the wedding with my passengers before hearing his decision to drive or not that night.

BOB CREAGER
Bob was an articulate young man of 18 who knew a lot about the Amish from his driving experiences. His passengers were from Lower Michigan. He was from Centerville, near Kalamazoo. He shared with me a booklet he found interesting, entertaining, and useful, *Van Riders Handbook*, printed by Brookside Publishing in Millersburg, PA. Another book is *Driving the Amish* by Jim Butterfield and published by Herald Press (www.mph.org).

BILL POHLE, NEIGHBOR DRIVER
Bill was a lively, cheerful, gregarious senior citizen who seemed to know everybody in the wedding party and local Amish at the dinner. His wife told me he is always that energetic and that she has a hard time keeping up with him. I could not either, and arranged to interview him this summer.

In contrast to the positive nature of Bill, some other drivers were not as friendly toward the Amish. I asked one at the wedding if he was going to witness the service. He replied, "I am a driver and I don't want anything else to do with them."

Another said, "They are cheap. They don't tip very well or not at all. They pay to the penny but not over."

I received a letter from Bill's wife on the 27th of December 2002. She said his health was failing and he was no longer able to drive or write a letter.

MICHIGAN TAXI DRIVER

Jim Belyou, a hearty retired Irishman from Mt. Pleasant, Michigan, sat in a chair at the Wautoma, Wisconsin, Amish quilt and furniture auction tent on a sizzling 92 degree summer day. He had brought a family from the Clare settlement of 75 families and four church districts near Mt. Pleasant in the center of the state to the auction and to visit. Jim retired two years ago from a paper route with over 300 customers, bought a 15-passenger van, and printed bright red and white business cards: "Amish Shuttle Service USA and Canada." These he gives out at churches and relies on his reputation to get him business along with a few ads in local papers. His longest trip was to Colorado for which he charged 55 cents per mile and negotiated a fee for layover time. Another destination was to Aylmer, Ontario, for a wedding near London and another to Kitchener near Toronto for an ordination of a bishop. He makes many trips to northern Indiana. His customers sometimes provide a room in an Amish house for sleeping, but he usually eats out.

Leaning back in his chair and shifting a toothpick in his mouth with his tongue, he confessed he got bored waiting for the Amish when he first started out in his business. Sometimes his wife, Sue, came along for company. He has not read Jim Butterfield's book, *Driving the Amish*, about the author's experiences driving Amish in Ohio's Holmes County. Belyou has no desire to write about his experiences. During this whole conversation, a delightful 12-year-old Amish girl sat nearby, listened intently, and engaged us in conversation. Her personality was as interesting as Jim's interview.

PART I *Wisconsin Settlements*

Chapter 15

NEW GLARUS

A DYING HISTORICAL SETTLEMENT

STATE OF WISCONSIN vs. YODER

A significant court case took place on December 1, 1970 in the Wisconsin Supreme Court. Appellants Jonas Yoder and Adin Yutzy, of the Old Order Amish religion, and Wallace Miller, a member of the Conservative Amish-Mennonite Church, were convicted of violating Wisconsin Compulsory School Attendance Law. Their children had graduated eighth grade and refused to enroll in high school for the next term. The adults were fined $5 each.

Historical traditions of the Amish and Mennonites were used in the case to point out the cultural background of the Anabaptists. John A. Hostetler's book *Amish Society* was referred to, as well as the Dortrecht Confession of 1632 containing religious practice. Salvation is the root of the Amish religion and public high schools do not lend themselves to that end and are too worldly. Parents' rights are also at stake.

The U.S. Supreme Court in Wisconsin vs. Yoder heard the case one year later. Justice Warren Burger delivered the opinion of the Court. Justice Douglas alone dissented. Powell and Rehnquist took no part in the consideration of decision. That case can be found on the web at http://caselaw.lp.findlaw.com. John A. Hostetler was a prime witness. The decision on May 15, 1972 for all the United States was that all Amish and Amish-Mennonites were exempt from compulsory attendance law that required enrollment in high school, i.e. beyond the eighth grade.

SURVIVING AMISH IN NEW GLARUS

There are only three households of Amish left in the New Glarus area. On May 25, 2002, I visited two of them. Kathy Bruin was weeding along the road and I stopped to ask for help. She was from New Glarus and gave me directions to one Amish household, that of Jay Kramer. He lived with two sisters on a rundown, unpainted wood farmhouse. Three dozen or more Holstein cows and several buggy horses were packed into a half-acre pasture along Argue Road. Part of the barn had collapsed. The yard was filled with old farm machinery and equipment. A rubber-tired manure spreader and tractor were near the barn. It looked like none were in working condition. Kathy said he used a rubber-tired tractor in the field, unusual for Amish. His brother John and sister Elizabeth Hershberger were the other Amish residents. None were listed in the 1996 or 2002 edition of the *Wisconsin, Minnesota, & Montana Amish Directory*. Elizabeth is the settlement scribe to the *Budget* newspaper and makes entries occasionally. She gets a free subscription and postage for being a scribe.

VISITING SENSITIVE SUBJECTS

Jay and I visited on the front porch of his house. It was filled with tools, a kerosene heater, hardware, and a friendly beagle. Jay was clean-shaven a few days ago, he said, and wore a green sweatshirt impregnated with oil and grease grime. He obviously enjoyed fixing things and carried a pair of pliers in the pocket on the side of his pant leg. He was less than six feet tall and had a sturdy build. His grip was firm when we shook hands. His speech was friendly, deliberate, and measured to find the proper expressions when it came to delicate matters. I suggested appropriate words, which he generally accepted. This was especially true on the topic of why the settlement disintegrated. The word I had offered was "friction." That friction came from the leadership, he said, after agonizing to say it. Jay stared into the field as he spoke and leaned on the porch railing with his forearms.

"Do you like staying here?" I asked.

"Yah...yeh! This is what I like to do. My brother John and sister are just down the road. I like it here."

I told Jay that I was writing a book and would like to use our conversation in it. It was all right with him and he hinted he would like to read it. "I'm curious as to how you English look at us, what you think of Amish."

"Give me your address and I'll send you one when it is published," I said.

As I moved down the steps of the porch in retreat, Jay found another topic to talk about. He seemed to enjoy the conversation and company. I felt sorry for him and stayed longer than I intended. He gave me directions to his sister's house north of County Road W, and I wished him well and left.

ELIZABETH HERSHBERGER, SCRIBE

I spotted a gray Amish church bench wagon in the backyard of a small, gray slate-sided house shaded by towering silver maple trees. A golden-colored kitten walked toward me on the sidewalk that led to the house. Its mewing demanded my attention, and I knelt down and petted the animal. Then I knocked on the back door. Stepping back, I could see in the window to the kitchen. A barefoot, dark-haired woman wearing a dark blue soiled dress rose from a chair and came to the door. I explained my visit with her brother and asked if I might interview her. She declined quickly, so I wished her well and left. Later that week, I looked for her articles in the *Budget*, and found a few short ones. It seemed like a lonely existence and I wondered why the family had not moved to another thriving settlement. Perhaps on my next visit I would find out.

PART I Wisconsin Settlements
Chapter 16
HILLSBORO

TRUCK FARMING

A clerk in the Ben Franklin store in Hillsboro gave me directions to an Amish farm on Hwy 80 south of town. The name Borkholder was on the rural mailbox. Nobody was home.

The long gravel drive up to the house had not been used very much. Ruts from washouts dug one-foot ditches that were filled with rock and debris. Two midget sentinel dogs greeted me with barks and growls but never attacked as I walked up the porch to the front door. Knocking brought no response. The inside reminded me of my great uncle's farm. It was plain, simple, drab, and old-fashioned. There were no traditional Amish blue curtains or shades. What looked like a summer kitchen in the backyard was vacant. A 150-foot long metal garage with sliding doors housed a tool room and workshop at the south end. Behind that was the machinery shed of bleached-weathered wood guarded by a dog inside who barked a warning as I approached. Another garage size building that looked like a schoolhouse sat atop the rise to the west. Grass had overgrown the walk to it. The barn had another miniature sentinel dog tied inside to give fair warning to intruders. Four other outbuildings and a windmill and cistern on a high point dotted the landscape. A bridge over a creek looked of questionable strength to hold my car and it rattled as I drove over it. The property did not appear to be well kept by anybody's standard and certainly not Amish norms.

OMAR MILLER ORGANIC FARM

I stopped at a root beer stand to ask for directions to another Amish farm. The carhop could not recall any Amish farms in the area, but knew of some near Wilton where she lived. A tavern is usually a good source for information and was my next try. The patrons seemed reluctant to share any information during the time it took me to drink a cool refreshing beverage on this 90-degree day. They made snide remarks about the Amish beards that made me reluctant to believe anything they would offer to help me. I left and drove south on Hwy 82. As luck would have it, I saw fresh buggy tracks in the soft gravel shoulder. I followed them right to the Omar Miller organic vegetable farm.

Omar and a son were in a 300-foot long field lined with white rows of remme material over tender plants. This material was a gauze-like mesh that kept the plants from burning in the sun. As I drove up the football field length drive, Omar and his five sons and daughters gathered in the yard at a safe distance to see and hear what was going on. I presented my purpose for being there and began asking questions.

"How many families are in this settlement?" I asked Omar.

"There are about 90 homesteads, but not necessarily all farms," he replied. "Some men are carpenters."

"What's your church count?"

"Well, there are seven churches in the community, but only five bishops. So, two of them take two districts. There's eight schools with about 20 scholars in each and one teacher in each."

"Where can I find a bulk food store in the settlement?" I asked.

"Well, there is one off Hwy 82 west three miles to County Road V."

"V like in Victor?" I asked.

"Yah, V. My front teeth are missing and some of the sounds don't come out right."

"Don't worry about that. I'm hard of hearing at my age, so I probably didn't hear you right," I replied. He seemed somewhat embarrassed, and I hoped I had not offended him with my response. But he chuckled and some of the older kids standing around had Cheshire cat grins on their faces.

"What do you grow for a cash crop on this farm?" I asked.

"Well, there are cucumbers, squashes of all kinds, some beans, peppers, and cabbages which are sent to LaFarge and Spring Green co-op markets and wholesalers. There's an organic dealer in LaFarge," he added. His answers were getting longer and more relaxed.

I said, "Yes, I know the organic plant there. We get milk, butter, and cottage cheese from LaFarge that is sold in Pick 'n Save grocery stores." Just then, his wife rode into the yard in a two-wheel cart. Omar said she had just come from the bulk store on V.

Thanking him for his information, I wished him well for the coming summer growing season. He had not offered his name, so I did not ask, but I noticed it on the mailbox as I left the gravel driveway on my way to the store on V.

THE STORE ON V
Omar's directions were correct. A collie-like dog sauntered toward me with head down and no particular interest in me. A sign on the store door said "Hours open, 8 to 5. Sales after 5 add 15% to the price." I was there at 4:55 p.m., but nobody was in the store. Not liking to be English in the store alone, I went back outside to find someone. A small one-horse gasoline engine running a water well pump was so sooty that I could not read the model name. But it was the only thing moving, so I went back in the store. A sign on the counter said to ring the bell for service. It was a regular

doorbell, but I did not hear anything ring. I was wandering through the aisles when a twentyish Amish lady peered around the corner and stared at me.

"I'm sorry, are English folks allowed in here?" I pleaded apologetically.

"Well, I guess it's O.K." she replied in a very soft and nearly offended voice.

"I found this directory of Amish communities that I'd like to buy." It had names in alphabetical order of Amish who subscribed to *Die Blatt* newspaper and their addresses. It was a real find.

Now she was standing next to me. "Well, you might find this book interesting. It is about an English boy, Joas, who goes to an Amish school. It was written by an Amish woman in this settlement." Now she turned into a saleslady and I knew I was welcome. A large, tall strong looking older Amish man peered around the corner of a shelf. Thinking he was another customer, I told the saleslady that she could take care of him. It was not necessary. Her father heard the doorbell and came to handle the sale, but left when he saw she was handling things.

She did ring up the sale for $11.44 and I talked about my book-writing venture. As I left, she said, "This has been very interesting!" I said I would be back sometime in summer. Her mother had arrived in another two-wheeled cart and greeted me confidently and cheerfully. The turnabout from caution to acceptance was rewarding.

YODER'S ENGINE SERVICE

One hundred yards to the south of V on Hwy 82 was a sign on the road and buildings looking like Amish architecture. The sign read "Engine Repair and Sales." As I drove in, two small barefoot Amish children were playing in the gravel drive near the 800 square foot metal-sided building that housed the business. A sheepdog-like animal with gravel on its back strolled by. Inside, James Yoder, son of Erwin according to the business card, was taking care of a customer. The English man, who drove a sporty silver convertible parked outside, wore John Lennon style glasses and a New Zealand safari hat, a spectacle if I ever saw one. His mannerisms were dramatic as he spoke with James, head nodding, arms waving, finger pointing, and voice pleading like a father admonishing his child. James was taking it all in stride and seemed to relish my intrusion.

"I'm writing a book about the Amish in Wisconsin and visiting all the settlements. I wonder if I might be able to ask a few questions about your business," I stated.

"You might want to talk to my father. He's in the barn milking. I'm sure he'd like to talk with you." James was enthusiastic and out from under the Lennon lover's domineering talk. We exchanged a few comments about an upcoming documentary television program called "Devil's Playground." It disclosed the "rumspringa" (literally, running around) time of four Amish youth in a 90-minute exposé. Then I headed for the barn.

An opaque plastic curtain hung across the barn door, probably to keep the cold out and the heat in. I could hear conversation on the other side and walked down the aisle looking for the father, Erwin. Slightly over five feet tall, he had a wandering right eye and sparse dark hair. His buttoned short sleeve shirt showed the work of his day. He was hand milking, nestled against the belly of bossy and sitting on a makeshift stool. I squatted down on a stool in the aisle and started the visit. I told him my purpose and he began talking. He had 16 shorthorn cows about the size of Jerseys. Their full-length tails were tied to a wire above them to keep from swishing in the face of the milkers. Some cows were all rusty red while others were spotted red and white. Another variation was pepper-and-salt color. I said my Amish friend in Marion had the spotted red and white variety, which I heard were called "Mennonite Holstein." It is a joke and he chuckled.

"Shorthorns are easier to care for and they produce higher butter fat. We get a premium for it. We get about $10 a hundredweight for the milk. A milk can holds 80 pounds. That's lower than what we have been getting. We have a co-op which is owned by an English—you know English, don't you?" He was on a roll and continued hand milking. It attracted James to join us and two other adolescent brothers and a bunch of smaller children who crowded around me on the 9-inch high stool. One small barefoot two-year-old girl stuck her finger on my left forearm like you would touch a snake, to see if I was real. Nobody else talked but Erwin and me for 45 minutes.

"What's going on out there?" Erwin exclaimed. Two boys ran to the barn door as horses galloped by. "Must be the weather—storm coming. They get nervous when a storm is coming."

"How did you know something was wrong?" I asked.

"I could hear them galloping outside. That's usually a sign something is up."

A squirrel-sized dog on my right side was enjoying my petting while a larger lemon yellow longhaired dog on my left side was content with my scratching his head. What a photograph this would have made, I thought.

Erwin said the *Wisconsin State Journal* had been there four years ago and took a photograph of his younger son retrieving the mail. It ended up in the article titled "Amish on the Move." Erwin was building a chicken coop that he could move around for "pasture grazing" that was part of organic farming. He used his cows to alternately graze and keep the grass down to three inches, and then brought in the chickens. The two natural fertilizers were rich for the soil, part of organic farming. He knew of Luthy's book, *Settlements that Failed* that describes the failings of Amish settlements over the years. I asked him if he was a preacher, but he was not. He added, "If we all read the good book things might be better." That was in response to my question of whether my classes on the Amish were worthwhile. Anything that will make living on this earth more enjoyable and peaceful would be worth it, I decided. We have something to learn from our Amish citizens.

It was an enjoyable visit and I thanked James and Erwin for their time and hospitality. I checked beneath my car to see if any kittens were under it and gauged my exit being watchful for the two girls playing near the driveway. Erwin reassured me that they would be all right. He was alert and aware of everything that was going on around his farm.

PART I *Wisconsin Settlements*
Chapter 17
HILL POINT

LAZY QUIET TOWN

South of Hillsboro on Hwy 42 is the small town of Hill Point. This is a lazy, quiet town with no freeways nearby. As I arrived at its center where the fire station is located, a young, tall Amish man was leaning against a telephone pole talking on a pay phone. His bicycle leaned against the same pole. I pulled over to ask him where the Amish families lived.

Instead, I went across the street to the Villa Inn, a bar and restaurant that is run by Donald Mutterer and his wife for the past 17 years. They were sitting on the front porch on this hot June early evening. I was hungry and thirsty, so I ordered a cold ham and Swiss sandwich and 50 cent glass of Miller High Life on tap. Don added some potato salad and pickle and chips. I was the only customer in this neatly organized bar. All the Green Bay Packer helmet pour spouts on the booze bottles were facing the same direction. Nothing in the place was out of symmetry. I wondered how he felt about the Amish in the community or anything that disrupted the customary status quo.

MORE THAN HORSE SHOES

"I don't really mind the Amish, but they do cut up the road in the summer when the asphalt is hot and their horses' shoes dig holes in the road. Then the road crews have got to go out and repair. We have asked them to switch to soft shoes in the summer, but they refuse. I do not have anything against them, they are hard workers, but they cost us money in taxes. Besides, they do not contribute anything to the community. But they are better than some of the riffraff that are moving into town lately," he said, while holding his slim brand cigarette between his first and second fingers. His thin arms and frame reminded me of my uncle who looked the same, smoked and died of emphysema. A friend on the porch had retired from driving a truck that picked up bulk milk from farms. He told about the Amish (he pronounced it "Aymish") group of young boys who came into town with a boom box that they hid in a haystack back home. He also saw the same boys at the ballpark in their buggy drinking Miller Lite until 2 a.m. "But, the clan does have nice homes. And they are hypocrites! The hired hands lived in mobile homes provided by the owner with electric appliances that they used," he said.

Donald, changing the subject, said there were three schools, one on G, and the others to the east of town. He seemed to be trying to maintain a civil discussion in my presence.

Just then, three young Amish boys came walking into town. They wore medium blue shirts with buttons down the front. I went out to greet them. They told me a school and their home were on County Road G to the south of Hill Point. The leader did the talking. He said there were 36 families in the settlement. A buggy went by with a young male wearing uncharacteristic blue jeans and white Nike shoes. With night falling, deer migrating, and four hours yet to drive, I bid good day and drove south on Hwy 82 toward G.

Along the way, I passed the three boys and beeped my horn. A half mile further were four Amish girls in bare feet walking abreast on the other side of the road. Were the boys following them? Turning on G for the shortcut detour Donald had given me, I was able to see the huge school building and large home of the leader of the three boys.

Villa Inn was the focal point of my research in this settlement. It had all the elements I needed for balanced coverage—Amish, non-Amish, and opinionated.

PART I   Wisconsin Settlements

Chapter 18
GREENWOOD

On this initial trip to Greenwood on a Saturday late afternoon, the town was dead. A small restaurant at the edge of town was busy, so I went in to find out where the Amish were. The clerk gave me directions to a Mennonite farm up the road. It turned out the English-owned farm had been sold to Mennonites, but the owner still occupied it and was milking with the help of a hired hand. Larry Stamp was 63 years old with a leaking heart valve. He had a stubble beard, bib overalls, a faded baseball cap, and knee-high rubber boots covered with cow dung. He praised the smartness of the Mennonite farming practices but admitted his pole barn needed repair or replacement soon. He marked several Mennonite farms on my Wisconsin Gazetteer map and we parted.

As I drove north on Hwy 73, I saw what looked like an Amish or Mennonite schoolhouse with all the windows broken. Could exuberant Mennonites or perhaps local angry citizens have done this? A bit farther, a group of 18 young Mennonites and Amish were playing volleyball in a farmyard. I saw several other Mennonite farms along the Highway and another schoolhouse on Hwy 29 as I turned east in search of Interstate 39 south on my way home. It was now early evening, the sun painted long shadows across the landscape, and I had had a full day. I looked forward to some home cooked food in Westfield and a four-hour drive home.

FINDING A FRIEND
Locating the Amish can be difficult, if not impossible. With the aid of directories, the task is simplified, but not

solved. The Amish move frequently. Addresses in rural areas are usually fire lane numbers and postal service numbers. The *Wisconsin, Minnesota, & Montana Amish Directory* is the best guide. The 2002 edition came out in August. However, the previous publication was 1996, six years old. The Directory includes hand-drawn maps of the settlements or by sections if it is large. Some settlements do not have artistic cartographers. It appears that bishops compose the maps and affix their signature to them.

Another means of locating the Amish is to ask in the town nearest to the settlement. That was the case in trying to find Melvin Yoder in Greenwood. A local waitress directed me to two Amish farms.

"Just go west on County G to the top of the hill and you'll find the first one. Go another mile and you'll come to the second one," she said. And she was right. But the first farm was the Schwartz and not Yoder. But Menno Schwartz, cousin to my Amish friends in Marion, knew where Melvin lived and gave me directions that were 90% correct. Central Avenue was hard to find, but find it I did. Then the fire lane numbers came into play. There it was, the Yoder farm. His son, Eddie, lived next door on the same farm.

Eddie was in the back yard preparing a sprayer for the field. His slender build and reddish hair and misaligned front teeth made him distinctive. He was pouring a white liquid in a 50-gallon translucent plastic drum on a two-wheeled cart. Perhaps it was Malathion, a weed killer or insecticide. A one horsepower gasoline motor was mounted in front of the tank with valves and hoses leading to and from the tank. Six-foot arms were folded over each other like a resting Monarch butterfly with spray nozzles spaced nine inches apart. These would be extended to cover several rows of plants in the field. Patiently waiting, a team of Belgian horses was hitched to the rig. Eddie allowed me to photograph the rig while he and a young son retreated to a building out of camera range.

In a refurbished shed with new cinder block below and old rafters and roof above, I found his father, Melvin. Before I went through the doorway, he exclaimed, " I know, I should have answered your letter. I know. You've got my book." It must have been telepathy. The book was the *Amish Directory* he loaned me at the Amherst quilt auction. Melvin was tucked away at the side of the 6-foot low ceiling beyond a table saw and clutter. Two dogs begged for my attention, and the black Labrador got most of it. Melvin showed me a small end table with folding sides he had made on his router, band saw, drill, and planer. He hoped to market it somewhere.

Melvin is a 5'4" tall rotund man with a Santa Claus girth and chuckle. Even his clear watery eyes twinkle. He has a crisp, quick sense of humor and easily retorts to my teasing comments. He allowed me to photograph the shop. His two executive type swivel chairs at his disheveled desk in a corner got my attention. He took my snide remark about the desk being messy for a CEO in stride, replying with some of his own.

He said he bought several quilt tops at the Amherst auction, but his wife did not like them. He will bring them to another auction to get rid of them. It is the luxury of any retired man to spend time at auctions. A cool breeze wormed its way through the shed, a relief from the 90-degree furnace outside. Melvin was in a good place, his castle, and workshop. What more can a man ask for who has a humble heart?

PART I *Wisconsin Settlements*
Chapter 19
SPENCER, AND LOYAL

NEW ORDER AMISH

SPENCER

Northwest of Marshfield is Spencer. It serves as a hub for a cluster of Amish and Mennonite farms—Stratford, Unity, Chili, Granton, Curtiss, Edgar, and Thorp. Spencer is home for the sect of New Order Amish that use tractors in the field. Most Amish, if they do use tractors, use them for stationary power sources, with long belts for threshing machines.

LOYAL

Loyal has been in the newspapers recently. The city folks seem to be perturbed by the horse droppings (the article headline called it "Do-Do") left behind when the Swartzentruber Amish buggies are in town. As I drove through the town May 18, 2002, I did not smell or see any deposit in the street. In Kingston, the Amish there voluntarily shovel and sweep the "horse-apples" off the street every Saturday.

One Swartzentruber mother I visited west of Loyal on Hwy 98 said she did not know any way to remedy the situation. Suddenly, half a dozen Holstein heifers ran out of the barn and into the yard. The farm boy in me instinctively reacted and waved them off while the mother and three children did the same to return them to the barn. I noticed the house and other buildings on her farm were somewhat more crudely constructed. Her blue dress was soiled from her work cleaning chickens. She smiled often through misaligned and missing front teeth, but was a cheerful and friendly person.

Having met the Swartzentrubers in Pennsylvania and in Fennimore, Wisconsin with similar, more primitive or first century church ethos, I speculated that it was not the horse droppings that may have upset the citizens of Loyal, but the sect itself. Perhaps they feared property values would decline because of "unsavory" neighbors living in the area. I found this sentiment in the Cashton area. There, Amish bought cheap, unproductive, and depleted farmland with dilapidated 1860 barns, homes, and outbuildings and made a go of it. Was it "do-do" or "don't-don't" driving the citizens of Loyal?

I had stopped at this farm on the pretense of buying eggs that I saw advertised on the road. Buying something is the easiest way to gain access to folks. However, the last carton was short two eggs, so a responsible girl was sent to fetch two more. When she returned, I teased her asking if the eggs were still warm and if she had to reach under the chicken to get them. Mother and child laughed and sensed the humor of my teasing. After paying 80 cents for the brown eggs, I drove out past a tiny child in a dark coat and black felt hat sitting on a rock. His face was sullen as though he was bored, but he waved. I waved back enthusiastically and hoped it brightened up his day.

I visited another Swartzentruber Amish east of Loyal on Hwy 98. A large homemade sign near the road offered woodcrafts, lawn furniture, and baskets for sale. At the rear of the house was a red vertical sided metal woodworking shed. An engine in a closet sized building attached to the shed ran the equipment inside.

Dennis L. Miller saw me in the doorway, shut down the machines and engine, locked the beagle inside, and greeted me. He was a man in his 30s, trim, in a blue pullover Nehru-collar short-sleeved shirt. Broadfall pants and two-strand suspenders were the standard. A stutter developed in his speech as we talked, sometimes locking him in silence. But we continued our conversation, including the horse "Dodo" I read about in the paper. Dennis said it would be dangerous to dismount from a buggy to sweep up the droppings without someone holding the horse. He had no other solution.

Then he asked me a favor. "Would you help me find a wholesaler to market the lawn furniture I built?" I said I would. "The furniture includes gliders, swings, tables, benches, and rockers." At this time, he was supplying Spokeville Lawn Furniture in nearby Spencer with products. He gave me a sheet with neatly typed columns of items and wholesale prices. Anxious to return to his work, he left. The barn and other buildings were eerily silent. No person or animal was in sight. No equipment was standing in the yard or fields. Perhaps he was alone on this farm.

Fox Farm Near Loyal

The Swartzentruber Amish woman directed me to a Mennonite farm near Greenwood. It was the Fox Farm. The mailbox proudly displayed their name, Fox. Three 60-foot Harvestore silos stood sentinel over the barnyard. An eight-wheeled Ford tractor hitched to a fertilizing rig stood idle in the yard. This was a progressive operation. I rang the bell next to the back door, which was covered with a wrought iron security gate. A Mennonite woman in a blue print dress and a small white head cover came to the door. She answered a few questions about the area, but was busy with crying children, so I thanked her and went on my way.

PART I   Wisconsin Settlements
Chapter 20
ATHENS, BOYD, CURTISS, OWENS-UNITY

THE BELTLINE

DIRECTORY INFORMATION
At the beginning of each settlement listed in the *Wisconsin, Minnesota & Montana Amish Directory 2002* is a brief history of the early formation. Pioneer settlers and dates of significant events are noted. Name, year of birth, community of origin, a list of the ministry, date ordained as deacon, minister and/or bishop, and date of death, if applicable are provided. Schools are also listed with teacher(s) named, grades taught, and number of students (scholars). This *Directory* was the source of information for some of this and the next four chapters.

BELTLINE COMMUNITIES
Traversing the midsection of the state is a line of communities along State Hwy 29. They dominate the terrain from Wausau to Chippewa Falls. Mixed in with Amish settlements are various sects of Mennonites including Conservative, Independent, Bethany, Weaverland Conference, Sheldon, Nationwide, and Unaffiliated. Among the Amish, there are Old Order, New Order, Swartzentruber, and Amish-Mennonite.

ATHENS
Athens was settled in the early fall of 1990. A group of men from Spring Run, Pennsylvania, came to Wisconsin in search of farm bargains and a good milk market. By the twos, threes, and then eights, families came to buy farms.

One year later, a wedding was held. There have been five since, with three couples taking up residence in Athens. The first funeral was in 2002 for a "special child," with burial on land provided on the Graber farm.

Home schooling was practiced the first year. Then a trailer on Levi Yoder's farm was used for a school. The third year a new school named Shady Pine School was built on the Beiler farm. Lumber to build it was scavenged from a burned out house and donated to the settlement.

There are now twenty-eight households or families (not all households are a family) in the settlement with three schools, two in operation with 50 students. The largest family has 13 children, three of them being married.

All but three husbands are farmers. Carpentry, woodworking, retail, and repair shop are the vocations of two husbands. One is simply "retired."

Mennonites live in the Athens area. Some are in the Nationwide Fellowship with two ministers, one deacon, and one bishop. The *Budget* scribes, the Martins, tell a heartwarming story of their family of 12 children that survived a fire that destroyed their house. They lived in a Catholic convent in town for four months until they moved into a new house built and furnished by neighbors and Christian friends.

In the *Die Botschaft*, a national Old Order Amish newspaper, scribes Daniel and Mary write in their own words:

"Oct. 7 Greetings to all readers. Looked pretty frosty out this morning. The first "real" frost we had this fall. Still not a hard one. Church was here at our house for son Davids yesterday and be at son Samuels next, communion. Visitors yesterday were John and Sam Hertzlers of Mechanicsville, MD. Our daughter Sarah, the Henry Yoders of Wulff Valley, WI moved to Lowville, NY last week. I went along then came back with the driver. I spent part of Thursday at brother

David's barn raising then started west again. Stopped at Mary's parents at Romulus, NY for the night. Gahobt eich vol, Daniel and Mary."

In the *Budget* newspaper, scribe Mrs. J.M.S of the Milan Area writes: "Oct.15—Worthy mention is the start of the third day with clear, blue skies, after many rainy days in past weeks. Farmers are struggling in muddy fields to get their silos filled. Our area families are starting their home schooling with David Planks having 3, Earnest Schwartzes 2, Andy Masts 4 and Alvin Borntragers 2. Some a quite a ways from the school and would need transportation and with low milk prices, this is the way for this year. We got our wood pile replenished on Fri. with our children and grandchildren's help. The Lambright family of Whitehall were also here and assisted. Christ Borntrager was an accidental tractor victim lately and was laid up. A bald eagle is seen around the area at present, and also David Planks are entertaining a skunk family or vice versa."

BOYD

I have been told that there are over 200 Mennonite families in the Beltline area. I was unable to locate any Amish families, but there is a scribe, Mary Martin, on "Stony Lonesome Road" in Boyd. She describes herself in the *Who is Who in the Budget* as a Nationwide Fellowship Mennonite and "just a common mother with a common family living a common life."

CURTISS

There are no Amish listed for Curtiss in the *Amish Directory 2002*, but a *Budget* scribe is in *Who is Who*, Jerry and Elizabeth Stutzman, who are retired. Their eleven children have all "left the nest" and range in age from 21 to 40.

A deacon and a minister for the Unity Nationwide Fellowship live in Curtiss. They are both Martins.

OWEN-UNITY

This settlement spreads out from near Owen (County N) to near Unity (Hwy 13). There are 17 families (all but two are farming) listed in the *Amish Directory 2002*. One teacher is listed living on Cloverdale Road and has been its sole educator since 1992. Jonas Zook is the scribe and operates a retail store.

PART I Wisconsin Settlements
Chapter 21
AUGUSTA, FAIRCHILD

FARMERS, WOODWORKING, & SAWMILLS

In Augusta, there are six church districts with about 20 families in each. A hand-drawn map of roads numbers family locations as well as schools, a cheese plant, and a cemetery. Each family listed documents husband and wife's dates of birth and marriage and a listing of their children and their birth dates. A symbol "A" after their name indicates they are living at the home of their parents. The symbol "B" indicates single and living away from home. It does not indicate if they left the sect. The symbol of married is the letter "C". The date of death, if applicable, appears also.

The number of children in each family may average about seven. One family had 18 living children. Eight were still living at home, and the remaining ten were married, including one set of twins. Three other families had 14 children, mostly married. There are seven schools operating, three being added in school term 2001-2002. Most teachers are from Augusta and Fairchild. All were women except two.

My companion on this excursion was a student from my Amish class, Mary. Born and raised in Augusta, she knew the area. The preponderance of sawmills was the first anomaly that struck me. At least 36 families listed sawmill, woodworking, flooring, sawyer, or lumber as the occupation solely or with farming or another occupation. Mary said a local lumberyard brings logs to these sawmills to be cut to order—planks and four inch square by eight-foot long posts. Much of the red metal shed construction and layout was identical throughout the settlement. Why argue with a good thing? If it works, don't fix it.

As Mary skillfully navigated through the settlement, zigzagging over the non-parallel roads, I tried to log businesses and Amish homes on my Wisconsin Gazetteer map. The black dots became so close and thick they appeared as flyspecks on a windowsill of a barn.

Names on the mailboxes seemed to be repeated often. However, upon closer observation, there was a slight variation. Because the first settler in 1978 was a Borntrager family from the Cashton settlement as well as the next two families with a total of 21 children, it is no wonder there are so many of their names on mailboxes.

COUNTRY MARKET

The Country Market was on County Road M in the heart of the settlement less than a mile east and three miles south of Augusta. They prized "Old Fashioned Quality" and printed it on their business cards. They sold bulk foods and spices, baked goods, and woodcrafts. The store was a separate building set farther back from the road than the house and was nearly overlooked except for a small roadside sign. No mantle lanterns were lit when we were there, nor was there any heat on the chilly day. As we left, the friendly middle-aged Amish clerk brought in pieces of wood to build a fire in the cast iron stove. I bought a small solid cedar box for my daughter-in-law's birthday and looked at the harmonicas for sale, tempted to buy. I was surprised to see them in such a conservative settlement. I have seen only two Amish children with mouth organs, and they were both "special children" allowed to have them as amusement for themselves.

Mary knew of the Hershberger Woodworking shop where the one auction each year is held outside its door. On

County RR and Hay Creek Road, the building has a convoluted collection of cubbyholes and rooms filled with finished and unfinished furniture. The "office" walls are plastered with work orders, sales receipts, catalog pages, and related price lists. Paper and plastic wrapping litters the never-swept floors.

Across from the Hershberger shop was the Miller farrier or blacksmith. Four English pickup trucks hitched to horse trailers were stationed in the circular drive adjacent to the barn. With only one other blacksmith listed in the *Amish Directory 2002*, and buggy horses (Standardbred) requiring new shoes changed every six weeks, this was a profitable business. Some math calculations may bear this out. There are 108 families in the settlement, each with at least one buggy and horse (some may have as many as three). A horse is shod eight times each year. That amounts to 864 customers a year. At $20 for each shoeing (shoes are $20 extra), that is $17,280 a year. However, with Amish having no health insurance, one swift kick to a farrier from a dissatisfied horse and one could spend that entire amount quickly in our English health system.

.

From the *Budget* scribe Amos in his own words;
"Oct. 7 Now the sun is shining so bright, everything is turning out right! Yes, it seems so good to see the sun and blue skies! And then there were these boys that went "pigeon catching" this one evening with the two seated top buggy and two horses and were at Andy Yoders and going out the drive, and horses started to run and one kicked and tugs unhooked. Then the brakes were slammed on and neck-yoke unhooked and the pole went in the side bank and broke off and buggy flipped on road and horses took off without buggy. Boys got up and started home and stopped at Ed F. Borntragers to see if he could take them home. He had no horse in barn so they walked the 1? miles home

figuring the horses are at home. No horses around, but boys go to bed and sleep. Next morning, Ed goes out to let the cows in from pasture, hears a groan, listens, hears more groans, then investigates and finds these two horses in a mud hole on east side of road, tangled up in harness. One horse on top of other. One horse had to hold up head out of water to breath. Hollers for help and Joseph Mast and boys help to get the horses untangled and up!! May Gluck es verstand! Amos F."

PART I   Wisconsin Settlements
Chapter 22
CHETEK AND NEW AUBURN

ISOLATED

Located near the southern border of Barron County in rolling clay and sandy loam soil in northwestern Wisconsin, Chetek was founded on October 18, 1974, as an Old Order community. There were never more than 11 families at a time in the settlement up to 1990, and a maximum of 19 to date. One school is currently operating with 14 students. Most families are noticeably smaller than other settlements. The cemetery and Sunny Meadow School are situated southwest of Chetek along 4th Avenue at the junction of County I and A near the Red Cedar River.

New Auburn's 27 families straddle State Hwy 53 fifteen miles south of Chetek. Family size is larger than Chetek, filling Twin Lake (opened in 1999) and Sunny Meadow Schools (opened in 2000) with 29 and 27 scholars respectively. Early families did home schooling. Occupations are clustered around day labor, carpentry, sawmill, and pallet shop. Only three list farmer, one clock repair (the first settler), and one harness maker shop.

The Chetek scribe for the *Budget* has served for 15 years. She suffered a tragic loss of her husband and two oldest daughters, aged seven and nine, who were killed in a buggy-train accident in Whitehall. She moved to Amherst and married a man whose wife had died of cancer. They lived in Indiana briefly and then moved back to Amherst for eight years. That settlement disbanded by December 7, 2000. I helped the last family move. Then the scribe moved back to Chetek.

These tragedies are common in rural areas. Mobility is common within the Amish community. However, moving to another settlement usually reconnects relatives and friends, not strangers as in the English business-driven relocations. Chetek is a small settlement and was hard to find, as witnessed by one of the students in my Amish class at the University of Wisconsin-Waukesha. Judy Wisniewski wrote to me of her "searching" experience and sent along a map of Barron County marked up with her route. Here is her story.

"Dear Richard,
After our class at UWW ended in October, I took the opportunity to visit friends in Rice Lake, WI. We decided to look for the Amish in the area. Touring on a Monday morning helps locate their farms by just looking for clothes hanging on the line to dry. Just south of Chetek, we found 4-5 small farms and a schoolhouse on 4th Avenue and 20th Street. These were probably Old Order Amish. Finding Amish in the Spooner area is almost impossible. From an article in the *Budget*, the scribe was talking about lightening knocking out her modem. Finding non-motorized and non-electrified farms might be a problem. We couldn't find any. We did find one store selling Amish furniture on Hwy B in Barron. They got most of their goods from Ohio. Cheryl Whiteford called and told me that you met my friends, Edna and Emmon Schmucker. One of their sons has an auction around July 4th every year—lots of fresh doughnuts, too. My Rice Lake friends just reported seeing two buggies crossing Hwy 29 in the Thorp, WI area. There is an auction in that area in the spring. I think it may be in Stetsonville.
Sincerely, Judith L. Wisniewski"

PART I Wisconsin Settlements
Chapter 23
PLATTEVILLE AND CUBA CITY

BUDGET and DIE BOTSCHAFT

South of Livingston on Hwy 80 is Platteville. Amish have not submitted their congregation listing or map for publication in the *Amish Directory 2002*. Although there are *Die Botschaft* articles that appear from time to time, nobody from Platteville is listed in *Who is Who in the Budget*. Finding these settlements becomes difficult, so I have included articles from their newspapers to tell their story in their own words.

Sunnydale Road
"Sept. 29 Dear readers far and near. While relaxing for a bit before calling it a day, I will see what I can get accomplished in this letter. Chores are done for another day and I think we are both glad. Our first heifer we raised freshened today. And to make a long story short we will just say she didn't want to cooperate and it took quite a bit longer till we were done. Council services were held today with the test being Matthew 18. It is hard to believe we are at that time of year already. The episode with the heifer turned out much better this morning than last night. So we have hopes that she will improve. The white washer is here this morning so the barn is getting it's annual cleaning. If only it would stay so nice and clean. Bill Pohle, another driver has been diagnosed with cancer. If I have it correct he had it before. His daughter also has cancer. Those

of you who know them might want to send him a card. Well, my work doesn't get done by itself so I should get to work. Life is a coin. You can spend it any way you wish, but you can only spend it once. Sincerely, David and Lisa"

"Sept 30 Hello to all of our friends who read. We are having a warmer spell again with 72 degrees at 5:00 in the morning. Our *gmay liet* gathered together at Ike Stoltzfuses yesterday. We had *oddings gmay*...preached by Sammie and Elam Allgyer. It was nice to have Puds Sams among our group also! It is als so precious to have others parents come to church. There is some excitement in the air with wedding plans being made at Israel's Jakes in Fennimore. Their Katie getting Bennie Lapp's Henry for her husband. Their special day is planned of Oct 24. A load of our people went to a "special school meeting" on Saturday in Kingston, WI. It takes "special parents" to raise "special children." Wishing you all God's blessings...Emanuel and Mayme"

Cuba City, Wisconsin
Platteville District
"Oct. 7- Dear Botschaft Readers, Greetings of Love in Jesus Name. And now it's Oct. already. Had a low of 37 deg. This morn. But don't think we had any frost. So we still have lots of string beans from the garden. Anybody still want some? Council services were held at Isaac Stolzfus on Sun. afterall. So now we plan on having communion at Leroy Allgyers on Oct 15. Two wks. later at Henry A. & Nov. 10, to be here. Come join us. Henry & we are changing around as we planned on

going to PA for a wk. & the load we want to go with starts on the eve. Of Oct 25. So how many of our friends & relatives will we get to see then? Noah & Rachel"

<u>Author's Note</u>

This internal communication mechanism through newspapers is what helps to keep the social group together and up to date. Farmers glean weather information from valley and ridge farmers. Homemakers share garden abundance with others. Support is found in kind notes for "special children" parents. Church locations and special meetings keep everyone aware and informed so they can be responsible to the congregation.

PART I Wisconsin Settlements
Chapter 24
MONDOVI AND DURAND

DIE BOTSCHAFT

The Mondovi settlement started in March 1991. Folks
came from Pennsylvania and found a real estate agent who
did not take the Amish seriously until they had surveyed the
farms for sale and returned to the agent's office ready to do
business. Groups of five and six families emigrated at a
time. The reason is cheap land relative to where they came
from. Amish from Wautoma, Blair, and Augusta helped this
initial wave to unload the household goods and farm equipment from semi-trucks.

A minister and bishop were among the early settlers
from Delaware, Missouri, and Pennsylvania. By fall of the
first year there were ten families established.

Some unusual incidents are recorded in the *Amish
Directory 2002*. A four-year-old girl fell and inhaled a kernel of corn into her lung. She recovered. A twin had heart
defects requiring surgery at eight months old in New Jersey.
A two-year-old fell against a line shaft receiving burns and
scratches. A young boy climbed out on a tree limb that
broke sending him to the ground and receiving two broken
wrists and injuring his spleen and liver. Two cows had to be
sold because a neighboring boy used them for target practice with his BB gun. A year-old boy with "weak lungs"
inhaled kerosene fumes and died in a Rochester, Minnesota
hospital a week later. There was a stillborn, a victim of cancer,
and a buggy and semi truck accident, killing an Amish woman
in the buggy. She left eleven children to be cared for.

There are 73 families living in Mondovi as of April 2002. The Mondovi *Budget* scribe, Naomi, has served for thirteen years. She has thirteen children and her husband, David, operates a furniture shop. She also reports for the Durand settlement that started in 1991. She wrote their congregation has "67 households plus two widows living alone." Naomi and David were married in Delaware and moved to Pennsylvania where David's parents lived. Family ties are strong. She writes, "One son, Willis (20) lives here but not at home. Sad to say, he has left the Amish faith."

From the *Die Botschaft* comes this scribe's report; "Oct. 7-The busy month of Oct. here. Harvest moon-pumpkins, apples, colorful trees. Rust, orange, yellow, gold all blended together. I need to find me some squash-acorn is my favorite-I did raise 2 small ones. Middle church was at Paul E. Stutzmans. Will be there Oct 20 for council meeting with Crist M. Millers furnishing the eats. Going back to our visit to Kingston to a wedding, I met Elizabeth Miller who is in a widow circle letter with me & others. Always nice to see a face now along with our letters. Another thing on my mind this morning is these ads & shops who want quilts & crafts on consignment, all be careful, don't send items by mail unless an Amish store. Two of us here are left out quite a bit by a store in Pepin when in PA we lost at a NY store, with sad stories. They are so nice to start with, but they also know Amish don't sue & take advantage of this. 20 items have disappeared for me in the last few yrs. Now she goes to other areas so be sure & not wait too long for money. Blessings to all, prayers for the ill & heavy laden. It takes courage to grow old gracefully. Could be worse. Sara B. "

PART I   Wisconsin Settlements
Chapter 25
MEDFORD AND CURTISS

A RELATIVE CONNECTION

Joe Lehman from Sumner County, Kansas, founded the Medford settlement in 1920. Joe Chupp from Reno County, Kansas, followed shortly after him. Some think Medford was the first settlement in Wisconsin, but it was Exeland in Sawyer County in 1909, according to David Luthy of Aylmer, Ontario, Canada. Exeland is now a Mennonite congregation.

CONTACTS AND CONNECTIONS

I was put in contact with Verlon U. Petznick through my 96-year-old aunt Clara. He lives in Wausau and his father and Clara were first cousins. Verlon's brother owned a farm near Athens and east of Medford that was sold to an Amish family named Stoltzfus or Stutzman on Bungalow Road off County A. Verlon said in his letter to me (just as he wrote it) that "German Baptists (like Mennonites)" lived on a farm near the Stoltzfuses. They had eleven children.

Verlon's friend, Joseph Adamzak, lives "right among the Old Order Amish community," and "hauled milk from the Amish people back in the '40s. He would take our family around the Amish farms esp. Sun. to find the church mtg. Places. That was back in the '30s. Wilfred, my brother, cut cattle horns for years for the Amish in that area, and when his barn burned the 2nd time, they helped, and the ladies helped Carol with cooking. Some of them came for Dad's funeral back in 1973. Quite some memories. My mother would take me out of school about 50 yrs. ago to attend

Amish auctions."

I am beginning to appreciate just how many English folks do know something about the Amish. More and more frequently, I hear of folks traveling through the "touristy" Amish and Mennonite communities, but they rely on stereotypical or commercially propagated images of their lifestyle. It is easy to fall into a nostalgic, sentimental, or idealistic scenario of these "plain people."

PART I   Wisconsin Settlements

Chapter 26
LANCASTER

WITNESSING A WEDDING AS A GUEST

Nestled in the hills and valleys of southwestern Wisconsin is a cluster of Amish settlements: Beetown, Bloomington, Fennimore, Lancaster, and Livingston. I was invited to attend a wedding there on Thursday, January 31, 2002. At 8 a.m. I drove my Amish family friends from Marion to the bridegroom's parents' house near Beetown. It had snowed the night before and the ground was covered with two inches of bright sparkling fallout. The overcast sky kept the temperature near freezing. It was a dreary day for a wedding, but Amish farmers are used to being with the elements whatever they bring.

The wedding ceremony would be in the old farmhouse. A large room had been added, perhaps in anticipation of this event. The addition measured 30 by 40 feet with a door and six windows that flooded the room with diffused light. The groom's father greeted two carloads of guests, four vans loaded with eight to fifteen relatives, and a yellow school bus with a collection of friends and relatives from two distant settlements. Local Amish came by horse and buggy. Women and small children retreated to the house to help in preparations. Men and young boys gathered in the damp and cold barn. The men stood along the gutters in the center. Younger boys congregated casually inside the front door of the barn, peering out when vehicles arrived.

I had been to a church service before in another settlement and met with the Amish men inside the barn. There I had been greeted and had engaged in quiet conversation with the Amish man next to me. At this settlement, however, I was not greeted and felt that I was intruding, so I left the frigid barn and retreated to the relative warmth of the basement of the house.

Abe had informed the groom's father that I would like to witness the wedding service. Shortly before it began, the father offered me a seating place on a bench in the corner of the men's room. Women were seated with their daughters in an adjoining room. The beige pinewood benches measured six feet long and eight inches wide, enough for average size buttocks. Folding legs at either end, enabling easy storage of the benches in a wagon that carries them from farm to farm for church services, kept me sixteen inches off the floor. I wore a dark blue blazer, dark pants, and dark tie in order to be as inconspicuous as possible among the dark, somber Amish suits. At 8:45 a.m., Abe escorted me upstairs along with the older men. They sat on the back benches along the wall that provided the only backrest in the room besides mine. The younger men were seated last; young sons aged two through ten sat with their fathers.

As men filed into the benches, they were handed the *Ausbund*, a hymnal used by Anabaptists since the 16th century. It is the oldest Protestant hymnal in continuous use. We sat without conversation until the *Vorsinger* or *Vorstimmer* (lead hymn singer, or in Pennsylvania called a *Forsinger*) began by announcing in German hymn 74. The Vorsinger sang the beginning of each new line in a "trembling falsetto" (*Amish Society*, p. 213). Then the rest thunderously chimed in and I was enveloped with sound. The pace was extremely slow with syllables sung with four or five close notes. The next hymn was number 131, *Lob Lied*, always the second one sung at any church service. It took thirty minutes to sing the two hymns.

Then there was a long silence before the elders conducting the service and wedding party came into the room.

They had been upstairs receiving last instructions and prayers. The bride and groom were escorted by their attending couples, or *Newesitzers* (side sitters) in Pennsylvania German, and were seated in chairs facing each other. Six elders sat in chairs at the head of the wedding couple. A visiting Bishop, brother to Erma, conducted the ceremony. Another Bishop delivered the first sermon of thirty minutes in Pennsylvania German. During the second sermon by Erma's brother, several men's heads bobbed and eyes closed in deep meditation. Out the window next to me, I could see Amish women parading to the outhouse in the back yard. Some went singly and others in twos and threes, as women are wont to do. Children were shuttled from mothers to husbands and back. Fathers took sons out to the barn for relief.

VORSINGER

The Vorsinger sitting next to me had his hands full. He referred often to a small booklet that contained the words and melodies of the hymns in the *Ausbund*. The melody is displayed on a musical staff but not by quarter, half, or full notes, only relative pitch. One melody can be used for many hymns. The note values are not denoted in the hymnal so they must be memorized, causing less than synchronized sound. After the first sermon, his wife sent over the Vorsinger's two sons to him. A box of crackers accompanied them and juice-filled sipping cup. Soon the two-year-old became drowsy in his father's arms. I offered the father part of my bench for the five-year-old, enabling room for the two-year-old to lie down next to his father and sleep. A large Tupperware container filled with soda crackers and homemade cookies was circulated to fathers with children. A clear plastic water pitcher and a cup were also passed to the thirsty without disruption. The treat seemed to pacify the youngsters, as I heard no cries or outbursts from them during the three-hour service.

The preaching elders stood in the doorway between the men's and women's rooms and turned to each as they spoke in Pennsylvania German. Their mannerisms were similar. As they turned from one room to another, their eyes became fixed on one or two spots on the walls and never on individuals. Then their heads would turn down toward their folded hands and their speech became muffled. They cleared their throat often, adjusted their glasses on their nose, stroked their beard, and scratched their head. Words flowed from their mouth with only brief pauses. They used no notes or podium.

Suddenly, a prayer was commanded and every man in unison crouched off the bench, turned 180 degrees, knelt, and put his chest on the bench where he had been sitting. Some cradled their head in their hands. Some younger unmarried men were not as moved and kept their heads up and gazed around the room. Then the Bishop read a prayer from *Die Ernshafte Christenpflicht*, a small black covered book of prayers in German for mornings, evenings, weddings, funerals, communion, and other occasions.

The humble kneeling reminded me of the German word *Gelassenheit* (submission). Men submit to the Ordnung, guarded and maintained by the ministers, bishops, and deacons, boys submit to their fathers, wives submit to their husbands, and all resign themselves to God's will. Other core beliefs and values included in *Gelassenheit* are self surrender, yielding to others, self-denial, contentment, calm spirit, obedience, humility, thrift, and simplicity. What more can a humble person be?

One tender moment that I saw was the Vorsinger tapping the cheek of his drowsy son lying on his lap. When the father stopped, his son reached up and grasped his father's fingers and renewed the tapping on his cheek without ever lifting his head or opening his eyes. What a trusting, confident bond between father and son.

Married men wear beards. One unusual observation was of a clean-shaven father. He had only a small tuft on his chin and perhaps never shaved or grew facial hair. He seemed more passive and gave less direction to his sons than other fathers.

Another unusual sight was of the groom and his attendant. Their eyes were closed for most, if not all, of the ceremony while they were seated. The groom also wore the same "mutsa" suit commonly worn at church with no distinguishing special clothing. His bride-to-be wore the common plain, light blue calf-length dress, white cape over the shoulder, and white apron. Her attendant and other women in this settlement wore the same. She sat motionless throughout the ceremony except when taking vows. From my vantage point, it seemed that the bride, groom, and Bishop kneeled, stacking hands of each, one on top of the other, and the official betrothal words were spoken. No rings were exchanged, nor an embrace or kiss.

During the second sermon, twenty youth, later identified as servers at the meal to follow, came into the room and sat in the reserved section behind the wedding party. At the end of the marriage performed by the Bishop, the food servers left for the bride's parents' new home nearby.

After the last sermon, seated elders "affirmed" the message in Pennsylvnia German dialect. Then another kneeling and prayer were followed by two hymns. A slight genuflection was observed during a prayer. Four unmarried men served as hostlers and left the room to prepare the buggies. They would drive the bride and groom and attendants to the dinner. Then the men left in reverse order of their entrance. The ceremony was over and it was on to the dinner.

DINNER

I warmed up my Honda and waited for my passengers

from Marion. The hostlers drove the wedding party out the drive and onto an upgrade highway to the bride's family's new home. The gravel driveway steeply dropped to a bridge over a creek, turned left, and then ascended the side of a hill to the house yard. A light snow was falling, covering the gravel with a white blanket. The forecast was for more snow by nightfall. One driver monitored radio notices carefully, as his guest was to return to Michigan and another to Kentucky that night.

Inside the house, the cooking/heating stove radiated thawing heat. The aroma of food mixed with warm air wafted through the huge 40 by 50 foot room. Tables lined the outside walls and the walls of a center structure of bathroom and stairways to the basement and bedrooms upstairs. Ushers escorted guests to the proper table position. Drivers were placed at one table in view of the wedding party seated in the corner of an outside wall. When all were seated, a call for prayer silenced us. When the caller finished and lifted his head, so did we, like dominoes falling. Then the food bowls and platters were started at the head of a table section on both sides. Each person took what he or she wanted. A server collected the dish at the end of the table. That dish would not return.

It was a feast that I, as a single man, would call a banquet. Baked skinless chicken with a light coating was first. Mashed potatoes and gravy followed. Then came creamed corn, potato salad, bread and butter, mayo, pitted prunes, strawberry tapioca, dressing (ground chicken and bread crumbs), noodles, vegetables, and carrot salad. For dessert, there was apple pie, chocolate pie, box cake, mints, coffee, and milk, and later, when the tables were cleared, a bowl with a variety of candy bars and candy. It was a menu straight from the Stephen Scott book, *The Amish Wedding*. Preparation of each item was assigned to a person and posted on a kitchen cabinet. Recipes must have been theirs.

Most cooking was done on another stove in the basement. Pitchers of water pumped from a hand pump in the kitchen were abundant on tables and refilled often. After the meal, folks walked around greeting relatives and guests. There was no music except the singing of songs taken from the Sunday night sing songbook. Some went upstairs to the bride's bedroom to see the small number of gifts on the bed. More would be received in the next few weeks when the new couple would visit relatives from both families in the area. This would be their honeymoon.

To accommodate the crowd of nearly 150 persons, two particleboard outhouses were built near the house. The seating area was Styrofoam insulation with two appropriate tear-shaped holes cut in it. I had been in a lot of outhouses, but none with this innovation. The insulation was softer than hardwood and warmer. It was the last stop for some guests before traveling home with their drivers. However, a blizzard was in progress, and some drivers decided not to drive that night and they and their passengers would have to find places to sleep and eat. Those with buggies and horses could make it home, even in the dark at 10 p.m. My passengers were ready to leave for a relative's home in the community where we would sleep. The father said he knew the way, but his son countered with other directions. The father was right.

The snow was accumulating on the ground and the country roads were disappearing with the drifting. My Honda Accord clawed its way through drifts and finally up the drive at our destination. Shown to my bedroom on the second floor of the old farmhouse, I was surprised to see electric lights guiding my way. The farm was being rented from a non-Amish landlord, thus allowing the use of electricity for house and barn. Two young girls were sound asleep on the bed I was to have, so their mother carried them off to another room. Outside the wind whined, but inside the furnace fan purred as I pulled the warmed sheet and blankets around my neck and drifted off in record time.

We headed for Marion and home for my passengers the next morning over plowed roads and with bright sunshine. The father needed to make one stop at the Swartzentruber Amish Coleman lamp repair shop. One more stop was for lunch and another, as the sun was setting, for fishing bait that the son would use the next day. The Amish wedding had been an unusual and unforgettable experience I will treasure.

PART II Feeder States
Chapter 1
INDIANA, OHIO, PENNSYLVANIA, AND KENTUCKY

GOSHEN, INDIANA

I had been to the Elkhart, Indiana area before, so I knew where the Tourist Information Center was. I asked if there was a Mennonite run bed and breakfast in the area where I could stay for the night. There was Royer's B&B south of Elkhart on County Road 38. The tourist attendant showed me the rooms of Royer's B&B on her large screen computer which was able to scan or pan the rooms visually. I was impressed not only by the technology, but by the impressive ambiance and the fact that Mennonites were into this much "worldliness." There was even a photograph of Raymond and Barbara in the tourist brochure with Raymond casually reading a paper and Barbara standing ready to serve him a cup of coffee. The attendant phoned Royer to assure room availability, and then put me on the phone with Barbara so she could get information and a credit card number, an easy way to check out a customer's authenticity. It was getting dark, so I had timed this well. Twenty minutes later, I was turning into their driveway.

What an entrance! Tall trees lined the driveway and large light powdery snowflakes drifted lazily in front of my headlights. On the right were three ramshackle old buildings. Old is important and revered as it maintains tradition of past generations. I later learned that Raymond had moved them from nearby sites to preserve a part of history. Working construction in his "productive" days, he knew how to move such buildings. A curving lane brought me to the main building, their private residence, and business office. Barbara greeted me at the door with a smile and handshake. She spoke slowly and softly with the confidence only a mother of nine children can project. Soon Raymond entered and we exchanged greetings. I knew it would be an enjoyable stay.

Barbara showed me my bedroom on the second floor facing the howling north wind that had picked up during the day. The cover on the bed was a brightly colored Amish quilt that she removed, saying it was only for show. The room was filled with heirlooms and knickknacks collected over decades. It reminded me of the other Mennonite B&B I had stayed in several times before, with Bill and Carol Giersch in Lancaster, Pennsylvania, which was also filled with trinkets and bric-a-brac. Was there something about Mennonite women that destined them to collect trinkets? After unpacking, I went downstairs where Barbara was doing a crossword puzzle and Raymond was stretched out in a reclining chair. We made small talk for an hour, and I bid them good evening. The living room lights were out shortly afterwards.

The next morning, Raymond knocked on my door and announced, "Breakfast in 30 minutes, Richard." The meal would be served in the summer kitchen and dining hall across the drive. Raymond had built the structure to accommodate the large number of guests they had. It included a small room that displayed several quilts, books, wall hangings, and crafts for sale. Raymond began breakfast with a lengthy prayer that covered all the bases. Snow was falling, and Barbara remarked it reminded her it was pumpkin pie making time. For breakfast, she had made hot applesauce, coffee cake, scrambled eggs, American fries, whole-wheat toast with preserves, and sausages wrapped in a ribbon of dough like pigs in a blanket. Raymond offered to read me something from a paperback book he had perused during the meal. It was scripture from II Peter 1:5-8,

"Make every effort to add to your faith goodness; and to your goodness, knowledge; and to knowledge, self-control, perseverance; and to perseverance, Godliness; and to Godliness, brotherly kindness; and to brotherly kindness, love."
I made a note of it in my notebook. I asked if I could photograph them in her kitchen, and Barbara quickly put away some things to tidy up a bit. Then it was time for me to do some photographing outside.

Snow was still quietly falling. Raymond invited me to see the log cabin building that he had moved from its original site some miles away. A queen sized, four poster bed dominated the first room. An Early American motif decorated the bathroom with a lion-clawed tub and a porcelain washbowl and pitcher on an antique wooden washstand. Opening the upstairs bedroom door, I was greeted by two king sized beds, side by side, that took up the entire width of the room. Another femininely furnished bathroom was off the bedroom. I photographed the rooms after consulting with Barbara and offered to send the photos for her use. I showed Raymond the wide-angle lens I had, which would make it easy to get into tight places, such as the bathroom, and include almost everything in the photo. He had never seen one and found it humorously distorted the view. As we said goodbye, Raymond gave me a book by an Amish man, Elmo Stoll, *Give Me This Mountain: a Selection of Views and Values.* The editor of Family Life periodicals for over two decades, Mr. Stoll had died in September of 1998. The book, printed in 1999, contains his articles selected by his family.

GRABILL, INDIANA

As I drove through the Goshen countryside, I photographed some of the atypical Amish farmhouses along the way. Unlike the ordinary Wisconsin Amish farmhouses and buildings, they had an old European architectural style. Goshen College was where a student in my Amish class once worked as a librarian. Barbara Royer had suggested driving Hwy 30, as it went through the heartland of Ohio. But first I wanted to see Grabill, Indiana, and the place that Bernd G. Langin wrote about in his book, *Plain and Amish: an Alternative to a Modern Pessimism.* I saw the popular book for sale at EssenHouse Restaurant in Middlebury, Indiana, as well as in Berlin, Ohio. A Mennonite tour guide, Steven Troyer, at the Mennonite Information Center in Berlin, cautioned me about the sincerity of the author, a journalist by profession, as well as about the story, because Langin had concealed a camera to take the photographs that appear in his book. This reminded me of the incident when I had the chance to photograph a barn raising in Cashton five years ago. I felt that taking photos would be too intrusive, so left the site without ever tripping the shutter. But I am getting ahead of my own story, or better yet, just starting it.

VERIFYING REPORTING

I drove down Interstate 69 to exit 116, and then up state Hwy 1 to Leo and then on to Grabill. How fortunate to come across Langin's book while on my journey. Here I was in the very town, burg, or hamlet (whatever they call it), where he lived with the Amish. They accepted him because he could speak German fluently. Raymond Royer confirmed this fact.

An Amish man in Grabill knew about Langin. I met him on Cuba Road, the very road on which Langin had lived, and came upon it by accident. (Or is that called serendipity?) As I was photographing a farmhouse, I looked up only to see a street sign that designated "Cuba Road." The Amish man was riding in a "courting" buggy with a very undisciplined young colt and was on the wrong side of the road, which enabled me to call out to him and ask where the road to Harlan was. He replied, "Next road, left."

I followed his direction and pulled over to the side of the road to photograph the farm buildings I had passed. Several Amish children had just been dropped off by a yellow school bus in front of their house. There is a growing trend for Amish to use school bus service. As luck would have it, my direction giver was in the viewfinder when I tripped the shutter. As he turned on the road where I was, his frisky colt slipped on the wet, snowy macadam and nearly went down. The colt was so skittish; I exclaimed in my own culture-tainted habit, "I'd better let you go. Your horse seems uneasy." The man replied, "He's just a colt. Thank you. Thank you." The thought that I had given him permission to go in my habitual "telephonese" phrase seemed ludicrous to me afterward, just as his unreserved double thank you seemed overdone. (Or did he do it deliberately to accentuate my impudence?) As I reflected about the brief exchange, I wished I had taken more time to ask if I might talk with him when he finished his run with the colt. I might have obtained much more insight into the settlement's reaction to Langin's live-in with them and his writing about it. It was an opportunity lost but an experience gained, nonetheless. After a few more photos, I embarked for Bellville, Ohio, and a rest at a Comfort Inn.

HOLMES COUNTY, OHIO

I chose Bellville, as it was at the head of the scenic road leading through Clear Creek and the Mohegan Memorial State Forest and eventually Amish country of Millersburg, Berlin, Walnut Creek, and Sugar Creek. A light snow was still falling lazily as I sidetracked to the town of Shreve to have lunch at an "Amish" restaurant. A ten-mile detour later, I found the restaurant and learned that the waitresses were Mennonites and two English brothers owned it. The owners provided a service of bussing their help to and from work. My waitress was not aware of bussing Amish school kids in Ohio. They walked to school, she said.

ENGLISH TURNED PLAIN

After being a tourist for a while in a few stores in Berlin, I took advantage of some shafts of sunshine to photograph farms. At the Mennonite Information Center, I met Steven Troyer. Our common experience was meeting Scott Savage, author of the book, *Plain People*. I had met Scott in Shorewood, Wisconsin, in Harry W. Schwartz Bookshop where he was promoting his book. He was a librarian by profession, but gave up the hectic lifestyle to become a Quaker. He married another librarian and lived with his family near the Amish settlement in Barnesville, Ohio, in the southeast corner of the state. He dramatized his withdrawal from the English world of materialism and mechanization, or rites de passage, whichever way you wish to perceive it, by walking to Columbus, Ohio, the capitol, to turn in (retire) his driver's license, never to drive a car again. I was eager to see for myself where Scott was living and to observe the Amish in the area.

But it was not to be. I had no idea where Scott Savage might be, but judging from the map, I felt certain that locals would know of the Quaker author. My first stop on Sunday morning was at a small, cinder block store in Bellville. Three local residents were discussing the recent burial of the daughter of a famous person. Hearing my plight, they phoned the postman to see if he recognized the Savage name. No. On to Barnesville and the corner coffee shop. No. But they did give me advice NOT to take the scenic route I had romantically planned. The scenic drive along the Ohio River and West Virginia border was too hilly and would take more time than I had allotted for this leg of the trip. A Texas-booted and Stetson-hatted man said some corners on my planned route were so sharp you could see your own taillights. So, it was on Interstate 70 that I headed for Pennsylvania and "The Big Valley."

KISHACOQUILLAS VALLEY, PENNSYLVANIA

The process of finding Amish settlements is challenging. The following descriptions will give you an appreciation for the way I searched for this settlement. For me, luck played a large part.

The drive was fast, and I almost missed exit 13 off of I-70. I had read about this country in *Rosanna of the Amish*. It is a classic true story written by Rosanna's youngest son. An Irish girl raised and finally adopted by an Amish woman in the Big Valley, Rosanna becomes Amish. Settlements were near the towns of Huntingdon, Allensville, Belleville, Lewistown, and Reedsville, there in the 19th century when the story unfolded. Because it was Sunday, I was not in luck to meet any Amish in town, nor did many people know their whereabouts or even the story of Rosanna. The only interesting information was to be found in the Comfort Inn pub, where the barmaid said the Amish all came into town on Wednesdays for the farmers' market. The cook's brother had married an Amish woman who had abandoned the communion of the Amish.

The front desk clerk at the Clarion Hotel, Tammy Mountz, was able to provide information as to the location of Amish settlements. She also gave me a map of the Big Valley in detail. She suggested calling Mr. Clair DeLong, a local who was a graduate of Penn State with a major in sociology and who had served as county agent and befriended the Amish in Big Valley while fulfilling those duties. Mr. DeLong claimed to be a consultant to a movie director for the filming of "Trial by Fire," a documentary about the Amish, because of his experience working with the Amish in the area. Our phone conversation was interspersed with gurgling coughs and wheezes, but he managed to get out a time we could meet to answer my questions. I would wait at the hotel for him.

My expedition to Amish country was filled with coincidence and good luck. My next phone call also brought results. Photographer Bill Coleman, and book writer from State College, Pennsylvania, lived nearby. His book, *Amish Odyssey*, is filled with photos of the Amish in the Big Valley. I had emailed him about my visit to Pennsylvania to see the area where the story of *Rosanna of the Amish* took place. Bill's brother Carl was home and gave some great information. He gave me John E. Sharp's phone number at the Mennonite Church USA Archives that I had driven past two days before. John not only knew about Big Valley, he had lived there. The most exciting news was that he knew John A. Hostetler, author of *Amish Society* and other books, and said that Hostetler was now living in Goshen, Indiana. I had lost track of him for two years since my phone conversation with him when he lived north of Philadelphia. "Ring me up anytime," was his closing comment, in the old telephone parlance. Now I would have a chance to meet him personally in Goshen on my return trip home. Then John E. Sharp offered another bonus.

He knew the farm where Rosanna had been raised. He described in detail where the roads were, their name, where the creek and dips in the road were, and the color of the house and barn. His description of the farm was exactly as we found it. Clair's guess as to the color of the house was correct. Later I found a sketch in *Rosanna's Boys*, written by Joseph W. Yoder in 1944. It confirmed that the other house at the site was probably the grandawdy house (grandparents). These were wonderful finds and fulfilled every hope I had before this trip began. And it was all a matter of luck beyond my powers. And it did not end there.

Yoder makes an interesting observation in the book that describes the Amish as he sees them.

"While their hospitality is very free among themselves, Amish to Amish, stranger or acquainted, they are not so hospitable to non-Amish. This is due to timidity, known sometimes as inferiority complex. This inferiority does not arise from a consciousness of weakness but from the feeling that the Amish do not know the rules and amenities of non-Amish or polite society. Sometimes, too, there is a self-protecting feeling toward strangers of the outside, because the Amish do not know exactly what the outsider might be up to. But when the Amish once know people and have confidence in their honesty and integrity, their hospitality extends to all alike." (p.73, *Rosanna's Boys*)

Tour With Clair DeLong

Clair arrived at the hotel to pick me up. Sensitive to my genuine, authentic, and sincere interest in the history and life story of the Amish, he offered to show me an extensive area of Big Valley. It was an opportunity for him to share his life story as well. He said John A. Hostetler was born near Belleville, another unexpected bonus piece of information. Clair prided himself for serving as trustee with seven Amish men from three diverse groups ranging from liberal to conservative. He was entrusted with custodianship of the checkbook for the account. We talked about my dilemma over the ethical question of photographing Amish folks and about Bill Coleman's books filled with photos from the settlements. I later heard that his subjects had abandoned the Amish community, but continued wearing the traditional Amish clothes and driving buggies.

224 Amish in Wisconsin

We passed a barn portrayed in the novel *No Strange Fire*, by Ted Wojiasik published by Herald Press. John E. Sharp wrote the introduction. Then we passed a creamery that Clair was instrumental in setting up that collected milk from Amish and non-Amish farmers. He explained the range of funeral practices, from embalming to clothing, and talked about the cemetery, the latter becoming our next stop and my next photograph.

Clair talked about weddings and a phrase that came from II Corinthians that guides us not to take from the earth more than we need and to give back to it in full measure. It is also part of the Koran. Another subject was the work of the Mennonite Central Committee in canning meat in a portable trailer for distribution to needy people all over the world. He showed me B&Bs, some run by Mennonites, that were in the heart of the Valley and started me daydreaming about living here for a month just to observe the plain people in this quiet and beautiful area. I made note of the phone number of one B&B, Far View Farm, which he recommended. I phoned the Glicks (Mennonites) and received their brochure. Then Clair showed me the ostentatious, worldly people's homes in an exclusive section of the Valley. These were $700,000 homes on $100,000 lots, quite a contrast from the modest Amish life. Clair said one Amish farm was assessed at $150,000 for about 120 acres. He knew because as county agent he was consulted. The tax was commensurate.

We shared a discussion about inbreeding in such a stable settlement. Clair pointed out that the Nebraska Amish in the Valley have only five family names from which they descend, and that some were intermixing with a "rival" Amish sect, the more liberal Renno sect. As for their survival, he felt their faith was strong enough to ward off the earthly world, and that "their God is less immense than our concept." Clair's legacy will be carried on by his protégé,

Chris Hostetler, who is equally committed to the preservation of a people, the Amish.

HARRODSBURG, KENTUCKY

While researching the Shakers at Pleasant Hill, an Elderhostel program, I came across a bulk food store north of Harrodsburg on Hwy 127. The large neatly lettered sign on the highway read: "The Kountry Kupboard, Bulk Food Store, Spices, Dried Fruits, Bakery, Deli." A group of Amish-Mennonites (they are more Mennonite than Amish in their lifestyle) was sitting at a new wooden picnic bench having lunch under the large overhanging eaves of the front of the store that resembled an old western town saloon. The men all wore bright blue shirts and dark suspenders, and the women wore dresses of the same color. The women did not wear a bertha, a triangular shawl worn over the shoulder covering any "advantage" in front. Their head cover was white, but not the light gauze-like material of the Amish.

The inside of the store was bright and the shelves neatly ordered. Anthony Suarez, owner and co-manager, greeted me with a wide smile and Hispanic accent. His home is in Costa Rica where two of his Mennonite brothers are missionaries. He was obviously proud of his new store, which was built in June, after having moved from the city of Harrodsburg. In a newspaper article of Sunday, April 8, 2001, he said "We found [Hwy] 127 an asset. Business tripled when we moved here." Main attractions are fresh sweet-cream butter and fresh-baked breads, rolls, cakes, and pies. I bought jars of pickled okra and blackberry jam from Amish plants in Lancaster, Pennsylvania and Wallingsford, Kentucky, respectively.

I returned to the store the day I started for home. I purchased a book, *The Amish In America: Settlements that Failed, 1840-1960,* by David Luthy from Aylmer, Ontario.

This settlement is growing in Mercer County. The Amish came from Flemingsburg and the tally is 15 or 16 households and 13 complete families. All drive automobiles and use cell phones, which hang from the men's trousers in English fashion. On my way out, Enos Martin, who was managing the checkout counter, pleasantly bid me farewell, while Anthony offered me a free lemonade from the cooler and a box of freshly baked frosted rolls to enjoy on my journey home.

One of my fellow "scholars" in the Elderhostel program, Dick Harshburger from North Manchester, Indiana, told me about an Amish child that had been admitted to a hospital. The children's ward used Raggedy Ann printed gowns. The parents requested that a plain green gown be used for their child in keeping with their congregation's custom, its Ordnung. Dick himself, a retired economics professor, belongs to Church of the Brethren, a group that formed in 1908 from the German Baptist Brethren, a sect of the Anabaptist movement.

PART II Feeder States
Chapter 2
LANCASTER, PENNSYLVANIA

HISTORIC AND TOURISTY

Most students of the Amish and the public at large probably know the Lancaster/Amish connection. In my estimation, it is the most commercialized tourist settlement in the country and the longest surviving, as it was first settled in the early 1720s to 1790s. Although I had visited here a half dozen times, this visit provided a new optimistic perspective on the question of the survival of the Amish culture. The preponderance of farms clustered in this concentrated geographic area lent itself to the feeling that community and solidarity were intact. These buildings alone had stood for over three or four and up to seven generations with no signs of decay. The clothing of these plain people was universal, neat, and timeless.

With the plethora of tourists comes dollars, shared by the English entrepreneurs who own the shops and the Amish who make some of the artifacts and provide the ambiance as they drive through town in their gray-covered buggies and black garb. They are also employed in some shops, though there are more Mennonites than Amish. Their successful image is enhanced by the economy as made evident by the 220-page "Lancaster County Business Directory 2000," which is a compilation of Amish owned and operated businesses, including DavCo Family, Inc., which produced the Directory. The directory even lists a phone number and more surprising, a web page address.

All of what I saw, I saw for the first time. My rose-colored glasses were no longer tinted by sentimentality, but

228 Amish in Wisconsin

enlightenment. These Amish were adapting to the economic needs for their survival, a la the modification of their Ordnung (the unwritten ground rules of their church group headed by its leadership composed of a bishop, deacon, and preacher.) Bulk milk tanks, allowed by the leaders some 20 years ago, keep the milk cool by refrigeration and bring more dollars on the market as Grade A milk for drinking, rather than lower priced Grade B milk used only for cheese products. In contrast, the Big Valley Amish (who settled in central Pennsylvania around 1790), were, as Clair DeLong stated, "comfortably just living out their lives." They had no bulk milk tank. In my opinion, the economy is reflected in the well-maintained barns, outbuildings, buggies, and houses.

Upon entering Lancaster, I headed for my favorite watering hole, the Lancaster Dispensing Company, for a Stroud Reserve amber beer and sandwich. The pub is just off the city center square, where a tall obelisk pierces the dark sky and is surrounded by statues of soldiers from the Civil War seemingly guarding it. The huge red-bricked market building was closed, but on another of my visits here it was open to hundreds of folks buying produce, honey, peanut brittle, wall hangings, and quilts supplied by mostly Amish entrepreneurs.

My Mennonite hosts at the bed and breakfast, Bill and Carol Giersch, were as friendly and personable as ever. Bill and I shared some religious talk, especially his hope for a part-time assignment at a local Mennonite church as pastor. It had been his desire to become an evangelistic pastor for a long time. (His installation was November 18, 2001 in Watsontown, PA, near the Susquehanna River.) Carol had directions for me to the Herr House, the first Mennonite home in the area (1719), which held the longest continuous Mennonite church services in America. She also gave me directions to an Amish bookstore where I could buy the

Martyrs Mirror, a collection of 4,000 accounts of early Anabaptists who paid the ultimate price for their stubborn adherence and allegiance to the movement and to their Lord and Master. One of the book's uses was to imbue in the youth the heritage of their families. Its subtitle is "The story of seventeen centuries of Christian martyrdom from the time of Christ to A.D. 1660."

MARTYRS MIRROR

The author of *Martyrs Mirror* was Thieleman J. van Braght, a Dutchman. The first American edition was translated from Dutch to German and was printed at the Ephrata Cloister, Pennsylvania, in 1745. (This was French and Indian War times.) This pietistic group wrote hymns and lived a sparse existence. They were known to give medical attention to both English and American soldiers wounded in the Revolutionary War. The first English edition of the *Martyrs Mirror* was published in 1837 at Lampeter Square in Lancaster. The second English edition was published in London in 1853, and the third in 1886 in Elkhart, Indiana, near the current large Amish and Mennonite settlements. There have been eleven English printings to date from Herald Press in Scottdale, Pennsylvania and Waterloo, Ontario (a large Mennonite settlement).

When I bought the *Martyrs Mirror* at the Gordonville Book Store, I asked the two Amish shopkeepers if they read much of the book. They offered minimal admissions, but they sold a lot of them, they said. I reflected that the most published book in America is the Bible, and it appears it is not read much either, judging by the newspaper accounts of violations of its word. My Mennonite pastor friend, Lawrence Kratz, in Waukesha, Wisconsin, confessed that he had not read from *Martyrs Mirror* in a long time. It is not a pleasant book to read with its grueling accounts of torture, cutting out of tongues, burning at the stake, and drowning.

These tactics were used to curtail the spread of the Anabaptist movement in Europe in the 16th Century.

It may appear that we are a long way from home, Wisconsin, but my intention is to show the binding commitment of these folks to their faith. The common threads, despite slight differences in settlements, are that they are in the world, but not of it, and that their life on this planet will be the measure of their salvation in eternity. To be able to understand the Amish in Wisconsin, I need to observe them elsewhere in the country. Through this ethnographic exercise, I know them a little better and appreciate them a lot more.

Serendipity is real. Some call it coincidence or synchronizing. On December 23, 2001, I was sitting at a restaurant breakfast counter and intuitively offered my Amish Insight business card to a senior man next to me. He said he had lived in Lancaster for many years and would consent to an interview after the holidays. Much of my trip seems to have been directed by coincidence. As I left Lancaster on Hwy 340, a large number of gray-topped Amish buggies (color is significant in identifying sects) were parked at a farm/business. The business shop had a closed sign in the window, but I noticed many blue dressed Amish women in the windows of the large house, all with their head cover on and their backs to the window. I photographed several buggies and then discovered and photographed another large collection of buggies on the other side of the house, all gray-topped and identical in appearance, if not brand new. It was a wedding, verified at the nearby English-run restaurant.

PART II Feeder States
Chapter 3
ARTHUR AND ARCOLA, ILLINOIS

ENTREPRENEURSHIP

ARCOLA

The Arcola Chamber of Commerce describes this Amish settlement as being founded in the 1860s, fifty years before any Wisconsin settlement. "Some 300 families still practice this unique way of life exemplified by 1) strength of faith, 2) family bonds, and 3) commitment to community." They all belong to the same church, unusual for this large size Amish settlement. The Chamber's brochure states there are approximately 100 Amish businesses in the area. By contrast, in Lancaster County, Pennsylvania, an Amish and Mennonite business directory fills 200 pages!

The Urbana News-Gazette newspaper in its June 16, 2000 issue counts "approximately 4,200 followers of the Amish faith" around the adjacent area to Arthur, Illinois. This is the fourth largest Old Order Amish community in the nation. That is half the number in all of Wisconsin. The article is titled "Selling Country Charm (and eggs) Illinois Amish Country: A place where quaint shops abound." Levi Beachy, the storeowner interviewed in the article, now calls the tourists customers. This entrepreneurship is a foretelling of the changes awaiting the Amish in the next generation.

Finally, the article features Mennonite Brethren Conrad Wetzel, curator of the Illinois Amish Interpretive Center (www.amishcenter) in downtown Arcola (1-888-45AMISH). He provides maps of the Amish businesses in the area and provides visitors with explanations and information about the Amish faith and way of life to prevent them from making gross faux pas. We Elderhostelers met Wetzel as part of the Elderhostel program at the University of Illinois-Champaign/Urbana the week of May 20, 2001. I do not know of any Amish interpretive center in Wisconsin. Yet, there are 8,000 Amish in the state. The largest settlement in Cashton has more than 260 families. Arcola has a center that includes a museum, small theater, and a film of the Arcola/Arthur area entitled "In the World But Not of It." Gifts, books, videos, and guided tours of Amish homes and farms are available. Conrad Wetzel leads the tour of the Interpretive Center. His Mennonite background serves him well for explanations and answers to audience questions. He asked us to "learn about the Amish, and perhaps more important, to learn from the Amish." He promotes the Mennonite Relief Sale the last week in August each year to raise money for disaster relief worldwide. Forty-five such sales are held in the United States and Canada raising over 5.3 million dollars annually

ARTHUR

Our first stop on the Elderhostel tour arranged through the Interpretive Center was for lunch at the Yoder farm. Three other carloads of guests joined our group. Each person paid about $15; some of the fee was kept by the Center, leaving about $10 per person for the Amish. There were 24 for lunch seated in a long narrow room of the house, netting the Amish about $240. Several of these lunches were provided weekly, conceivably earning $700-$1,000 per month during the spring, summer, and fall months. The tours provide necessary income for semi-retired farmers or factory workers.

The practice of supplementing family income with non-farm activity has been spreading westward from its origin in Lancaster County, Pennsylvania. Perhaps it will be curtailed when it reaches the buttes and valleys of LaFarge, Ontario, and Evansville, Wisconsin. Our state may be the last vestige of isolation for the most conservative Amish who want to avoid the exposure to American culture. It becomes increasingly difficult to keep their beliefs and lifestyle in sync.

The inside of the Yoder house was clean and uncluttered. Ceilings and walls were painted glossy white. The large, bright kitchen had solid oak cabinets, with a modern stove and refrigerator fueled by propane. A large panel in a wall was hinged near the ceiling enabling it to be swung up and out of the way, opening another room for church services. A home may need to hold 20 families, about 120 persons, for services. Outside, wooden buildings were all painted white. Several pieces of machinery, some with pneumatic rubber tires, were stored neatly out of sight behind a shed. Only liberal sects would use such tires. An ingenious modification was made to a seed driller using a 12-volt battery to power a hydraulic pump to lift and/or lower the driller to the earth. Buggies were parked inside a shed along with 10-speed bicycles.

Three houses may be on one farm, one for the son and his family, a second for his parents, and a third for his wife's parents. The uniform neatness of farm buildings and homes in this community speaks highly for the Amish effort to present a good impression and dispel inappropriate stereotypes of these plain people.

At the Levi Schrock farmhouse, Edna May, his wife, led us through the immaculately clean dining room, trimmed in dark pinewood. Five children were raised in this house; two remained Amish and three became Mennonite. Most "falling-away" Amish who become Mennonite stay in the area. A coal stove for winter use was along an interior wall. Several glider rocking chairs were placed about the room. A desk was wedged between two windows with a mantle chime clock above it. One small bedroom was off the living room, with a tiny bathroom adjacent. Running water supplied the entire house.

CONRAD WETZEL GUIDED TOUR

The afternoon was filled with surprises and exposure to a unique lifestyle. Conrad maneuvered us through the rural roads over the Kaskasia River and past the Edgewood Buggy Shop and a bicycle shop. We saw one of the 18 "parochial" schoolhouses; this one accommodates special children. We passed Kaufman's Cabinet Shop, owned by a bishop, and a school and meetinghouse of the Beachy-Amish sect. A man named Beachy owned the Beachy Grocery Store, but he was not of the Beachy-Amish sect. In the store, I found tins of ground-cooked beef, beef chunks, and boneless chicken and turkey. The food was processed at the Grabill Country Meats plant in Grabill, Indiana. It reminded me of my Army days and K-rations.

We learned there were 24 Amish bishops in the settlement, an indicator of its large size. Conrad explained that banned Amish might join any of the five area Mennonite Churches, and thus that sect had grown to nearly 1,000 in this area. No Mennonite descendant is a member here, just Amish converts.

We saw no horse collars on two buggy horses that were hitched at a store. Instead, a wide leather band with a cushion material stretched across the chests of the horses. The preacher in Bonduel, Wisconsin used this type, a custom that followed his emigration from Ohio. An open buggy with pneumatic rubber tires and a station wagon rear seat for the driver caught my eye as it cruised silently down the road. The driver looked anything but Amish. He may have been a wannabe. "For the Amish," Conrad said, "being more alike is more important than being different."

Because this land is very flat and once swampy, the fields were injected with drain tiles that fed to a drainage ditch. Conrad pointed out another school, a cabinet shop, a health food store, and a massive furniture distribution building owned by Mr. Mast, a former Amish. The Otto Center, named after the man who donated the land for it, houses a school and place for auctions for Amish, Beachy, and Mennonites.

The cemetery was behind the Otto Center on donated land. Simple concrete tombstones were of uniform small size, no more than 24 inches high and 18 inches wide, with inscriptions on the far side that included name, date of birth and death, and number of years, months, and days lived. A fence surrounded the half-full graveyard with approximately 200 interred within.

The Country Shoe Store advertised Red Wing Shoes, a product of Red Wing, Minnesota, on the Mississippi River near La Crosse, Wisconsin. Near it was a quilt shop, and beyond that, Howard Plank's Pro Hardware Store. Here they sold everything in the line of hardware, plus broadfall denim pants for $34.50 and coats for $54.50 made in Ohio. Amish women make most clothing at home, not in factories. We passed a bookbinding shop and the casket maker's farm where beech wood is the wood of choice. A local newspaper, the *Echo*, kept families informed about church schedules, which farm or place services would be held, funerals, weddings, and other helpful information.

Next, we toured the Willis and Dorothy Helmuth farm. The milk house was equipped with a bulk tank and the barn with vacuum lines for the DeLaval milking pails. A commercial creamery in Decatur picked up their milk on Monday, Wednesday, Friday, and Saturday. It was used for ice cream. Willis said it took him 30 minutes to milk 16 Holstein cows with three pails. Red Holsteins were his preference if he could afford them or find them. I thought of the Amish family in Marion, Wisconsin, that had 21 of them. Willis said the 70 herds in the settlement were down to 45 in two years because farmers are not earning enough to rely on milk for sole income, despite the raise from $10 per hundredweight to $14. He said the abundance of milk from Canada imports was filling the market since the trade agreement. He is aware of world affairs through the Decatur newspaper and networking with others in the settlement.

Willis said the cabinet and furniture shops both helped and hurt the Amish. They provide jobs but take fathers away from the farm and family. Outside jobs may provide needed income, but the disruption of an absent father in a family of six can be more costly. His 13-year-old son, Lester, told him to take the job at the factory, and he would run the farm. He told of letting his son take four horses and plow a 5-acre field. This kind of eagerness on the part of Lester will keep the young generation farming if they can improve the economics.

Conrad said the woodworkers get together once a year in Arthur to discuss their industry and meet other enterprising Amish. One such woodworker is blind and owns a pallet production shop. Conrad's comments led me to believe that this is a vibrant and growing community. Families are not leaving the community for greener pastures. Those in the middle of the conservative/progressive lifestyle are adapting to the economics of the times, and those on the extreme conservative side leave. Amish homes that we saw were clean on the outside and the yards clutter-free and trim. The crops of corn in the field looked healthy, as did their cattle and horses. These folks appeared happy and friendly, and generally better off than many Wisconsin Amish. One must remember that they have been in Arthur since 1865 when Moses Yoder, Daniel Yoder, and Daniel Otto purchased farms from the English who were already here. The first Wisconsin settlement would form 45 years later. The Arthur Amish have even adapted by sending one-third of their children to the local public schools. They have started almost 200 businesses with some employing other Amish. This is change at a measured pace and perhaps fast enough to keep families and faith intact.

PEOPLE OF PRESERVATION

The third morning we saw a video titled "The Amish: A People of Preservation." It describes the Lancaster, Pennsylvania settlement, narrated by John L. Ruth, author, and graduate of Harvard. He is now a Mennonite minister and Conrad Wetzel's brother-in-law. Conrad characterized himself as an "advocate for the Amish." He described them as "people of intention," that is, they intend to follow the rules of the group and faith by deliberate choice. He also used the term "shared memory" to describe the bonding that children experience when they do the same things their parents did as youth. However, this is the first generation to make a break from the past with many innovations and changes. Conrad's examples included the expanding woodworking shop business, Amish "snowbirds" going to Sarasota (a winter retreat for Amish and Mennonites), drivers taking families to nearby Decatur for supper, the opening of natural soap shops, and refrigeration repair businesses. It is a time of change for the Amish in this settlement.

ATWOOD

North of Arthur is Atwood. We visited the Village Craftsman, furniture, and woodcraft store where Ronnie Schlabach showed us the process to build a custom chair. One was destined for an Illinois State Supreme Court Justice. Ronnie rents the building and all equipment runs on electricity. (Remember the Salemville Cheese plant in Kingston operating the same way?) A network of sub-contractors works cooperatively together. They supply components of furniture, rather than a single shop completing a whole project. Ronnie has the only Amish furniture shop in the city of Atwood. He did not mind me photographing him while he demonstrated making an inlay. It is the first time I have been invited to include an Amish person in my photos. Mel Rose Quilts was our next stop. This quaint small white clapboard house had belonged to the grandparents of the owner, Rose. It contained the wood burning cooking/heating stove of Rose's parents. Her mother lived here until she was 105 years old. A dozen quilts on a bed were "turned back" (a special way of folding and displaying quilts) for our viewing and potential purchase. None was purchased, so it was on to our last stop for the day.

TECHNICAL CAREER
Lynn Miller, 23 years old, is an articulate, intelligent, and personable Amish single man. He lives with his parents and operates a propane refrigeration repair service. His skills were honed in Iowa, where he worked as an apprentice for three months. He uses solar and wind generators to run equipment and charge batteries. A portable night-light of his design is sold at a local Amish hardware store. His greatest concern for the settlement, he said, was "the trend toward individualism and materialism." One example was the push for tractor use in the field. "The Ordnung was not

a shield to hold others out, but to keep Amish in," he said. As a single male, he is not eligible for the lot, the selection process for religious leaders. He said their bishops are elected from their ministers. When there are problems, they are brought to a minister. If a resolution is not found, a meeting with the district might be held at the end of a church service. Discussion could be held with other districts before action is taken, as in shunning. Asked what it meant to be Amish, Lynn said it was to keep the faith. He described the process for baptism when adults generally between 16 and 20 years of age decide to join the congregation and become Amish. Our group was impressed with this man. By the same token, an Amish man told Conrad he is impressed with the people that come from the Interpretive Center. "They ask more intelligent questions," he observed. That has been the goal of all my teaching about the Amish.

SYMPOSIUM

FRAKTUR AND LIVING PLAIN IN THE
MODERN WORLD

I was among Amish, Mennonites, Hutterites, and other interested English at this gathering in early February 2002. The Illinois Amish Interpretive Center located in Arcola sponsored the Fraktur session Thursday evening. Fraktur is a combination of calligraphy and decorative folk art that survives from the Middle Ages. Monks of that period made ornate Bibles in Gothic German, with enlarged first letters of each chapter entwined with garlands, animals, and religious symbols. Wedding certificates and other documents were emblazoned with fraktur. In Dublin, Ireland, I saw the illuminated manuscript of the *Book of Kells*, one such ornate Bible that reflects this art form. According to John L. Ruth, Franconia Mennonites who settled on the

Wissahickon River in Germantown (now a part of Philadelphia) were the first to revive the tradition. Schoolmasters produced small leaflets with words of encouragement and praise for student achievement. Students practiced their penmanship and alphabet, producing samplers that could be pasted on the inside cover of a book. Doylestown, in Bucks County north of Philadelphia, exhibits local fraktur, as does the Mennonite Heritage Center in Harleysville, Montgomery County.

In his lecture, historian and author John L. Ruth said the tradition was nearly extinct by 1850. He and his wife, Roma, were promoting a revival of fraktur. The Interpretive Center, which housed this session, had a display of early 1800s samples. The next day Roma conducted a workshop on basic design and painting fraktur. Hutterites were also known to produce the stylized printing, but John made no mention of Amish practice, nor have I even seen or heard of it in Amish quarters.

AMISH AND HUTTERITE HYMNS AND SONGS

Merle Gingerich is an Amish resident of Arthur and he called on several men to be Vorstimmer. He would lead the singing on Friday evening. They declined, so he led the singing. Four Hutterites from North Dakota also participated. Conrad Wetzel, a "Dunker" Brethren and curator at the Interpretive Center, was moderator. An audience of nearly 50 local Amish attended. John Ruth provided insight into the hymn translations from German to English. He said he had been privileged to read two stanzas of a hymn at graveside services for John A. Hostetler, prolific author and scholar of Amish and Hutterite societies.

Merle read from *Songs of the Ausbund, volume I,* number seven, "Als Christus mit seiner wahren Lehr," which is sung by most congregations. Michael Sattler, an early Anabaptist who was tortured with hot irons and his tongue cut out before being burned at the stake in 1527 in Rottenburg, wrote the hymn. Others wrote the core of the hymns in the dungeons of the Passau Schloss, a castle in Bavaria. Sattler's trial and death are described in grisly detail in the *Martyrs Mirror*. Merle admonished us several times when singing these songs to remember the forefathers who suffered in order to pave the way for Anabaptist religious freedom.

Songs sung on Sunday service are slow with a somewhat wailing sound. I had heard them at an Amish wedding and at an Amish Sunday service. The four Hutterites at the symposium sang these same hymns back home, but faster. They demonstrated several stanzas of many songs throughout the evening. At the social following the program, many from the audience surrounded the singers. It appeared to me that the Hutterites were a novelty for the Amish, as Amish are for the English. This meeting of Mennonite, Amish, and Hutterite may have rekindled and revitalized the Anabaptist bond between them, just as John and Roma Ruth were trying to revive fraktur.

CASKET MAKER

Before the Saturday afternoon session started, my traveling companion, Mary, and I arranged with an Amish man, whose name shall not be used at his request, to visit his brother, a carpenter who made caskets for the settlement. There had been a rush on them the week before with six deaths. Because this community is large, 4,000 persons, the casket maker, as did his father before him, stocked up to a dozen of various sizes, from infant to behemoth. He allowed me to photograph the three-deck vault of caskets as well as a casket he pulled out to photograph in the light of the wood shop.

Beech wood is the preferred material, stained, and lacquered a mahogany color. A coarse packing material, excelsior, is laid in the bottom and white cotton cloth lines the interior. The head part of the casket lid is hinged and folds back toward the feet to facilitate viewing. Pallbearer's handles are bolted to the sides. At the shoulder, side planks are bent by sawing several vertical slots one-quarter inch deep and bending the board. Two small ornate old wooden folding three-legged stools passed down three generations are placed under the head and foot of the casket during the wake, service, and last viewing at the cemetery. The carpenter brought out an infant's casket and a wooden vault for me to photograph. Four caskets in the process of being finished were piled one on top of the other in the shop area. Several planks were glued together and held by clamps to form the bottom of a large casket. Beech boards were bundled together as stock at the back of the shop. This wood is provided and the cost borne by the collective settlement. The casket maker charges $300 for his services. The only other expense is for the funeral director for embalming. The cemetery is on donated land and gravediggers volunteer their labor. The carpenter's wife summoned her husband and two sons for lunch and invited me to join them at his brother's house.

BARN RAISING

One of the intentions of the symposium was to illustrate the change that is taking place in the Anabaptist communities. Andrew Kaufmann, semi-retired Bishop in Arthur, was the foreman for barn raising. He shouted the orders to the crew and admonished no one to talk to insure safety. He said barns are no longer built with 12 x 12 inch timbers, but with 2 x 6 inch trusses. The portable saw and modern equipment made the old tools obsolete. To show how the massive sections were raised into position, Andrew built a small model and had three men play out the roles as helpers to his commands. Nearing ninety years old, Andrew admitted his memory was not as good as it used to be and he no longer "raised barns."

He was adamant that parents must instill strong faith in their sons. As a draft may be forthcoming, and if deferments are expected, young men will need to profess their faith convincingly to the draft board. The Anabaptists have been non-aggressive, conscientious objectors throughout history. To break the tradition and take up arms would mean sure shunning by the congregation, but only those who are baptized members. Shunning is not applied to unbaptized men.

HUTTERITE CHANGES BY THE DECADES

Tony Waldner, a young man from Fordville, North Dakota, described the changes in his Hutterite colony. The changes in the 450 colonies are visible in decade intervals. That is, slight changes are unnoticeable. Farm equipment is the most up-to-date. Computers are used only in the pig house to maintain business records and never in the schools. However, in a documentary film made in Saskatchewan, one scene showed a computer being used in a home by a young girl playing Pac-Man. One person is responsible for Internet traffic. A Council does decision-making for the colony business every morning. Family size has dropped from an average of 12 to 5. Snaps have replaced hooks and eyes on clothing, collars are evident on coats, and bright colors abound in men's shirts and women's dresses. Individual education beyond the eighth grade is possible. Tony was sent and paid to get his teaching degree and serve as colony teacher. He said religious services are shorter and more English is displacing German. Unlike the Amish who avoid political matters, the Fordville colony has two of the three members on the Township Council. With 90 eligible voters in the colony, they have a majority block in

244 Amish in Wisconsin

the township. Having been to two Hutterite colonies myself in Saskatchewan, I knew that the changes are dramatic and progressive.

LUNCH IN A MODERN AMISH HOME
Mose, our host, invited us to his house for lunch. The long table seated four boys, three girls, and their parents, the two of us, and a special adult nephew. The food was bounteous and traditional. Grace was silent and the conversation primarily between parents and guests. It was Saturday; the entire family was present because school children were home and others were not working. After lunch, Mose had to show off his basement engineering marvels. A wood and coal-burning, non-electric furnace circulated heat and drew cold air by convection from the house. His plumbing was modern copper tubing and the water purifier and filtration were upgraded. A water heater supplied hot water for kitchen and a modern bathroom. A sump pump used a diaphragm rather than impellers enabling it to run dry without damage. He was proud of his work.

Most revealing about the settlement was the dramatic changes from farming to entrepreneurship that have kept this settlement growing to 4,000 persons and prosperous since its inception in 1865.

BICYCLE SHOP
The bicycle sales and service shop housed in a metal-sided building was owned and operated by a senior citizen Amish man. He and his wife were engaged in a conversation with a friendly English couple as I walked into the shop. When the owner asked what he could do for me, I responded that I was at the fraktur symposium. His wife said that she had seen the announcement in the local newsletter. That seemed to break the ice and the wariness often exhibited by Amish until they figure out what you are

up to. A series of repartees followed between the owner and me in good jest. Eventually, he offered to have us meet his brother who lived next door to answer my questions about the congregation.

His shop was stocked with two dozen bikes hanging from ceiling racks and another dozen bikes and tricycles on the floor. Small parts for bicycles, such as tools and tire repair tool kits, were hooked to a pegboard. In a repair section cordoned off from the rest of the shop, a bicycle was inverted in a fixture to repair a chain derailleur. Rubber overshoes in manufacturer's boxes were neatly displayed on shelves.

In his retirement, this Amish man continued to earn a living without any social security benefits and contributed to his community by providing a service.

PART II Feeder States

Chapter 4
PILGRIMAGE EAST

NEW PERSPECTIVES

Shortly after Valentines Day 2002, I began to pack for a five-week excursion through Amish country in Indiana, Ohio, and Pennsylvania. Two days before I was to leave, bronchitis struck. The next day I got pinkeye. Was there an omen in this? Packed with pills and drops, I "hitched up my wagon" on Sunday, February 17.

RESPECTS TO JOHN ANDREW HOSTETLER

Goshen, Indiana was my first stop. I wanted to pay graveside respects to John Andrew Hostetler, author of many Amish and Hutterite books. John Sharp, Mennonite archive historian in Goshen, had emailed me the obituary and would know the location of the grave. He offered to drive with me to the Violet Cemetery in Goshen. We saw an unimproved lot and walked toward it and then stopped so John could get his bearings. While he did, I looked down at the tombstone for the grave I was standing on. It was John A. Hostetler's. I photographed it and my mission at this stop was accomplished.

BRETHREN CHURCH OFFICE

Along the way, I saw an office building across the street from the Ashland College campus in Ashland, Ohio. Curious about this sect of the Anabaptist fraternity, I inquired at the Brethren Church office. I was introduced to Mr. Richard Winfield, editor of the *Brethren Evangelist*, a newsletter of the Brethren Church. Formed in 1708 in

Schwarzenau, Germany, this pietistic group later split from the German Baptist Brethren and became known as the Dunkers, as they literally dunked their baptized into river or lake water. There are now over 11,000 members in 120 congregations. (For more, read *Brethren Society* by Carl F. Bowman.)

HOLMES COUNTY, OHIO

My second "hitching post" was Mt. Hope, in Holmes County with the largest concentration of Amish in the country. Hoping to find an Amish home at which to stay, I inquired at Marty's Shoe Store. Marty, the Amish owner directed me to Bishop David Kline. I had bought his book, *Great Possessions*, just hours before. The roads to his house twisted like a serpent and rolled and dove like a roller coaster. He could not put me up, but cordially agreed to a visit at 7:30 that evening. I arrived to find him searching for the Orion constellation with a stargazing telescope on a tripod. It was a dark cloud-clear night, and a friend had joined him in the search. David offered me a place in the house to wait for him. Grandchildren played in the room and paid little attention to me. His daughter came in and said hello, as did his wife.

The two astronomers were unsuccessful in their search for Orion, and David turned his attention to my interview. He is a very gregarious, intelligent, cheerful, and optimistic person. As bishop, his greatest task is to resolve differences, disputes, and confrontations within his flock. He said commercial photographers would take photos of the Amish that may be intrusive, but that he, David, "does not own Mt. Hope, Ohio." Some things are better ignored than contested, was my conclusion.

He emphasized the unique local control of the community under his wing, so to speak, and not a national committee to decide issues. He said the youth and young adults continue to use the German dialect in everyday conversations. A common language binds its speakers together. He knew Scott Savage, a librarian converted to Quakerism in Barnesville, my next destination. David read Scott's *Plain People* newsletter, connected with the Luddite land conservation movement. I subscribed to it after hearing and meeting Scott at his book signing and promotion at the Harry W. Schwartz Bookshop in Shorewood, Wisconsin. David said Holmes County is densely populated because the soil is good for farming, resembling that of Lancaster County, Pennsylvania. He looks for oak trees to tell him the soil is limestone laden and good nutrition for crops. He clarified some fine points of the Amish wedding ritual that I had witnessed several weeks previous, such as the vows portion, and directed me to the Book Shanty in Mt. Hope for a pamphlet describing the vows.

My final question was "What will the Amish look like 100 years from now?" His answer was quick and direct, that they would be "assimilated" into the general culture. This was not a depressing statement but a reality, in his judgment. I could not have agreed more with him after seeing the massive influx of Amish businesses in the area. These businesses are markers of survival carried out by a very resourceful and flexible people.

Finally, he encouraged me to write this book and to tell the stories of my experiences in local taverns near Amish settlements. Here is where I seek and get reactions, not always pleasant, from English neighbors. My theater acting experience and a naïve approach to my questioning fosters sincere and oftentimes hateful responses from them. They often "let it all hang out" in some kind of cathartic regurgitation. Some locals out of fear, jealousy, bigotry, prejudice, and discrimination hate Amish. That hatred will be heated up, I suspect, when the next military draft is called up and

Anabaptist youth seek Conscientious Objector status.

BUGGY, SLEIGH, AND STAGE COACH RESTORATION

I like to think that I do not take a trip; I let the trip take me. Wandering off the beaten path is often exciting and rewarding. Today I set out to find the Swartzentruber Amish and found a buggy shop instead. Although Amish did not operate it, the restoration of ancient sleighs, Conestoga wagons, Amish buggies, and stagecoaches was impressive. Dilapidated shells of sleighs took on like-new brilliance and certain nostalgia of the old days and old ways of living, a time when things went smoother and slower and one smelled the roses along the way. It is a time that some people dream they could return to, and they find the Old Amish ways a reminder of that wish. I watched as these artisans painstakingly applied u-shaped tacks to the upholstery and masking tape to the body for painting stripes. A local artist painted a winter scene on the back of a two-seated sleigh reminding me of the Budweiser Clydesdale horses on Christmas cards. A & D Buggy Shop even had a web site to advertise at www.a-dbuggy.com in Millersburg, Ohio. The "A" is for Alvin, the owner, who allowed me to photograph over 30 units waiting to be reborn, a three-year backlog.

I photographed an Amish cemetery bordering a narrow road. A symbolic empty Bud beer bottle marked a passing redneck's disdain for both the Amish and the dead. I bought a root beer at an Amish bulk food store along County Road 345. According to a road sign, baskets were for sale, so I checked them out but bought none. They were similar in design to the baskets sold by the Swartzentruber Amish in Viroqua. Then I was on to Berlin, Ohio, less than 10 miles south and the heart of tourist territory.

My only purchases in Berlin were a prescription for my bronchitis, a book titled *Home Remedies from Amish Country* in Sommers General Store, and Unker's medicated salve. Motherly and persuasive clerks who cared about my respiratory affliction pushed the salve on me. It reminded me of the mother of my Amish friend in Marion who made menthol, camphor, eucalyptus, and pine needle smelling concoctions for colds from a recipe that she learned from her mother.

MY MENNONITE HOSTS

Martin and Ruth Yoder, Conservative Mennonites, were my hosts at their bed and breakfast near Mt. Hope. The log cabin building was appointed with pristine antique Red Racer sleds, leather football helmets, and fishing rods from the 1920s. An 1840s traveling chest was designed with the domed top to prevent other heavy chests being placed on top, thus ensuring it was the first to be unloaded. Martin was a Mennonite minister and retired teacher who built the B&B as a kind of spiritual retreat center. He practiced his craft on me the first night when we had a 90-minute counseling session ending with his beneficent prayer. The place was recommended by another Amish Bishop I talked with as it was nearby and his daughter worked there as housekeeper. The Bishop insisted that Martin provide transportation for the young girl to and from work at the B&B. Martin capitulated in order to get trustworthy and reliable help. Such is the interplay between Amish and Mennonites.

SUGAR CREEK, OHIO AND THE *BUDGET* NEWSPAPER OFFICE

Curiosity drove me to see how the *Budget* is assembled. The editor, Fanny Erb-Miller, escorted me to the galley room where the columns of print are pasted up to make a photocopy-ready text for the printer. I saw raw copies of settlement scribes' writing of current happenings on lined paper provided by the *Budget*. Scribes also received stamps for weekly mailings and a free year's subscription to the paper for their service. Only three women at computers are needed to compose the articles to columns of type for the weekly periodical. This unusual paper attracted the curiosity of the *New York Times*, which published an article about the *Budget*.

BARNESVILLE, OHIO

Scott Savage, librarian turned Quaker, described his new Amish lifestyle in his book and I wanted to see how it was working out. The idyllic did not seem to coincide with reality. First, he was not home on the farm. He was working. Furthermore, his neighbor had to drive him to work at a technical college. Had he really abandoned the hectic, modern life I wondered? Was he able to provide for his family from his farm-grown food?

His wife answered the door cradling an infant in her arms, and four or five siblings anchored to her skirt while we talked. In the shadow of the mantle lamp that hissed from the ceiling in the living room, they looked to me like poor Amish. I came with an idyllic hope that this venture of theirs was as glowing as Scott had written about it. But in reality, it did not appear so to me. Had his writing in the book obscured my vision? Can American Christians make the transition to minimalist living? Amish wannabes would do well to study Scott's experiment before they attempt to convert.

LANCASTER, PENNSYLVANIA AND NEW LIFE HOMESTEAD B&B

My long-time Mennonite friends, Bill and Carol Giersch, greeted me with hugs at their New Life Homestead B&B and another night's stay. Bill was now pastor at Beaver Run Mennonite Church near Harrisburg, and Carol helped with groups and other functions. They were starting another "new life" together, and I foresaw them selling the B&B and moving closer to their church. I was happy to see them so happy. They told me about a "mud auction" being held at the fire station the next day to raise money for the Strasburg engine house. They call it a mud auction because it is held each year in the spring when it is normally wet. This year was a drought, and a serious one for farmers.

The auction would provide wonderful photo opportunities. Hundreds of Amish would be there and the weather forecast was pleasant. A tent full of Percherons, Belgians, mules, and Standardbred were auctioned in the cordoned-off street with 50 Amish lining one side within my camera rangefinder. In a large metal building used for the quilt auction, I asked a young Amish father where he got the list of items for sale. He offered to have one of his sons go up to the auctioneer's stage and get one of the listings. I said to the young son, "Get two and I'll give you a quarter." (It reminded me of Scrooge offering a half a crown to a boy in the street to buy a goose at the corner butcher for the Crachett family.) Both sons went and each brought back a listing, so I had to give them each a quarter. Two ten-year-old Amish boys had bright orange plastic cap pistols they shot off from time to time, perhaps imitating the animal trainer in a cage at a circus. Another had an imitation Nokia cell phone that played all the Looney-tunes of the real ones. Is this a sign of worldliness in the next generation of Amish?

Multiple auctioneers worked the crowd in a dozen locations simultaneously. One handled lawn mowers and bicycles near the engine house. Another sold 12-foot wide rolls of rugs. Two auctioned off dry food products to groups of Amish women, such as breakfast cereals and baking and cake mixes from the back of two semi-trailers. Two separate men took bids for farm machinery—used, new, and rebuilt.

Two alternated to sell the horses to a predominantly Amish male crowd. Another sold hand tools near the horse tent. The scene took on the atmosphere of a 12-ring circus. After three hours of this intense activity, a roll of 36-frame film exposed, a hot dog and cold Sprite, I was ready to leave.

LANCASTER, PENNSYLVANIA AND LINCOLN HAUS B&B

Verna Fisher is the innkeeper at the Lincoln Haus B&B where I stayed for two days. She is a school bus driver for the city public schools, is single, and in her 40s. She is also Amish-Mennonite. Her more liberal sect allows her to do the things she is doing, i.e., drive a vehicle and use a portable phone in her quarters lit with electric lights. She works for the owner, Miss Zook, who is Old Order Amish, a strict sect. Thus, she does not drive a car. Before hiring Verna, Miss Zook lived in the innkeeper's quarters without electricity or portable telephone. The only phone, in the outer lobby of the inn, was for business. Nearing her four-score years, she met a widowed Amish man her age and in a few months married and moved in with him. Miss Zook may sell the B&B, and Verna has always wanted to own it. Do these events break your stereotypical perception of what Amishness is?

ELDERHOSTEL AT BLACK ROCK MENNONITE RETREAT

The five days at the Elderhostel were filled with speakers, food, and field trips educating us about the Amish, Amish-Mennonites, and Mennonites in the Quarryville area and Lancaster County.

Merle Good and his wife Phyllis own the "Peoples' Place." It is an excellent bookstore in Intercourse, and a fascinating educational center for the Anabaptists' story. The Goods are Mennonites and told us about quilts, history, and lifestyle (including food at weddings) of Amish and Mennonites. They spoke of peace and service issues and clarified misconceptions and myths about the plain people. Four misconceptions that Merle listed were 1) Amish are a dying group, 2) Amish are old fashioned, 3) Amish are against education, and 4) Amish never change. Merle also listed four myths that the Amish do not believe, which are 1) Faith is a delusion, 2) Commitment is a sign of weakness, 3) Machines bring people together, and 4) More of anything is attainable or obtainable.

One startling statistic shows how rooted one family is in Lancaster County. One Mennonite family extends over nine generations. However, the number of children in Merle's family has changed from 19 children in his grandfather's family to seven children in Merle's father's to two in Merle and Phyllis' family.

Phyllis attested to the tension she felt between humility and success in her business. She told of the tradition that food has among the Amish; it is an expression of love and affection with homemade noodles and garden raised vegetables. Recipes are tailored to their rural setting (use of gardens), extended families where volume is needed, and the active community life where meals need to be prepared for hundreds of people on Sundays after church service and other events. Food for Sunday church meal includes 25 loaves of "store bought" bread, three pounds of butter, and 40 "schnitz pies." For a wedding, the shopping list may include 35 roasting chickens, 38 loaves of bread, 20 quarts of peaches or pears, 10 pounds of sugar, five layer cakes, and much more. Some principles guiding cooks include: do not waste anything, food is to be enjoyed, even indulged, and eat seasonably, that is, whatever is ripe.

According to Phyllis Pellman Good, the Amish did not bring quilts from Europe. They originated in the United States. She said the years between 1880 and 1940 were years of excellent quilt making. Wool and cotton were used then, whereas synthetics are more common now. She called the quilts "displays of affection." Quilts sold at auctions made women a significant part of the Amish economy. The quilts were named according to their patterns, such as Log Cabin, Sunshine and Shadow, Roman Stripe, Center Diamond, Hole in the Barn Door, Double Four Patch, Double Wedding Ring, Railroad Crossing, Broken Star, and Jacob's Ladder. Appliqué designs are also used for quilts sold to the public, but not for Amish homes. They would be too fancy for an Amish bed. I have seen quilts sell at auction in Wisconsin settlements from $200 to $1,200. Women and antique shop dealers seem to be the buyers of most quilts. When the economy is down, so are the bids for the quilts and bargains can be had.

Stephen Scott, a published author and Old Order River Brethren from Elizabethtown College, helped us understand the clothing that differentiates Brethren from Old Order Mennonites and Amish. The basic guidelines come from scripture: not to be conformed to this world (Romans 12:1-2), and to strive for humility, simplicity, and uniformity. For example, ministers wear coats called a frock that have no outside pockets or turned over collar. Scott's book, *Why Do They Dress That Way?* describes in detail the reasons for their dress.

Louise Stoltzfus, scholar, published author, and single, talked about women's fashion and education among the Amish and Mennonite. She was raised Old Order Amish until age 16, then became New Order Amish, and presently is a mainline Mennonite. ("The best of all worlds," she said.) She described the parameters of fashion as neatness, comfort, and simplicity, displaying them in her own dress. She said unmarried women wear white aprons, and purple is their favorite dress color. Synthetic materials are used for practical reasons. The use of a head cover for women is prescribed in I Corinthians 11:5-10.

Ann Lapp opened her home to us with her sister Rachel as guide. They are Amish-Mennonites who live on the family farm north of Intercourse in Lancaster County. The amenities were shocking for those of us aware of traditional Amish homes. Thick carpeting, framed photos of family portraits on the walls, and automobiles and pickups in the garage shattered our image of plain people. One of their sisters is in the Mennonite mission colony in Ascension, Paraguay. The division, complexity, and change that are taking place within the Anabaptist flock are unending and embroiled in tension and controversy, unlike the simplistic and idyllic sentimental image often held by many Englishers. The fluidity of motion from one sect to another enables the kinds of choice parents have in public charter schools and voucher programs. The times, they are a changin'.

BIG VALLEY AND BELLEVILLE, PENNSYLVANIA

Twin Oaks B&B would be my home for the next seven days. Innkeepers Norm and Sarah Glick became generous hosts with substantial breakfasts and homey accommodations, as well as providers of helpful information and directions to persons and places.

It was in this valley two years before that I found the home of Rosanna (*Rosanna of the Amish*). Clair DeLong, a retired county agent for Mifflin County, took me on a tour of the unusual Amish settlements in this valley and found Rosanna's home in Belleville. The river meandering through this valley, the Kishacoquillas, was enough to draw me to this place.

I had hoped, naively, to meet some of the Old Order, Renno, and Nebraska Amish, but their privacy prevented it.

Except for seeing white covered buggies of the Nebraska, yellow top buggies of the Byler, and black top buggies of Renno on the roads, I saw and talked with very few Amish. Percy Yoder, a Mennonite and curator at the Mifflin County Mennonite Historical Society, arranged one meeting with Bishop John J.S. Yoder. Bishop Yoder's wife had died only weeks before and I felt awkward and intrusive as the strained visit progressed. It was a humbling, if not humiliating, experience for me. My ambition and expectations had overshadowed reality and sensitivity.

However, one rewarding disclosure was that Yoder's farm was one of the six barns in the area that had been torched by a disgruntled Amish man in March of 1992, 10 years ago to the month of this trip. Within 23 days, volunteer neighbors rebuilt all six barns. "Unknown friends" contributed over $600,000 to an account in the Kish Bank for materials. A movie dramatization was made of it, "Harvest of Fire."

Percy also escorted me through a Nebraska Amish sawmill operation. The noise of three diesel engines, a five foot diameter circle saw blade, and a shaker platform, prevented any conversation or distraction of the workers. On another day, he invited me to ride along to pick up four Nebraska Amish from a work site. That brief encounter was low key, humorous, and enjoyable, but without the depth I had hoped to have. I resigned myself to reading more book accounts, but at least I had a feel for the geography and history of this place.

BEACHY AMISH CHURCH SERVICE

At 10:30 a.m. on March 2, a warm 55-degree day, I attended services in the Valley View Amish-Mennonite Church in Belleville. The service had already started and the pews were filled, so I opened a metal folding chair from the anteroom and sat in the back. Men and women sat on

separate sides of the aisle. Women were dressed in light
pastel plain long dresses and white sheer prayer caps. Men
were dressed in black or gray suits without stand-up collars
or were in white shirts without ties. Some suit coats had
hooks and eyes. Sons sat with fathers. One young girl with
a white sheer head cover sat with her father on the men's
side. Three ceiling fans revolved slowly and hung from an
egg-colored, stucco-plaster domed ceiling with indirect
lighting. Where stained glass windows might have been
were plain windows and shades. A slightly raised pulpit was
centered on the aisle. A microphone jutted out at the visiting preacher, but the system was ineffective in amplifying.
The main sermon was an hour and a quarter long, followed
by a prayer. All who could, stood, rotated, and kneeled on
the floor in the pews with heads down. One hymn in four-
part harmony followed, without organ or piano accompani-
ment. I observed the holy kiss, lips to lips, exchanged
between the minister and another man at the end of the service in the back of the sanctuary.

The minister and his son invited me to the luncheon, a
special occasion because of a visiting preacher. It was held
in the basement with potluck casseroles, beverages, and
desserts. Matt Peachy, the high school teacher for the congregation, another young man, two observers, and I discussed, debated, and shared our religious experiences for
two hours. Matt also invited me to observe his high school
class during my stay in Belleville. I met Dan King, an elderly man and former minister of the congregation, who now
lived with his second wife in the retirement home next to the
church. His first wife, Sylvia, was the sister to John A.
Hostetler. My admiration and affection for John drew me to
this place and the people who knew him, and Dan King was
one of them.

ABRAHAM SAMUEL YODER, JR.

Percy Yoder put me in touch with Abraham (Abe)
Yoder. Abe was a slight, elderly, and lively Brethren in
Christ deacon who had left his father's Amish home in order
to fulfill his religious quest and salvation. He left the
Zook/Spicher Church, which is now Valley View Amish-
Mennonite Church. His narrow face was accentuated with
his short hair parted in the middle and a short beard pro-
truding from his chin. His Amish life in the Big Valley had
not answered the eternal questions he had when he reached
his 40th year of age. He converted to Brethren at a tent
revival in nearby Reedsville in 1954. His Amish brother,
coincidentally, farmed near Quarryville where I had just
attended an Elderhostel program.

Abe and his second wife, Mildred, were missionaries in
Zimbabwe, Africa, from 1993 to 1996 and managed a
guesthouse. Mildred now volunteers at the retirement home
where Dan King lives. Abe followed his father's proclivity
and wrote an autobiography, *My Walk with God*, a self-published book that he gave me. He showed me the cemetery
where his parents are buried. Before we parted, he also gave
me a copy of his father's book, *My Life Story*.

What I learned from Abe is that in a community with several religious sects living side by side, the opportunity to change
is enhanced for the disillusioned or disgruntled without losing
contact with their blood family. Some shunning is modified or
overlooked to maintain family ties. It becomes an amalgamated
culture with thin lines between Amish and Amish-Mennonite,
as well as Amish-Mennonite and Brethren or Mennonite and is
easy to move and obvious to everyone. It may also be the slip-
pery slope to oblivion for some sects. As the elders die out, so
will their clothing with hooks and eyes. I see a more rambunc-
tious youth with Nike air pump sneakers charging down the
court and new referees calling the violations with a slow or very
late whistle—or not at all.

BELLEVILLE MARKET DAY

Every Wednesday in Belleville, there is market day. Vendors sell tools, harness equipment, vegetables, poultry and rabbits, dishcloths, socks, and hundreds of other household and farm items. A weekly event prompts some vendors to construct buildings that are more permanent while others merely set up tables. Horses, cows, and pigs are sold in a county fair type barn on the square. In the parking lot, hay is sold by the truckload.

Amish farmers from the Kishacoquillas Valley are customers. Women buy produce and household items and load them in their buggies. Men buy pig runts and cart them off in their "pickup" open buggies. Young Amish men cruise into the market square in their two-wheeled black carts and park at the football field length hitching rack. White top and brown bottom buggies from the Nebraska sect Amish seem to contain produce, such as oranges and condiments. Yellow top and black bottom buggies belong to the Byler sect. The majority of buggies are gray-top Lancaster County style. Over a three-hour period, more than 50 buggies made their appearance at the hitching rack. I have yet to see any of the above-mentioned buggies in Wisconsin settlements. Yet, several Amish men here said families move to Wisconsin. Before moving, they probably sell their buggies locally and buy new or used ones in the destination settlement in order to conform to congregation rules and custom.

CONVERSATIONS WITH THE PATRIARCHS

On the final afternoon of my Pilgrimage east, I met with Clair DeLong. He is a friend of the Amish in Mifflin County and retired county agent. I had met him two years ago when he introduced me to the Big Valley and its history and folklore. He majored in sociology at Penn State, specializing in power structures and put that knowledge to good use in his work dealing with political and economic measures that impacted the Amish. He knew Joe W. Yoder, author of *Rosanna of the Amish* and John A. Hostetler, author of *Amish Society* and authority on the Amish. Both lived in the Valley. John's Master's thesis on the Amish in the Big Valley launched him into a career as professor at Temple University. Clair was a consultant in the production of the movie "Trial by Fire" and another movie taken in the Valley, "Harvest of Fire." Clair outlined the two divisions under the white buggy group (two Yoder and a Zook), two yellow top buggy groups (Byler and Peachy), and the most liberal black top Renno group. He estimated their total population to be 1,500.

Claire's assessment of the infamous arson of six Amish barns in 1992 totaled $1,000,000 in damage. As county agent, he assisted in the calculation of $600,000 to repair the damage and $400,000 to settlement deacons for collateral damage. Tonight he drove into a farmyard where one of the rebuilt barns stood and he chatted with the young Amish owner in Pennsylvania Deutsch. He told me the 22-year-old arsonist got eight years in prison (term up in August, 2002) and his girl-friend accomplice, 24 months. The boy had been known to burn corn shocks standing in the field, and his father had burned a barn. Does it appear to you there is pyromania or copycat neurosis at work here?

Clair is in his 80s and "is cutting back," but has groomed a protégé, Dave Filson, at Penn State College of Agriculture-Coop Extension, to carry on his work with the Big Valley Amish. When I asked Clair how he as county agent was able to penetrate the private lives of the plain folks, he said an Amish man once told him, "You told us what we could do, but not what we had to do." To both Clair and Dave's credit and legacy, they have accomplished a great deal for their people.

Tomorrow morning I will be on my way to Philadelphia to visit my brother and finish my Pilgrimage east with research at Swarthmore College. Then, it is homeward bound.

PART III Other Anabaptists

Chapter 1
HUTTERITES

THE MIDDLE WAY

Not as well known are the Hutterite Anabaptists. I include them in this book to clear up confusion over who they are, as the media is beginning to explore and publish articles and features about them. Richard Rodriquez, writer and essayist on the Lehrer News Hour on PBS, told about them in April of 2001. He was inspired by the black and white photographs from Laura Wilson's oversize book, *Hutterites of Montana.* These brothers and sisters of the Amish and Mennonites shun the modern world by living communally, as prescribed in the Bible's Book of Acts 2:44, predominantly on the vacant plains of Montana, Washington, North and South Dakota, Minnesota, and the Provinces of Manitoba, Saskatchewan, Alberta, and British Columbia. There are over 35,000 living in 382 colonies.

Larry Wenger, a Mennonite deacon in Lancaster County, told me that Hutterites are also living in New York State and in Farmington, Pennsylvania. Located on U.S. Hwy 40 near Ft. Necessity National Battlefield, the Farmington community has a factory that produces specialty equipment for health care businesses. To schedule a visit, I phoned Peter, who handles guests and tours of the factory. Classical piano music played while I was on hold. Not the ordinary Muzak, it showed class and a far cry from the minimalist phone booth at the end of the lane in some Amish settlements. They broke away from the Hutterites recently and are now called the Society of Brothers. Their origins were in Germany in 1920s led by Eberhard Arnold.

Differences in leadership styles caused the schism.

The Hutterites founder, Jakob Hutter, was an Austrian religious reformer and heretic who was burned at the stake in 1536 for his defiance of the Catholic Church. A scholarly treatment of the Hutterites is competently documented in John A. Hostetler's classic book, *Hutterite Society*. A more casual and personal near-autobiographical book is Samuel Hofer's *Born Hutterite*. A most dramatic story is Michael Holzach's *The Forgotten People: a Year Among the Hutterites*, translated from German. Michael's experience immersed him in the totality of Hutterite life, from religious lessons to milk hand. He quotes from *The Article Book* of 1577 a passage by Peter Walbot: "The more people own, the greater the need. For those who seek much will lack much and those who desire many things will lack much more. For where your treasure is, there will your heart be also." Michael, a Social Studies major in Germany, reporter, and freelance writer, met a sad end to his life in an accidental drowning. Jim Lehrer, the PBS television News Hour host, may well take his name from one of these Hutterite groups, the Lehrerleut. Lehrer translates to the German word for teacher. He is not a Hutterite, but an articulate and probing journalist.

<h2 style="text-align:center">VISITING A HUTTERITE COLONY</h2>

I visited two Hutterite colonies in Canada during the summer of 1997. At the Cypress Hills Colony, nestled in the far southwest corner of Saskatchewan near the town of Swift Current, I followed the "milk man," Walter Entz, for a day. He manages a dairy heard of about 40 Holsteins with a computer, a young apprentice assistant, and a modern, automated milking parlor. His quiet and humble demeanor is not unlike that of the Amish or Mennonites, nor are most of his religious beliefs and values, as one would expect from an Anabaptist brother. These three groups crossed paths many times on European soil in the 15th and 16th centuries avoiding religious persecution and slaughter.

Curious about Walter's situation, I called him in January 2002. Albert, an older colony handyman, answered the communal phone. We chatted for a while about the weather, that I was from the States, and had visited the Cypress Colony. The more we talked, the more friendly he sounded. Perhaps he enjoyed the diversion from his routine chores. He tried to transfer me to the barn where he thought Walter would be working, but was unsuccessful. He took my phone number and said he would have Walter call me. He never did.

About 90 brethren live in one-story, motel type buildings that contain the apartments of each family. Hutterites are communal, thus communistic as described in the Book of Acts. At Cypress Hills Colony, they raise 5,000 chickens in an enclosed building, and 1,000 pigs on 12,000 acres of moderately productive land. The silage, chopped up mature and green corn stalks, that Walter offered me smelled better than my morning cereal. The machines used to harvest this abundance include four brand-new Ford eight-wheeled tractors and four combines, an investment of about $920,000.

Though common in religion with the Amish, the Hutterites interpret the same text in far different ways. The liberal use of technology would send shivers down the spine of Old Order preachers, if not apoplexy. Yet, the two Anabaptist groups share the same roots of the 16th century Protestant Reformation.

PART III Other Anabaptists

Chapter 2
MENNONITES

GOSHEN, INDIANA

On my return trip from Lancaster and other points east, I arranged to stop at Goshen College, the Mennonite College in Goshen, Indiana. John E. Sharp, my contact person, is the director, Mennonite Church USA Historical Committee and Archives, Goshen, Indiana and North Newton, Kansas. He is also a native of, and very familiar with, Big Valley in Pennsylvania. Photographer Bill Coleman's assistant helped me contact him, and what good fortune it was.

John's office was impressive. The ceiling appeared to be 12 feet high, and seemingly propped up by bookshelves jammed with neat rows of books. Tucked in a corner was his small desk adorned with the professorial laptop computer. He entered my name in it, so I assume I am an entry in his archives for all time to come. He had a box filled with additional books on the Amish and Mennonites that he used in an Elderhostel course at the Amigo Centre, Sturgis, Michigan, and the Geneva Center in Rochester, Michigan during the summer. Sharing is a teacher thing, so he printed his course outline for me when I told him that I taught an Elderhostel course about the Amish in Wisconsin. The distinctive Amish-made rocking chair I was comfortably sitting in was a bent-hickory model, looking much like the Wisconsin model. I was comfortable being with John, and our conversation turned to the Amish culture.

The first question I asked was why he thought there was an increasing interest in the Amish people and culture.

He thought it was something idyllic, that the difference between our English lifestyle and the Amish represented a dramatic contrast that catches our attention and appears peaceful, quiet, and calm, unencumbered by the stock market fluctuations, wars over oil, presidential elections, kids ballet lessons and pj parties, or new fashion swings. This led to a second explanation that he called "symbolic fantasy," that their lifestyle was an alternative to consider. Any alternative would do, but this was the most extreme and secretive, therefore it must be the most valuable. It was "plain" and "simplified."

The third quality that John thought made the Amish idolized or put on a pedestal was sentimentality. Their lifestyle seems so gentle, tender, influenced more by emotion than reason, almost maudlin. Lastly, their values are lessons for living and give a sense of belonging, of community, and fellowship that had direction, especially in the face of the Y2K threats and apocalyptic horrors. Those religiously based values and virtues correspond to the increase in our religious participation. We "cocoon" ourselves in our homes and apartments, wrapped up in the web pages rather than the web of life. (See Donnermeyer, Kreps, and Kreps book, *Lessons for Living*.) But we do not know all we need to know to understand the Amish. Not many Englishers try to become Amish, and most of those who try, fail. Yet, the Amish hold out to us in their lifestyle something that we can adopt. A legacy.

My second question had to do with the life of Joseph W. Yoder, youngest son of Rosanna. Yoder was the author of *Rosanna of the Amish* and *Rosanna's Boys*. The stories take place in the 1800's in the Big Valley, located in central Pennsylvania. John E. Sharp is cited in the editor's note of the former book. He gave me a photocopy of Yoder, and one with Joseph's wife, Laura Lane, for my appreciation and archives. I experience a new and larger dimension of a story, especially from a bygone era, when I see the person who wrote it. To be present in the geography of the story is exciting. So, when I visited the Big Valley, I sought out and photographed the home where Rosanna was raised. .

Yoder had multiple allegiances to Anabaptist and then to English Christian churches. He was the product of an Irish mother in an Amish culture, which may account for his mobility between church groups. Or, he may have made the changes because he had been enlightened or denigrated, depending on your perspective. He tried to promote his view of how the Amish could change to better their lives.

Such is the excitement of research as expressed by Barbara Tuckman:

> "Research is endlessly seductive; writing is hard work. One has to sit down on that chair and think and transform thought into readable, conservative, interesting sentences that both make sense and make the reader turn the page. It is laborious, slow, often painful, sometimes agony. It means rearrangement, revision, adding, cutting, rewriting. But it brings a sense of excitement, almost of rapture, a moment on Olympus. In short, it is an act of creation."

AUTHOR'S FOOTNOTE

The September 5, 2001 *Budget* newspaper carried the death notice of John A. Hostetler on the front page. He was 82 years old when he died on August 28 in the Goshen General Hospital where he had been a patient for four days. His father, Joseph, and mother, Nancy (her maiden name was also Hostetler) preceded him in death; they were from Belleville, PA. John was a professor at Temple University in Philadelphia for 34 years. Married in 1949, his first wife died in 1951. Two years later, he married his present wife who resides in Goshen, Indiana. John is buried in Violett Cemetery. Memorial contributions are accepted by Goshen College for the Mennonite Museum Fund.

Hostetler testified in 1972 before the United States Supreme Court in the case "Wisconsin vs. Yoder," a case originating in Wisconsin's courts from New Glarus.

"He was the leading scholar interpreting Amish and Hutterite communities for many years," said Donald B. Kraybill, who followed Hostetler as director of the Young Center for Anabaptist and Pietist Studies at Elizabethtown College in Lancaster County.

"He was a constant advocate for the larger society to make the community hospitable for the Amish way of life," said Herman Borntreger, of the National Committee for Amish Religious Freedom.

His obituary in the Associated Press reported "Hostetler was born into an Old Order Amish family in Cold Water, near Belleville, Mifflin County. But his father was excommunicated from the Amish Church in 1929, and his family moved to Iowa." He became a Fulbright scholar and began teaching in 1963 at Penn State.

RICHLAND CENTER

Ella Hege, a Mennonite widow living in Rockbridge, eight miles northwest of Richland Center, was on her way to the mailbox when I phoned her on January 2, 2002, a frigid 15-degree day. She is the *Budget* scribe for the Richland Center congregation. Ella said there are also Hutterites living nearby in Yuba where she attends church. This is the first time I heard of Hutterites living in Wisconsin. Hutterites are Anabaptists, but they usually live communally in colonies. Yuba's do not. The colonies I visited were in Saskatchewan, Canada, where up to 120 persons lived on one farm in newer buildings resembling one-story cinder block motels with separate units for each family. (See Part III, Chapter 1).

In Wisconsin, Mennonites call themselves by many titles. Ella helped me construct this list:

•Bethany Mennonite (Church name in Marathon County)
•Wisler Church Mennonite (Some from Goshen, Indiana)
•Amish-Mennonite (Independent) (Some from Tampico, Illinois)
•Conservative Mennonite (Use tractors in fields, horse and buggy on roads)
•Weaverland Conference Mennonite (Similar to the Beachy Amish)
•Sheldon Mennonite Church (Independent, to Wisconsin in the 1930s)
•Mennonite Nationwide Fellowship (Conservative with cars)
•Mennonite/Unaffiliated
•New Order Amish (Technically Amish, but drive cars and use phones)
•Old Order Mennonite (Horse and buggy, plain clothes)

Donald B. Kraybill has written an informative book, *Anabaptist World USA*, that provides tables, graphs, interpretive essays, and directories of Brethren, Mennonite, Hutterite, and Amish congregations, settlements, and colonies in the United States. It further explains Ella Hege's list above.

A VISIT WITH MENNONITE ELLA HEGE

On Saturday, May 4, 2002, I left the LaValle Amish quilt auction mid-afternoon to visit with Ella in Rockbridge. Her small one story shaded home off Hwy 80 north of Richland Center was nestled next to a towering sandstone and pine tree bluff carved out by the Pine River. She was not home, nor did the fire warden in the corner store know of her whereabouts. So, I toured the small Rockbridge Park next to her house, walked through the natural tunnel in the bluff, and photographed a fisherman playing out his line in a pool next to the jagged layers of ancient sedimentary sandstone. Later I called with my handy cell phone, found her home, and drove next door.

A rotund, elderly, gray-haired woman, Ella greeted me at the sunroom door with a small-mouthed smile and bright clear blue eyes. She was dressed in her Mennonite head cover and faded blue and white vertical-striped belted sack dress. Her house was filled with bric-a-brac, flowers, and plants on windowsills, and a large quilt rack parked under the front picture window. The quilt was ordered and gave her needed cash and something to occupy her time alone. She told me of her ancestors from Switzerland who immigrated to America on the ship James Godwill in 1727. By 1863, there was recorded property ownership in Chambersburg, Pennsylvania, a town near Gettysburg and prominent in the Civil War. One has to wonder how they survived the war let alone their passive resistance to the military draft. Ella's husband had died in the 1980s after collapsing while delivering groceries to an Amish family. It is customary that Mennonites live symbiotically with the Amish, each benefiting from the services of the other in a cooperative community.

I told her of my plans to follow the migration route of the Amish down the Rhine River in Germany and France, the Alsace, Lorraine, and Palatinate regions. She gave me the addresses of four couples that had visited her recently, relatives who lived in Wissembourg, France. Four days later, I searched for the town in my *Reader's Digest Atlas of the World*, a remnant from my mother's estate, and I found Wissembourg. To my amazement, it was within a stone's throw from Zweilbrucken, Kaiserslauten, Saarbrucken, and

Kircheimbolanden, all towns on my itinerary! What providence! This kind of human contact in Europe was what I needed to encourage me on with confidence, enthusiasm, and passion.

"I hope to get to my roots in Switzerland some day," Ella sighed wistfully.

"Come along with me," I replied. She declined, as I knew she would, saying she hoped her son would be going in the near future and take her along.

I thanked Ella for her patience and helpful contacts in France as well as her own life story. She said she would help me in my research and writing this book in any way she could, and that I could call on her anytime. I let myself out, as she needed to ready herself for another gathering of friends at the Rockbridge Park. To remember the visit, I photographed her spring-green house next to the towering sandstone and pine tree bluff standing sentinel over my Mennonite friend in Rockbridge. Her faith had more than an earthly guardian watching over her.

Two weeks later, I mailed letters to the four families in her guest book. One week later, I received an email from Jean Hege from Wissembourg, France recommending two contacts for my trip. One was in Germany and the other in Pennsylvania at Masthof Press. He suggested a book published by them, entitled *Amish-Mennonites in Germany; Their Congregations, The Estates Where They Lived, Their Families*, by Hermann Guth. The book helped me by focusing on estate names within towns where the Amish had lived. They were renters on fiefs, not land owners.

WAUKESHA

MAPLE AVENUE MENNONITE CHURCH
Lawrence Kratz is the pastor of the only Mennonite church in southeastern Wisconsin. A native of New York

where he and his wife Clarice, a pastor, raised a clutch of children, they now shepherd the flock in the city of Waukesha, Wisconsin. Both attended seminary in Elkhart, Indiana. Their church is located at 346 Maple Avenue in a three-story corner house from the early 1900s. Just inside the front door, what used to be the living room is the main sanctuary. Folding chairs substitute for pews, a pedestal lectern serves as a pulpit. An upright piano stands against a wall. The room holds about 30 adults for a Sunday worship service, with a separate room for children. A kitchen in the back of the first floor stores dishes and 30-cup coffee makers. During the week, the building becomes a day care center. Funded partially by grants, it serves congregation members as well as non-members from the area, fulfilling one of the church proclamations, which is to serve others in need.

Lawrence lectured to my Amish classes at UW-Waukesha for several years. On one occasion, we met at his church. He is a tall, sturdy, soft-spoken, and thoughtful man who chooses his words carefully. His occupations include raising chickens and owning and running a dry cleaning plant. He currently operates a pastry and donut shop in Waukesha, supported by grants from the service clubs in town for his work with rehabilitation agencies. His workers are referrals from those agencies. Lawrence pitches in doing his favorite thing, turning over donuts in the deep-fry cauldrons.

He confessed that in the hustle of everyday life, it becomes more difficult to maintain the ideals of the Mennonite traditions. In this fellowship, clothing does not set them apart from the rest of us. Both married and unmarried males are clean-shaven. There are no horse and buggy riders here. But the conservative Mennonites resemble the traditional Amish in lifestyle. A glossy six-fold flyer describing the Mennonite church worldwide states, "For those who want to know more." What a dramatic difference from the Amish who caution knowing more, or worldly knowledge.

MANITOBA

JAKE PETERS, WINNIPEG

I met Jake on my way to Alaska at a campground in Winkler, Manitoba. The town, just over the border from Minnesota, is populated almost entirely by retired Mennonites. He was opening his travel trailer next to my campsite and offered me the local evening newspaper.

"What brings you to these parts?" he said in a soft, friendly way.

"I want to meet a Mennonite from the area as part of my research," I answered.

"Well, you're looking at one!" he exclaimed with a jovial chuckle.

Thus started a long friendship. Since 1998, we have maintained contact through mail and email. He gave me a treasured documentary book belonging to his father on the history of the Reinland area of Manitoba where his father settled. Other historical books he mailed to me included *The Growth of Foreign Missions in the Mennonite Church, Manitoba Mennonite Memories-1874 to 1974, Mennonite World Handbook*, and his self-published autobiography, *Approaching the Glory.* Although his wife is in poor health, he maintains a positive attitude sustained by his faith. He serves on a proselytizing committee for his Province Church, and his letters always contain short sermonettes.

It is through these chance meetings and personal contacts from other cultural or religious subgroups that makes them real and believable. What better way is there to learn and experience diversity?

NOVA SCOTIA

In June 1996, I drove my Volkswagen camper onto the ferry at Manitowoc, Wisconsin on my way to Nova Scotia Province. The boat trip across Lake Michigan was a forerunner of what I would see on the Canadian side of the great Saint Lawrence Seaway. But I was in search of Amish and Mennonites, not boats and ships. Clearing customs at Sarnia, I headed for London and the information center. Here I learned where to find Mennonites in Kitchener, Ontario.

KITCHENER MARKET
A farmer's market provided my first contact. It was under a makeshift tent fly made of a blue crinkly plastic material and propped up at the four corners by aluminum tent poles. The farmer wore a black fedora, black pants, and suit coat, white shirt, and no tie. I watched him attend to several customers buying his vegetables. He spoke softly with a minimum of words. The card tables on which he displayed his goods were restocked from his panel truck parked next to the tent.

When he was free of paying customers, I engaged him in conversation. I told him of my mission to meet Amish and Mennonites in Canada and that I was on my way to Nova Scotia. After answering a few of my questions, he briskly went into a litany of his beliefs. "I believe in one God, creator of all things. I believe in the Trinity. I believe in the New Testament. I believe we should not be yoked with unbelievers. I believe the wicked shall be punished." There were too many to write down at the speed he delivered them. Overwhelmed, or embarrassed, I bid good day and left him. He had better things to do.

Someone had told me there were Amish in Prince Edward Island Province. My search revealed none. Had I

subscribed to the *Budget* in 1996, I would have known if
there were a scribe there. In the December 12, 2001 issue,
on page 14, Mrs. Donald Plank, Mennonite scribe from
New Glasgow, Nova Scotia, describes a "...young conservative family who live on PEI, about an hour from the ferry.
They find it quite lonely, having no church where they feel
free to fellowship." Twelve other scribes from Ontario
Province wrote for this issue. I found some of these research
tools too late in my quest.

TRURO MARKET

Back on Nova Scotia, I found a contact in Truro. A lady
in the information center checked the computer for Amish
without results. Then she called a librarian friend who
directed me to the farmer's market being held that day. It
was here that I met the Dueck Mennonite family. Mrs.
Dueck was at a stand sorting out vegetables. As I
approached her, she was polite, but soon referred me to her
husband who was unloading more vegetables from a panel
truck. It is customary for males to speak with males in this
patriarchal society. Interested in my mission, he asked if I
would like to stay the night at their farm. I was ecstatic! I
was led to their Mennonite settlement west of Truro. It was
the Northfield Settlement, prominently displayed on the
map. The Bay of Fundy's highest tides were 10 kilometers
north.

Mr. Dueck apologized for not having a bed available in
the house. I had one in my camper and showed him. His
son, who lived with his wife in a small house near the
entrance to the farm, looked on as well and was curious to
know more about my amateur radio on the back table. His
brother was in Paraguay, where they all had lived, and was
a "ham," or amateur radio operator. He said if he had a radio
it would reduce his long distance phone bills. When I
returned home I sent a manual for him to prepare for the

license exam. Technology is not forbidden in this settlement.

A MEAL AND MUSIC

Mr. Dueck invited me for dinner in the house. The room had tables arranged in a square, open in the center. His wife sat on his left and young son to his right at the front table. His older son and daughter-in-law sat at a table at a right angle to the front table. I sat at the table to his left. The back table was filled with his three daughters. There was order in this family, and it emanated from Mr. Dueck.

The meal was modest and tasty. The soup was strongly seasoned, and when I got to the bottom of the bowl where the spices were, it seared my throat. Water gradually quenched the fire. Mr. Dueck began and finished the meal with silent prayer. Then the singing began. Mennonite hymnals were distributed to all. Mr. Dueck bellowed, "Who has the first one?" His oldest son called out, "Number 236." There was a moment of silence and pages rattling. Then Mr. Dueck began singing the hymn. Everyone followed except me. I did not know the hymn or melody. This procedure repeated two more times, as the family sang all verses of each hymn. Then Mr. Dueck turned to me and questioned why I was not singing. Feeling like a parishioner with my hand in the collection plate, I said I did not know the hymns.

He asked in a stern voice, "What is your religion?"

I said, "Methodist."

"What do you know about its beginning? What is it known for?" he said.

I replied, "John Wesley was its founder, and singing was highly revered." I had just put a silver foot in my mouth and cooked my own goose. They had a sinner in their midst. That was the end of singing. We all retired for the night.

FAREWELL

In the morning, I was invited for breakfast. Forgiven, I

suppose. Mr. Dueck had to drown a raccoon caught overnight in a trap. It had been raiding corn in the crib. I did not watch. Somehow, it was not respectful to God's beasts. Then he milked the only cow they had for their own use. I watched. After breakfast, the middle son in his teens wanted to show me the flock of barn swallows in the backyard. They swooped over the marshy area, sweeping insects into their mouths. I brought out my binoculars from the camper for him to use and a field guide for birds in the Northeastern States that I gave him to nurture his enthusiasm. On the front doorstep, I offered a straw hat to whomever it fit. Mr. Dueck said it would fit somebody and thanked me. He invited me to attend church with them with the caveat that it was in German. I was forgiven, but I declined, respectfully. Then with a smile Mrs. Dueck handed me an apple for my travels. They had provided a rich, surprising, rewarding, and thought-provoking experience.

FOLLOW-UP

On January 10, 2002, I found the Abram Dueck business card he had given to me on my visit in 1996. Curious about their life, I phoned them and talked with one of the daughters. She remembered me because I had signed their guest book. She also remembered the Roger Tory Peterson bird guide I had given her brother, Victor. I was astounded that either her memory was so good, or that I had made that much of an impression on her. She said her folks were at a warehouse sorting used clothing to be shipped to Germany and then on to Mennonites in Russia for distribution to needy families. She said her older brother, Karl, had moved away and built a new home for his family. It was a poignant conversation, renewing old memories of an exciting visit five years ago.

NESHKORO

The Spring Lake Country Store had been closed the last time I was here, because no business is conducted on a Sunday. This Saturday the store was open. The rectangular, brown painted store is at the intersection of County Road F and Z eight miles southeast of Wautoma in Spring Lake. The owner, Luke Ebersole, was busy at the back of the store packaging dry goods for the shelves. He remembered my letter and our telephone conversation asking about Mennonite churches in the Neshkoro area. His church is the Oak Ridge Mennonite Church located on Hwy S just north of Hwy 21 and a mile and a half west of Red Granite.

The store houses a bakery run by a Mennonite woman, Mattie E. Detweiler. She and three Mennonite women who assisted her were garbed in typical clothing. They wore a small white starched head cover. Their neatly pressed dresses were plain pastel color or faint print pattern and mid-calf length. They were busy with several customers buying fresh-baked loaves of bread, pies, Snickerdoodle cookies, and molasses cookies. As I bought the last package of molasses cookies, I spoke with Mattie. What surprised me was her intense eye contact and concentration as I spoke with her. It was intensely personal and disarming, especially with her attractive and angelic face and soft calm voice. I surmise this respectful encounter is a reflection of her faith that all persons are creatures of God.

I asked Luke if I could return another time and photograph inside the store for use in my Amish Culture classes. He approved, but I did not ask about photographing him. That will have to be asked on my next visit.

PROVIDENCE LEADS ME TO A DEACON
My friend Sandy wanted to drive on a quaint country

road south from the Spring Lake Country Store. Within a mile we came upon a sign near a mailbox: "God resisteth the proud, James 4:6." I thought this had to be a Mennonite family farm. A plain-dressed woman wearing a white head cover was hanging wash on a clothesline in the side yard. We drove in the long pea gravel driveway and parked in the back of the house. With her two young boys, she came over to us and exchanged greetings. I explained my visit to the area and wondered if she was Mennonite. She was, and she offered to get her husband to talk to us. Meanwhile, one young boy told us about their sheep in a nearby pasture.

Standing on the elevated porch looking down at us, her husband Ken Witmer appeared very tall. He wore dark pants and a checkerboard-patterned shirt. His full head of hair was wavy and black. His speech was slow, deliberate, and cautious. I explained my interest in the Amish and Mennonites. With that, he invited us into the house out of the chilly late April air.

His wife, Anna, directed the two sons and a daughter to clean up their books from the living room before we sat down on overstuffed furniture. A bookshelf in the wall was neatly organized with books stacked in order of height from left to right. There was no television. Ken now spoke in relaxed tones. For some of my questions, he referred me to Stephen Scott's book, *An Introduction to Old Order and Conservative Mennonite Groups*. Ken is in a photograph on page 207 where he is instructing at Messiah Bible School in Carbon Hill, Ohio. He said there are 15 families in the church where he is deacon. He praised Catherine the Great of Russia who provided safe harbor in that country for Mennonites under her reign. Following her death, many migrated to Paraguay, South America, where Mennonites still constitute a considerable population. Others migrated directly to the U.S. and Canada, as did many of those who went to Russia first. Ken said they had a prayer meeting on

Wednesdays and church service on Sunday at 11:00 a.m. As we were ready to leave, he went into his small tidy office illuminated by the computer monitor screen, opened a file drawer with hanging racks, and removed a book which he gave to me. It was *Marching On* by Mervin J. Baer, a "doctrinal history of the Fellowship Churches." He accepted a monetary donation for his church, we exchanged addresses and phone numbers, and he invited me to church service the next day.

While I talked with Ken, Sandy was chatting with Anna. She said their school had grades one through eight, the same as Amish schools. It was located in the old church building and had 20 students and two teachers. A man taught the upper grades and Ken's sister was the other teacher. Anna's daughter was doing 9th grade work at home and a boy in the community was doing 10th grade work at home and two days at school. They both brought their homework to the schoolteachers to review. At the age of 14, Anna came from Lancaster to Colby, Wisconsin where she met Ken, who was born in Canada. With five other families from the Unity Mennonite Church, they banded together to form the community of Oak Ridge Mennonite church of Redgranite, Wisconsin.

Outside, their flock of 32 sheep grazed with seven lambs along a slope leading down to a small pond, while the two sons played with a large bright yellow plastic bulldozer on the parking lot. Two cars and a van were also there. Along the drive was a 300-foot long garden with black plastic over watermelon plants that Ken raised "as a hobby." As we reached the road, I read the other side of the sign near the mailbox. It read: "A soft answer turneth away wrath. Proverbs 15:1."

NATIONWIDE FELLOWSHIP CHURCH SERVICE
As I entered the church the next day, an adult Bible

lesson was ending. The modern building had eggshell plaster walls and ceiling, stained oak wainscoting, plain windows, and cream-colored shades half-drawn. The six ceiling fans were not needed today. A rostrum in the front bisected the room, with men seated on the right and women on the left. The 12-inch high platform held an oversized lectern with a microphone in cobra-striking configuration. Behind this furniture was a wide bench with cranberry-colored cushions, the same as I was sitting on. Organ and piano were absent. No choir sang. A male lead singer (Vorsinger or Vorstimmer in German) started each hymn and each stanza, as in Amish singing. The hymnal was Mennonite and in English. Men wore black or dark blue suits with standup collars and no lapels, buttoned down the front over white dress shirts buttoned at the top and tieless. Women wore pastel or small print dresses, white head cover, and sweaters for warmth.

Ken presented the main sermon. It was titled "The Union of Sorrow and Love," using scripture from I Corinthians 13. The seemingly paradoxical title he explained by saying, "what costs the most are the most precious." He instructed the congregation to deny self, but not to the point of asceticism, referring to Luke 13:22 and 31. He referred to Hebrews 2:10 and Hebrews 5:8 and 9 to illustrate being perfected: "Although he was a son, he learned obedience from what he suffered and, once made perfect, he became the source of eternal salvation for all who obey him." He urged his flock to accept suffering (Luke 9:22) and not to be "nominal Christians." The Good Samaritan story in Luke 10:30-36 emphasized the compassion and suffering experienced by the Samaritan, the union of sorrow and love. Ken's final story was that of the Prodigal Son, whose father's sorrow did not hinder him from letting the son learn on his own, even to the point of desperation. Some would call this "tough love." Then a call to prayer prompted everyone to stand, turn about, and kneel on the floor with their chests on the pew in supplication, as do the Amish and Amish-Mennonites I have witnessed.

After the service, people stayed to converse with their neighbors. Michael Martin, a member of the church, came to the back of the room to greet me and say he heard I was writing a book on the Amish in Wisconsin. He also was writing a book. It is titled *Not of This World* and chronicles the Anabaptist history. He said he used prints from the *Martyrs Mirror* that are magnificent copper plate engravings of episodes of torture and slaughter of Anabaptists in the 16th century for their heretical betrayal of the Catholic Church. Several men joined us in friendly conversation including Ken, but women kept to themselves on their side of the room. The gathering was important to catch up with the news of other families and make plans for the coming week.

Ken apologized for not inviting me to stay for dinner the day before, but he did invite me to visit again and stay overnight with his family. It was a sign that I was trusted and that my interest in them and their faith was sincere. As we left the church, he and a few others headed for the prison nearby to minister to the prisoners, a sacrifice he made to share the love of his faith.

PART III *Other Anabaptists*
Chapter 3
AMISH-MENNONITES

MUSCODA & FENNIMORE

MUSCODA

Curtiss Kauffman is an Amish-Mennonite minister for the Pleasant Valley Amish-Mennonite church in Muscoda. He is also a scribe for the *Budget* newspaper. He has lived here for the past 20 years serving 108 members of the church. He was born Amish-Mennonite in Shelbyville, Illinois, 74 years ago. His wife died a year ago and he had to attend a niece's funeral the day after my visit. There are usually more funerals for folks his age than weddings. His parents were Conservative Amish-Mennonites living in Pigeon, Michigan, as well as Tampico, Illinois, and in Oregon. It was in Oregon that Curtiss met his wife of 13 years. She was a widow with one daughter. Together they adopted a son who is still living with Curtiss and has a lawn service in Muscoda.

Curtiss, which is his real name, is nearly six feet tall and has a solid frame. He reminds me of Burl Ives. His tousled short white hair is cut like any other Mennonite and he sports a trimmed white goatee. His left hand has been injured leaving only his thumb and first finger. Velcro straps secure his size eleven shoes and his pants are held up with suspenders. He is quick to chuckle at humor, exposing slight spaces between his front teeth, but serious in his conversation about his faith, church, and family. I had arrived at his home on Hwy 133W before he arrived, but he greeted me warmly.

Jacob Hertzler, an Amish man, was the first Amish

bishop in the United States, seven generations removed in Curtiss' genealogy and affirming his Amish roots. Curtiss showed me a self-published book by Larry L. Hostetler, *Descendents of Christian J. and Magdalena Hershberger* that affirms his claim. He also knew Ella Hege and her deceased husband, Noah, members of his church for a short time, who farmed in Muscoda and later joined a Mennonite congregation in Rockbridge. (My contact with Ella is in the chapter on Mennonites in this book.) Curtiss knew all this as a matter of course. It seems to be traditional to keep connections alive. He is a people person.

He told me about other related Anabaptist sects. The Beachy branch was in Missouri, Kansas, Oklahoma, Pennsylvania, Maryland, and Iowa, but not in the West. Horning Mennonites was another sect mostly in Pennsylvania, Indiana and Ontario, Canada, and Fennimore, Wisconsin, who originally came from Pennsylvania. These sects were named after charismatic religious leaders, just like the Swartzentruber. He showed me the *Mennonite Church Information 2002* book that lists individual members and their affiliation. His church meets every Sunday for two hours starting at 9:30 a.m. Bible classes are held on Wednesdays in winter for pre-baptized children 14 to 20 years of age. Since 1962, their Mennonite Christian Day School has met in a new building that doubles for their church services. The lot is used to choose preachers, but preachers choose the bishop from among themselves. They have their own cemetery and do not allow televisions, radios, or tobacco of any kind. Alcohol in the form of wine is used only in Communion.

He discussed the schism of 1890 when many divisions happened within the Mennonite flock. It is described in a book he and I both had read, *Traditions and Transitions* by Paton Yoder. Curtiss did not approve of persons who move out of a settlement as a way to resolve a dispute over the

Ordnung or a personality clash with the leadership. A book he recommended was *Up From the Rubble* by Dyck, which describes the horrible living conditions for the Mennonites in Russia in the WWII era. Our discussion ended, he escorted me out to my car, shook hands with me, and hoped for my safe drive. It was the hospitable way Amish folks said goodbye.

UNEXPECTED DIVIDEND

On my way to Fennimore to meet another Amish-Mennonite, I met an Old Order Amish man in Boscobel at a substantial 10 x 10 foot roofed, but floorless, roadside stand. He was selling starter flower plants and baby-sitting a five-year-old girl. His name was Newswanger. He was from a nearby settlement that formed in 1996 between Fennimore and Lancaster with 17 families on farms. His much-used straw hat was the style of the Lancaster, Pennsylvania, and Old Order Amish. I learned later that large numbers of Amish and "buggy" Mennonites are leaving Lancaster to take advantage of high priced land they sell and the cheaper land they buy in Wisconsin and other Midwest states. His coat was a style I had not seen before, with snaps instead of hooks and eyes, cotton coat instead of denim, and with a Nehru collar. Soft spoken, he showed interest in genealogy, so I showed him a book on Amish from Germany. He told me a short cut for the detour out of town and onto my next leg of the trip, and we bade good day as customers were arriving.

FENNIMORE

A mile south of Fennimore on Hwy 61 was the bulk food store where I met Nancy Martin. She and her husband, Ivan, were scribes for the *Budget*. They were Amish-Mennonites in the Weaverland Conference. Thorp and Granton belong to the same conference. Iowa, Missouri,

New York, Virginia, and Pennsylvania are the other states with Weaverland settlements. There are eight member families farming and 21 "scholars" in school, grades 1-7, in the Fennimore area. Nancy's family has seven children, the average for families.

The settlement formed in 1997 with families migrating from Pennsylvania. The young woman helping in the bulk food store was from nearby Platteville and belonged to the Groffdale Mennonite Conference that use horse and buggy. She also had a distinctive accent or dialect that came from her Swiss heritage. Nancy's group use cars, computers, fax, electricity, and, most interestingly, conference telephone calls for their church service on Sundays. Because they have no building or preachers, a phone call is made to a preacher in northern Missouri or Pennsylvania and a service is piped in on the second and last Sunday of the month. They also go to the Lancaster settlement semi-annually for Communion service.

The Weaverland Conference holds an annual meeting once a year in Pennsylvania for its religious leaders. Here the concerns expressed by the men and women of the settlements are articulated and suggestions made to resolve or remedy them. These concerns are generated twice each year in spring and fall after the Sunday church service in a council meeting. Only church members may attend, so non-baptized are excused. Some issues Nancy recalled were over computer use, email, and the Internet. Another was over the use of citizens band radio, CB. She said channel 19 had too much foul language for God fearing folks.

I mentioned that I taught classes about the Amish with the hope that we English would be better informed about the diverse lifestyles of Amish. For example, one English woman asked Nancy if she wore her head cover in the shower. Nancy said information is a two-way street. Amish can make use of knowledge about English culture as well.

She showed me the *Directory of the Weaverland Conference-Mennonite Churches, 2000.* She called it the "Church Book" for short. It lists alphabetically the names of members, family members, and other data. From it, she gave me the name of Amos B. Hoover, a historian who might help in my planning for research in Germany, France, and Switzerland in September 2002.

Nancy's store office accommodated our chat and an assortment of her children who drifted in and out during the hour. As with most offices, it had abundant unfinished and working papers decorating tops of file cabinets and desks. Clutter about the office was uncharacteristic of the shelves in the store that were orderly. I made a purchase, thanked Nancy for her willingness to take time to visit with me, and said good day.

I had a reservation from innkeeper Kathleen Polich at the Geiger House Bed and Breakfast in Cassville on the Mississippi River. The drive through the back roads due to a detour on Hwy 81 south of Lancaster was exquisite. The spring's yellow-green leaves and rich earth-brown contour-plowed fields made me slow down and enjoy the beauty of this part of Wisconsin. This is the "Driftless" area and the last glacier 10,000 years ago did not touch this terrain. I had to slow down; there was not a straight road on the ridges or valleys for as far as the eye could see. Deep valley roads resembled roller coasters. Picturesque pastures were dotted with black and white Holstein cows and rich brown Belgian workhorses. A recent book, *The Earth is the Lord's* by John Landis Ruth, describes the relationship of land and people. The title is befitting for the earth's caretakers, the Amish.

PART III Other Anabaptists

Chapter 4

OLD ORDER AND NATIONWIDE FELLOWSHIP MENNONITES

THORP AND WITHEE

Setting out to find the Amish in the Marshfield area in central Wisconsin, I was surprised and elated to find Old Order Mennonites instead. A brochure at the Marshfield Inn published by the Chamber of Commerce and Visitor's Bureau spelled out a self-guided automobile tour of the Old Order Mennonites from Spencer to Thorp. Our host at the Inn was Kate Hendricks, born and raised in Granton to the west of Marshfield. She gave me tips on where to find the Amish along Hwy 10. My mission now, however, was to visit the Old Order Mennonites by following the auto tour.

Matanatha Market

The tour guide directions were easy to follow, but the sudden 10-inch rainfall the night before had washed out three roads along our route and made for 180-degree turns. Small creeks fed into larger ones and the accumulated volume of water was too much for the five-foot high culverts. The earth below the asphalt roadbed was washed away and the road collapsed, looking like an earthquake had hit. After dodging washouts, I arrived at the market.

The store was closed. It was Sunday, and no business is transacted on this Holy Day. The brochure listed products they sell: spices, nuts, baking supplies, dry beans, gelatins, pasta, specialty flours, whole grains, dried fruit, chocolate products, cheese, cookbooks, and canning supplies. We saw the Bethany Mennonite Church along County Road F near the Eau Pleine River. It was later that I found out it was the Old Order church for the owners and operators of the market, Nelson and Melinda Weaver of the Weaverland Conference. As I was photographing the store building, a van drove by and into the farmyard next to the market. The passengers exited and walked toward me on the road. It was the Weaver family, cautious and curious of what I was doing. I greeted them and, to avoid any misunderstandings, quickly stated my business. Nelson had a slim, muscular frame and wore a plain white shirt, dark pants, and shoes, and was clean-shaven, with well-groomed short hair. He shook my hand with enthusiasm and with a friendly smile on his face.

They had moved from Lancaster, Pennsylvania in 1995 in search of cheaper land. This farm was 80 acres with another 80 that he rented out. It was not a dairy farm; cows were milked only for their own personal use. Instead, he raised heifers for beef. The Weavers took over the store business from a large family one year ago and built the new metal-sided store next to their farm for convenience. He said there were 250 Old Order families in the Marathon and Clark County area, a surprise for me. His family members remained silent during our visit, typical of Amish as well. It seemed like a good omen to meet such a friendly person at my first stop, and I was eager to move on to the next, Cloverdale Country Store in Curtiss.

Cloverdale Country Store

This store offered bulk and natural foods, as well as lawn furniture. Its ranch-style front was punctuated with hanging baskets of flowers. A refrigerated truck was parked on the side of the store. Heavy electrical wires drooped from the transformer at the road to the store. This Nationwide Fellowship Mennonite family uses more of the modern conveniences than Old Order Mennonite. Their family ties are tight-knit. When I phoned the store later, the woman told me she was a sister-in-law to Ken Witmer from Wautoma whom I had met a month before. Ken was a deacon for the Red Granite congregation near Neshkoro. I felt privileged to hear him preach in his church.

Down the road, church was ending at Aaron Nolt's farm. Horse and buggy was the mode of transportation for this sect, Old Order Mennonite. Horses were trim Standardbred, racetrack rejects. These buggies were distinctive with a four-inch metal awning over the front window. The body was square with sliding side doors. One buggy's rear brake drum was painted alternately red and white to alert automobile drivers of a non-twenty-first century vehicle ahead. A twelve-volt battery provided power to brake and head lights. Passengers nodded and waved modestly while passing as I admired the horse more than them. When all had left, Aaron walked toward us. His wife remained slightly behind and to the side of him. This is a patriarchal society. Do you know of any matriarchal society?

My friend Sandy was with me, otherwise, I guess Mrs. Nolt would not have stayed to hear the conversation. I asked her about some Old Time roses in her garden, but Aaron throttled her answer to a short one. However, she stayed for the rest of the visit.

Aaron said the farm was 80 acres and they milked 16 cows. He used steel-wheeled tractors in the field and had electricity in the house and barn. The house was heated hydronically with hot water and a circulating pump. The hot water was generated in an outside stand-alone furnace fed with wood, then pumped through pipes underground to the house radiators. It was the first time I had seen one of these systems in use on an Anabaptist farm, although I had seen them for sale at rural implement dealers.

Aaron had short-cropped black hair and no beard. His black chapeau was made of synthetic material, probably a plastic. His white shirt open at the collar was commercial looking and buttoned. His vest was black matching his coat, pants, and work shoes. But most intriguing was a slight accent that resembled the singsong lilt of Norwegian as he spoke. His wife's dress was long, dark, and of a lightweight material. She wore no apron nor bertha or cape. Her hair was up under a white see-through starched muslin head cover. The children in the buggies, most of them bare-footed, wore light-colored clothing. Two teen boys rode rubber-tired bikes.

I asked Aaron about their hymnal, if it was the *Ausbund*. He said no. When I asked where and when his hymnal was started, he somewhat sheepishly said with a chuckle, "Well, you got me there."

A long 60-foot garden paralleled the driveway. White muslin material covered the tender starter tomato plants. I said I had seen these covers in the Hillsboro Amish settlement, to which Aaron responded, "They are organic vegetable garden farmers there." His awareness of what was going on around the state was impressive. Perhaps if we English folks spent more time paying attention to our local politics and our communities as the Anabaptists do by design, we would not feel so overwhelmed with the wealth of worldly information via the Internet. Gardens and fellowship seem to be part of their plan for simplicity. Appetites and appearances seem to feed our plan for the good life. Could it be the Old Order Mennonites have it right?

HENE SUPPLY

The third stop on the tour was on Monday at the Hene Supply Store in Withee. State law requires three separate operations, so one of the stores handles hardware, a second sells bikes, and a third deals in bulk food and groceries. I photographed the collage of buildings as an open wagon filled with children pulled up to the hitching rack. Some call the open wagon a "hack" or "pickup wagon." There is no cover or cab, and the back is open with side rails to hold goods, milk cans, or other large items for transporting. I asked the Old Order Mennonite driver in his bright-checkered short sleeve shirt about the spirited horse. He had purchased him recently and had papers from New York to show his winnings on the racetrack, which was an indication of his stamina for pulling buggies. His five children never interrupted our conversation and seemed spellbound with what we said.

Inside the store in the clothing section where he tried on calf-high rubber boots, the driver told me two stories of how crooks dressed themselves as Amish to gain trust and innocence in their wrong doings. One robber mistakenly had a mustache, which the alert and knowledgeable taxi driver noticed and called police who nabbed the bandit. In another case, drug dealers were attempting to drive across the Canadian border, but the customs officer noticed the driver was also dressed as an Amish. Knowing the Amish do not drive cars, he notified police to apprehend the imposters. The Mennonite's children smiled and softly chuckled at the humor of the stories.

CENTRAL WISCONSIN PRODUCE AUCTION
Tour stop number four was a Mennonite owned building on Hwy O near Withee. On auction days, it bustles with buyers of farm fresh produce, bedding plants, pumpkins, fall decorations, crafts, shrubbery, nursery stock, and on special consignment auctions, quilts in May and September. A three-fold brochure advertises available produce by the month. Produce must be grown within a 100-mile zone to be "local grown." Others may sell on consignment. Nearby, a Mennonite newcomer from Lancaster, Pennsylvania, owns a butcher shop.

294 Amish in Wisconsin

MENNONITE FAMILY BOOK SHELF

On Monday, we stopped here to find new publications and meet the owners. I had photographed the road sign the day before to document the tour. Today I would ask if I could photograph the outside of the store, which was an extension of the farmhouse, a cozy building well landscaped with shrubs and flowers. Inside the store, we had to grope for books on the shelf for lack of lighting. Within a few minutes, Mrs. Irvin N. Shirk came to assist and apologized for not having the lights on. She was busy moving the store and their belongings across the street. Their son, living in a mobile home next door, was moving into the farmhouse and taking over the farm. Hearing my mission and knowing her husband's love for books, she went to retrieve Irvin. He enjoyed talking about new ideas and answering questions, she said.

A short man with muscular forearms and grip, Irwin grasped my hand in a friendly greeting. His colorful vertical-striped shirt reminded me of the Hutterites I saw in Arthur, Illinois, at a symposium. He was clean-shaven and had short black hair. The Shirks were Old Order Mennonites using horse and buggy instead of cars, but had electricity throughout the farm. His barn had room for 60 milkers, but old cows were being sold and carted away as we spoke. Heifers were raised in an "open barn" with roll-up canvas tarps on the sides. Irvin showed me a copy of the Directory of Old Order Mennonites in the Groffdale Conference that included an article he had written. It was a brief history of the Christian Mennonite church. We talked about farm subsidies; I asked how he financed his farm, to which he retorted, "The same you would." His father sold the Lancaster farm at a profit to buy the Thorp farm of 80 acres and now another 80 acres across the street. He would stay on as a "hired man" to help his son get started.

His books included religious, children's coloring, Laura Ingalls Wilder, Catherine Marshall's *Christy* series, cookbooks, dictionaries, thesauruses, and Concordances to name a few. Cards and gifts also filled the shelves. I bought *The Earth is the Lord's* by John L. Ruth, a 1,300 page volume on Mennonite history. It was priced right and I had been looking for it, having met the author personally and via email. It would be an ambitious undertaking to read it in my lifetime. I also bought two directories of local Mennonites and *God's Golden Children*, about kids with Crigler-Najjar syndrome. Irvin gave us a catalog of books in their store as we left.

HORST STABLES FAMILY RESTAURANT

The next morning we made our final stop at Horst for breakfast. Two miles south of Thorp, the Old Order Mennonites owned and operated this huge knotty-pined facility. Modern cooking grills and ovens lined the north wall. Our waitress was a Horst and was dressed in a long pastel print dress and white head cover. She engaged in conversation to the distress of some of her impatient customers. My order was scrambled eggs, sausage, homemade wholewheat toast, hash browns, and coffee. Under one roof was the restaurant and arena for horse auctions. Hungry horse dealers make good customers.

The owner, dressed in a checkered short-sleeved shirt and commercial jeans with suspenders, was clean-shaven with a standard haircut, and an intense facial expression. He showed us a jogging cart used to break horses with harnesses on a two-wheeled show cart. He met with two customers—a scrap iron metal collector and another large man who had opinions on all subjects. They were concerned about farm foreclosures, DNR incompetence in the deer chronic wasting disease situation, and terrorists.

St. Hedwig Church

This monolith of a building stood empty and boarded up off the road near Withee. Not a Mennonite structure by any means, but its blood-red brick symbolized the death of by-gone days when communities were homogenous and ethnically bound together. Here, Polish and Russian Catholics worshipped together for generations until individualism and progress bled them. A 60-foot tall glistening stainless steel bell tower held the surviving tower bells, still and haunting. I photographed the two in one frame, counterpoised. Will Mennonites and Amish fall to the same progress?

On the corner was a contrasting new Mennonite house abundant with flower gardens and groomed lawn. Next-door was the Thorcraft Custom Cabinet Shop, also Mennonite owned. You do not need much more than a horse and buggy to get to this work place. And home for lunch, too.

Adam and Ester Nolt

The Nolt Implement Repair Shop on Hwy X interested me. We turned in to investigate. A tall, balding Mennonite in dark blue pants and short-sleeved shirt greeted us on the walk outside the new house. His wife came out on the porch and invited us in. He did not hear or ignored her offer. She repeated it, and he complied.

Inside we were offered the overstuffed glider-rockers. Ester sat on the couch with a colorful throw in a yellow and white diamond pattern. Adam sat on a kitchen table chair. It was cool inside despite the 90-degree heat outside. A pleasant breeze moved past us. A new looking oak hutch was in the corner holding family Bibles, hymnals, and other books. Off-white linoleum glistened and was spotless. The spacious kitchen had light colored solid oak wood cabinets and a new wood-fired cook stove. Electric floor lamps in the living room and a ceiling lamp/fan in the kitchen were a stunning contrast to Amish homes.

Adam talked about water ram pumps used in place of windmill-powered pumps. We had read the same article about ram pumps by Joe C. Borntreger of the Cashton Amish settlement in the *Plain Interest* newspaper. We talked about the "overwhelming feeling of responsibility for the person chosen as deacon." Adam described the procedure they used casting lots for their leaders. It paralleled that of the Amish with the exception that Amish women have the right to nominate a person. Ester gave us the name of an Old Order Mennonite in Platteville whom I could meet to explore that settlement. She told us about Irma Leid who is the scribe for *Die Botshaft* newspaper and works in the Hene Supply store. Later, we would get the address of the widow whose minister husband had been killed in an auto/buggy accident. Irma was his sister.

We left as a customer arrived at the shop where Adam repaired and rebuilt farm implements. To be given hospitality like this as a stranger made me appreciate the warmth within this community.

"AMISH MAN DIES WHEN CAR HITS BUGGY"
This was the headline in the Milwaukee Journal Sentinel on June 7, 2002. My 95-year-old aunt Clara had clipped it out for me. Never did I think I would meet the widow. James S. Leid of Thorp was a 27-year-old husband, father, and deacon of the Old Order Mennonite church. His wife, Julia, was left to care for three children under five years old on an 80-acre farm with cut hay lying in the field. Relatives and friends from as far away as Lancaster, Pennsylvania, had supported Julia for a week and were just leaving as we arrived. Seven tractors, hay choppers, and wagons were in the field harvesting the crop and blowing it into the concrete silo. These were neighbor Old Order

Mennonite farmers pitching in to help in a time of need. It was a sad ending for a joyful and insightful weekend.

Permission was granted to photograph these Hutterite girls in their colony in Saskatchewan, Canada.

PART IV   References, Resources, Videos, Magazines, Booklets,Articles

REFERENCES, RESOURCES

This informal listing of books, booklets, pamphlets, magazines, newspaper articles, and videos was used in putting this book together and for the readers' curiosity and further investigation. Bold, highlighted entries are recommended reading. For used editions, try **www.abebooks.com**

•*Amish Society*, **and** *Hutterite Society*, **John A Hostetler, Johns Hopkins University Press, 4th edition.**
•*The Riddle of Amish Culture*, **by Donald B. Kraybill. A comprehensive and readable book explaining practices of the Amish people. Revised edition 2001.**
•*Amish Odyssey*, Bill Coleman author /photographer; email: amishphoto@aol.com www.amishphoto.com
•*The Amish, A Photographic Tour*, Carol Highsmith and Ted Landphair. Photographs of Lancaster County, Pennsylvania.
•*Amish Life, A Portrait of Plain Living*, John V. Wasilchick, with photographs by Jerry Erwin of Paradise, PA.
•*Lancaster County*, text by Ed Klimuska; photos by Kieth Baum and Jerry Irwin, with a forward by Donald Kraybill and Patrick Noonan.
•*Amish Ways*, Ruth Hoover Seitz, photos by Blair Seitz of Lancaster County, southern Ohio and southern Ontario, Canada.
•*The Amish*, Images of a Tradition, by Jan Folsom with black and white photos.
•*A Day in the Life of the Amish*, produced by Reiman Publications, Bob Ottum editor, with photos by Don Shenk, Julie Habel and Jon Paris and Amish folks.

•*Yonie Wondernose*, Marguerite De Angeli, child's story, published 1944. Gift of George H. De Jarlais.
•*Amish Home*, Raymond Bial, a photo essay.
•*Visit to Amish Country*, Raymond Bial, a photo essay.
•*Amish Houses and Barnes*, Stephen Scott, a photo/essay/documentary. Peoples Place Book 11.
•**A History of The Amish, Steven M. Nolt, with notes and bibliography. Good Books, Intercourse, PA 17534.**
•*Real People*, Amish and Mennonites in Lancaster County, Pennsylvania, by A. Martha Denlinger, Mennonite author.
•**The Amish Struggle with Modernity, edited by Donald B. Kraybill and Marc A Olshan with articles by Gertrude Enders Huntington, Diane Zimmerman Umble, David Luthy, Steven M. Nolt, and Kimberly D. Schmidt.**
•**An Introduction to Mennonite History, Cornelius J. Dyck, textbook. Herald Press.**
•*The Forgotten People, A Year Among the Hutterites*, by Michael Holzach translated by Stephan Lhotzky. A German reporter experiences being Hutterite.
•*Amish Boyhood Echoes*, Andy Yoder from Oconto, Wisconsin. Bay Impressions, Oconto, WI, 1991.
•*Lessons for Living*, A Practical Approach to Daily Life from the Amish Community, by Joseph F. Donnermeyer, George M. and Marty W. Kreps.
•*The Amish and the State*, edited by Donald B. Kraybill, professor of sociology at Elizabethtown College.
•*Amish Values; Wisdom that Works*, Ruth Hoover Seitz Photos by Blair Seitz.
•*Our People; the Amish and Mennonites of Ohio*, Levi Miller, an Amish born Mennonite from Holmes County, Ohio. (Sixth generation).
•*Mennonite Society*, Calvin Redekop, a Canadian Mennonite, writes from a sociological perspective.
•*The Amish School*, Sara E. Fisher (Old Order Amish) and Rachel K. Stahl.

•*The Puzzles of Amish Life*, Donald B. Kraybill. People's Place Booklet No. 10.

•*Living Without Electricity*, Stephen Scott, and Kenneth Pellman. People's Place Booklet No. 9.

•*Caretakers of Creation*, Farmers Reflect on their Faith and Work. Patrick Slattery, journalist from LaCrosse, Wisconsin contains the story, "Plain People," by Greg and Francine Molner from Hillsboro, Wisconsin.

•*Born Hutterite*, stories by Samuel Hofer, once a Hutterite, owner of Hofer Publication, Saskatoon, Saskatchewan, Canada.

•**The Amish in their own Words, compiled by Brad Igou from Amish writings over 25 years in the Family Life magazine. Herald Press.**

•**Rosanna of the Amish, Joseph W. Yoder (1872-1956). True story of an adopted Irish daughter raised by Amish in central Pennsylvania.**

•*America's Amish Country II*, Doyle Yoder and Leslie A. Kelly, photographer.

•*Songs of the Ausbund*, volume I. A history and translations of Ausbund hymns produced by the Ohio Amish Library.

•*Ausbund*, The Amish Book Committee, Lancaster, PA (original Luther translation in German)

•*Decorative Arts of the Amish of Lancaster County*, Daniel and Kathryn McCauley

•*Reinland; an Experience in Community*, Peter D. Zacharias. A centennial edition and gift from Jake Peters of Winnipeg, Manitoba, Canada

•*Mennonite World Handbook*, World Conference 1978, ed. Paul N. Kraybill.

•*The Growth of Foreign Missions in the Mennonite Brethren Church*, Gerhard Wilhelm Peters. 1952

•*Manitoba Mennonite Memories*, ed. Julius G. Toews, Lawrence Klippenstein.

•*A Modest Mennonite Home*, Steve Friesen, photos by John P. Herr.

•*The Quilter's Guide to Amish Quilts*, Jan Jefferson, Maggi McCormick Gordon and photos by Matthew Ward.

•*Toil and Peaceful Life*, Carl J. Tracie. Story of a Doukhobor village 1899-1918.

•**A Change and a Parting, Barbara S. Yambura, born and raised in the Amana colonies tells her story to Eunice Willis Bodine. The people of the Amanas are the Society of True Inspirationists, but are not Amish.**

•*Among the Amish*, Mel Horst, text by Elmer L. Smith. A photo essay.

•*Meet Mennonites*, Elmer L. Smith. A photo essay.

•*The Amish*, Elmer L. Smith. Photos by Mel Horst.

•*Lehman's Non-Electric Good Neighbor Heritage Catalog*, Kidron, Ohio.

•*The Budget Newspaper*, published weekly in Sugar Creek, Ohio. A compilation of letters from "scribes" from Anabaptist settlements, colonies and communities around the world. Interesting reading about farming, visiting relations for weddings, funerals and communions, etc.

•*Young Companion*, a magazine published by Pathway Publishers, Ontario, said to be used in home teaching and family reading.

•*Blackboard Bulletin*, another magazine by Pathway for family use.

•*Plain and Amish; an alternative to modern pessimism*, by Bernd G. Langin, 1994, Harold Press.

•*Rosanna's Boys*, by Joseph W. Yoder, 1987, Mennonite Board of Missions and originally published by Yoder Publishing Co., 1948.

•*Rachel*, by Mary Christner Borntrager, 1990, Herald Press.

•*Why Do They Dress That Way?* Stephen Scott, Good Books, Intercourse, PA.

•*Give Me This Mountain*, Elmo Stoll, published by the author's family after his early death in 1998. He was editor of Family Life newsletter.

•*Martyrs Mirror*, Herald Press. A 1300 page collection of martyr stories.

•*Harvard Encyclopedia of American Ethnic Groups*, Harvard University Press, 1980 with article on the Amish by John A. Hostetler, p122-125.

•*Lancaster County Business Directory 2000*, DaveCo Family, Inc. A 220-page directory of Amish and Mennonite businesses published by one.

•*Old Order Amish; their enduring way of life*, text by Donald B. Kraybill and photos by Lucian Niemeyer, 1993, Johns Hopkins.

•*Out of the Silent Past*, by Rhoda H. Campbell, a pamphlet. Feldser Printing, Lancaster, PA. 1950.

•*The Mystery of Jacob Amman*, by William R. McGrath. Amish-Mennonite Publications, Carrollton, Ohio, 1989.

•*Habits of the Heart*; Robert Bellah et al, University of California Press 1996.

•*Wisdom of the Plain Folk*, Donna and Robert Leahy. A photo/essay of Churchtown, Pennsylvania.

•*20 Most Asked Questions about the Amish and Mennonites*, Merle and Phyllis Good. People's Place Booklet No.1.

•*The Amish: the enduring spirit*; Leslie Ann Houslein. Photos by Jerry Irwin.

•*Pleasant Hill and its Shakers*, by Thomas D. Clark and F. Gerald Ham, Shakertown Press, Pleasant Hill, Kentucky, 1968.

•**Shaker Experience in America by Stephen J. Stein, Yale University Press, 1992.**

•*Why Some Amish Communities Fail: Extinct Settlements*, 1961-1999, by David Luthy, Pathway Publications, Aylmer, and Ontario, Canada. 2000.

•*A Typological Analyses of Social Systems*, essay #5, The Old Order Amish as a Social System, Charles P. Loomis, Michigan State College, 1948.

•*Amish Portrait*, by Walt Mauer, a photo/essay booklet published by Garden Spot Gifts, Inc. 1998

•*Approaching the Glory*, by Jake Peters, a Mennonite's autobiography (self published) Writeword Enterprises. Winnipeg, Mb. Canada, December 2000.
•*The Amish Wedding*, by Stephen Scott, Peoples Place Book No. 8, 1988.
•*Plain Buggies*, by Stephen Scott, Peoples Place Book No. 3, 1998.
•**Who is Who in the Budget, by editors of the Budget newspaper, Middlebury, IN 46540. Sold at Lark Country Store, Bonduel, WI.**
•*One Way Street*, by Elmo Stoll, Pathways Publications, LaGrange, IN, 1972.
•*The Amish in America: Settlements that Failed, 1840-1960* by David Luthy, Pathway Publishers, Alymer, and Ontario, Canada. 1991.
•*American Utopias* by Charles Nordhoff, Berkshire House Publishers, Stockbridge, MA. Originally published in1875 as *The Communistic Societies of the United States*. This edition published 1993.
•**On the Backroad to Heaven, Donald B. Kraybill and Carl F. Bowman, Johns Hopkins University Press, 2001.**
•**Our Heritage, Hope and Faith, Mary M. Miller, Carlisle Printing, Sugarcreek, Ohio, 2000. These are German and English translations of scripture, hymns and prayers used in church service.**
•**Amish Enterprise: From Plows to Profits, by Donald B. Kraybill, Steven M. Nolt. Johns Hopkins University Press, 1995.**
•*A Quiet and Peaceful Life*, by John L. Ruth. People's Place Book No. 2, 1985.
•**Amish Roots: A Treasury of History, Wisdom, and Lore. Edited by John A. Hostetler, Johns Hopkins University Press, 1992.**
•*Holy Bible* with comments by Dr. Martin Luther, (1768), published by Edwards Bros., Ann Arbor, MI 1952.

•*Commentary on the Whole Bible*, by Mathew Henry, Zondervan Publishing House, 1961.

•**Anabaptist World USA by Donald B. Kraybill and C. Nelson Hostetter, Herald Press, 2001. A database of statistics, directories of settlements and resources.**

•**The *Amish Children* by Phyllis Pellman Good and photos by Jerry Irwin, Good Books, Intercourse, PA, 2000.**

•*Great Possessions, An Amish Farmer's Journal*, by David Kline, Amish Bishop in Mt. Hope, Ohio. Wooster Book Company, Wooster, Ohio, 2001.

•**Old Order and Conservative Mennonite Groups by Stephen Scott, Good Books, Intercourse, PA, 1996.**

•**Brethren Society, The Cultural Transformation of a "Peculiar People" by Carl F. Bowman, Johns Hopkins University Press, 1995.**

•*Amish Communities and Business Directory* by Ottie Garrett published by Hitching Post Enterprises, Kalona, IA, 1996.

•*Tobias of the Amish* by Ervin R. Stutzman, Herald Press, Scottdale, PA, 2001.

•*Home Remedies from Amish Country*, Abana Books, Millersburg, Ohio, 2001.

•*Quilts Among the Plain People* by Rachel T. Pellman and Joanne Ranck, Good Books, Intercourse, PA, 1981.

•*Driving the Amish* by Jim Butterfield, photos by Doyle Yoder, Herald Press, 1997.

•*The Amazing Story of the Ausbund* by Ben S. Blank, Carlisle Printing, Sugar Creek, Ohio, 2001.

•Video, Holmes County: "It's Your Turn Now," by Holmes County Chamber of Commerce, 1999.

•*1001 Questions and Answers on the Christian Life*, Pathway Publishers, 1995.

•*Legacy of Michael Sattler* by John H. Yoder, Herald Press, 1973.

•**The Amish in the American Imagination by David Weaver-Zercher, Johns Hopkins University Press, 2001. Describes "the function of the Amish in American Society."**

•*Our Unitarian Heritage* by Earl Morse Wilbur, 1925, Beacon Press, Chapter VII, "Antitrinitarianism Among the Early Anabaptists, 1517-1530."

•*Amish-Mennonites in Germany* by Hermann Guth, Masthof Press, 1995. A description of congregations, the estates where they lived and their family genealogy. A translation from German to English. Ten appendixes contain letters from the 18th century. A photo essay of buildings, villages and estates where Amish and Mennonites leased.

•*Wisconsin, Minnesota, & Montana Amish Directory, 1996.* Compiled by Abana Book Service, Millersburg, Ohio. Printed by Schlabach Printers. A listing of family members in each settlement with hand made map plotting businesses and farms.

•*Wisconsin, Minnesota, and Montana Amish Directory 2002*, by DeVon Miller, Abana Book Services, Millersburg, OH 44654.

•*Tradition & Transition* by Paton Yoder, published by Herald Press in cooperation with Mennonite Historical Society, Goshen, Indiana. 1991. Documents Amish-Mennonites and Old Order Amish from 1800 to 1900, an often overlooked period which included "The Great Schism."

•*Joas Fights For Freedom* by Mrs. Elmer Lambright, Amish author from Hillsboro, Wisconsin, 2000.

•*2001 Address Directory of Amish Communities* compiled by Die Blatt newspaper, Shipshewana, Indiana.

•***The Shunning* by Beverly Lewis, Bethany House Publishers, 1997. A fictional story that takes place in Lancaster County, Pennsylvania.**

•*The Confession* by Beverly Lewis, Bethany House Publishers, 1997. A fictional story that takes place in Lancaster County, Pennsylvania.

•*The Reckoning* by Beverly Lewis, Bethany House Publishers, 1997. A fictional story that takes place in Lancaster County, Pennsylvania.

•*The Earth is the Lord's* by John Landis Ruth, commissioned by Lancaster Mennonite Historical Society and Lancaster Mennonite Conference. **Published by Herald Press, Scottdale, Pennsylvania, 2001. A 1389 page narrative history of the Lancaster Mennonite Conference, 39th in the series.**

•*God's Golden Children* compiled by Floyd and Katie Martin, printed by Brookside Printing, Millersburg, Pennsylvania, 2002. A compilation of stories of children with Crigler-Najjar syndrome. Pioneer Doctor Holmes Morton II of Strasburg, Pennsylvania.

•*Amish Wall Quilts* by Rachel Thomas Pellman, Martingale & Co., Woodinville, WA, 98072. Published 2001.

•*The Protestant Reformation: 1517-1559* by Lewis . Spitz, Concordia Publishing House, 1985, reprinted 2001.

•*Visits With The Amish: Impressions of the Plain Life* **by Linda Egenes, Iowa State Press, 2000. Observations of the Kalona, Iowa Amish settlement.**

•*Mennonite Tourguide to Western Europe* by Jan Gleysteen and reprinted by Wipf and Stock Publishers, copyright 2000 by Herald Press.

•*Extraordinary Groups: The Sociology of Unconventional Life-styles* by William M. Kephart, St. Martin's Press, New York, 1976. Includes Old Order Amish. The Oneida Community, The Father Divine Movement, The Shakers, The Mormons, The Hutterites, and the Modern Communes.

•*Amish Folk Medicine* by Patrick Quillin, Ph. D., RD. A paperback of "home remedies using foods, herbs and vitamins. Book World Services, Sarasota, Florida 1996.

Permission was granted to photograph these Hutterite
milkmen at a colony in Saskatchewan, Canada

VIDEOS, MAGAZINES, BOOKLETS, & ARTICLES

•"The Radicals," a video depicting Michael Sattler's role in the formation of the radical Anabaptist movement of 1525-1527. (www.visionvideo.com)

•New American Almanac Thirty Third Edition for the Year of Our Lord, 2002 by Ben J. Raber, Baltic, Ohio 43804, and printed by Gordonville, PA Print Shop.

•"Pennsylvania Mennonite Heritage," a magazine focusing on history, religion, culture and genealogy of Mennonites in Pennsylvania and published by the Lancaster Mennonite Historical Society.

•**"The Amish: A People of Preservation." A documentary video, narrated by John L. Ruth, Mennonite historian, filmed in Lancaster County, PA. Heritage Production, 1191 Sumneytown Pike, Harleysville, PA 19438.**

•*The Hutterites; to care and not to care*, video, 1984 RHB Productions.

•Family Bookshelf 2002 Book Catalog, printed by the Shirks, Old Order Mennonite family and owners. W8186 County Hwy. X, Thorp, Wisconsin.

•*The Diary*, a newsletter published monthly by Pequea Publishers, Gordonville, PA.

•*Die Botschaft*. A weekly newspaper serving Old Order Amish in U.S. and Canada published by Brookshire Printing, Lancaster, Pennsylvania.

•Mennonite Confession of Faith. Printed by Rod and Staff, Crockett, KY, eleventh printing, 1998. Contains Schleitheim and Dortrecht Confessions and Christian Fundamentals of a Conservative Mennonite sect.

•Oak Ridge Mennonite Church Statement of Standards pamphlet published by and for the Red Granite, Wisconsin conservative Mennonite Congregation.

•Ein Gesang-Buch Von Deutsch Melodies, a Second Edition song book published in German by the Groffdale Conference Mennonite Church, Earl Z. Weaver, coordinator, East Earl, Pennsylvania.

•Directory of Old Order Mennonites of Chippewa, Clark, and Taylor Counties, Wisconsin, 2000, 6th printing by O-W Enterprise, Withee, Wisconsin.

•Directory of Weaverland Conference Mennonites In Wisconsin, 2001, Second Edition printed by O-W

•Mennonite Countryside Tour, a brochure published by the Marshfield Convention and Visitors Bureau. A self-guided auto tour of Mennonite businesses in the Marshfield/Thorp, Wisconsin area.

•Amish Countryside Tour, a brochure published by the Marshfield Convention and Visitors Bureau. A self-guided auto tour of Amish businesses west of Marshfield along U.S. Hwy 10 in central Wisconsin.

•"Directory of the Nationwide Fellowship Churches," 2002. Published by Grace Press of Ephrata, PA. Contains statistics of the number of congregations and Ordained bishops, ministers and deacons, ministerial directory, congregational information and map to church site.

•Anabaptist and Reformed Walking Tours of Bern and Zurich, Switzerland: A tour Leaders Guide written and prepared by Samuel E. Wenger, 3 Fairview Drive, Akron, PA 17501, April, 2000.

•Mennonite Heritage Tour Journals, compiled by J. Lemar and Lois Ann Mast, printed by Olde Springfield Shoppe, Elverson, PA 19520-0171.

•Notes on Research Sources for Emigration Studies from Archives and Societies in Southern Germany, by Annette K. Burgert, 1993, a pamphlet published by AKB Publications, Myerstown, PA 17067-2642. Archives in Speyer, Kaiserslauten, Karlsruhe, Stuttgart, and Darmstadt, Germany.

•"The New American Almanac" Thirty-Third Edition, 2002, by B.J. Raber, Baltic, Ohio. Printed by Gordonville, PA Print Shop. Lists all ministers and settlement postal zip codes. Paperback.

•*The Mennonite Quarterly Review* **published by the Mennonite Historical Society, Goshen College, Goshen, Indiana, John D. Roth, editor, April 2001.**

•"Man Charged in Attacks on Amish," Milwaukee Journal Sentinel, November 7, 1995. See Michael J. Vieth case, www.courts.state.wi.us

•**"A Friend of the Amish Leads Unintrusive Tours," Chicago Tribune, August 20, 1999. Article about tour guide Kathy Kuderer of Down a Country Road, 12651 State Hwy 33, Cashton, WI 54619 (608-654-5318).** www.downacountryroadamish.com

•"Background Dynamics of the Amish Movement," by Leonard Gross, Goshen College, Goshen, Indiana, www.goshen.edu/~lonhs//GPUBLICATIONS/GROSS.html

•"Dinner with Amish Family Opens Doors," Milwaukee Journal Sentinel, Travel Section, August 27, 2000.

•"Amish Cooking Goes Back to Basics," Milwaukee Journal Sentinel, December 31, 2000.

•"The Old Order Amish: To Remain in the Faith or to Leave," by Thomas J. Meyers, Goshen College, Goshen, Indiana.

•"The Amish in Northern Indiana," essay by Samuel L. Yoder, Ed.D.

•"Amish Not Tied to the Land Any Longer," Milwaukee Journal Sentinel, October 23, 2000. www.amishnews.com

•"War brings different challenges to Amish," by Flynn McRoberts of Chicago Tribune, October 21, 2001.

•"Young Amish girl transformed by 21st-century gift," by Crocker Stephenson of Milwaukee Journal Sentinel, December 23, 2001.

• "Keeping the faith-against retaliation. Mennonites put aside vengeance for Sept. 11," by Mark Johnson of Milwaukee Journal Sentinel, January 1, 2002.

• Hutterite books- 1-605-334-0869 (Sioux Falls, N.D.)

• *Plain Interests*, A monthly newspaper published by Brookside Publishing, Millersburg, PA 17061.

• *Mennonite Weekly Review*, a newspaper, Newton, KS.

• *The Old Country News*, Elam Lapp editor, 420 Weaver Rd., Millersburg, PA 17061-9509.

• *Mennonite Life*, John A. Hostetler, professor of Anthropology and Sociology at Temple University, Philadelphia, Pennsylvania and former Old Order Amish. A booklet.

• Funds to defend the New Glarus fathers were raised by the National Committee for Religious Freedom in Livonia, Michigan, by Lutheran pastor Rev. William C. Lindholm. Their web page carried the *Washington Post* article. See http://holycrosslivonia.org/amish/mackaye.htm. Lindholm's extensive defense brief is also on the web site by adding the suffix /amish/case.htm and /amish/defense.htm.

• More information on Illinois settlements is available from www.arcola-il.org. More on Arthur can be found at www.ArthurIllinois.com and www.IllinoisAmishCountry.com or 1-800-72AMISH.

• The web site for The People's Place in Intercourse, PA is www.goodbks.com.

• Sam Hofer Publications vendor- 1-800-328-8411. Hutterite books.

• *The Schleitheim Confession*, translated by John H. Yoder, pamphlet, Herald Press, 1977.

• *Amish of Kishacoquillas*, by Samuel W. Peachey, Belleville, PA, 1930.

ORDER FORM FOR *__AMISH IN WISCONSIN__*

TO ORDER:

BY MAIL: (Send this form or a copy)
ADDRESS TO: Amish Insight
              Richard Dawley
              2249 S. Calhoun Rd.
              New Berlin, WI 53151
BY PHONE: Call 262-797-1858

Enclosed is:
 ❑ check   ❑ money order   ❑ cashier's check

Enter # of copies: _____ of *__Amish in Wisconsin__*

Enter the amount:$_____ payable to Richard Dawley

 ❑ $16.95 for one   plus $ 3.00 S/H= **$19.95**
 ❑ $33.90 for two   plus $ 6.00 S/H= **$39.90**
 ❑ $50.85 for three   plus $ 9.00 S/H= **$59.85**
 ❑ $67.80 for four   plus $12 00 S/H= **$79.80**
 ❑ $84.75 for five   plus $15.00 S/H= **$99.75**

(Optional, in case of questions)
Enter phone number: _____
   and email address: _____

SHIP TO:_____

ADDRESS_____

CITY_____

STATE_____ **ZIP**_____